HOW TO
Read & Interpret a Birth Chart

HOW TO
Read & Interpret
a Birth Chart

GUIDEPOSTS FOR UNDERSTANDING
NATAL ASTROLOGY

LAURIE FARRINGTON

foreword by Theresa Reed

WEISER
BOOKS

This edition first published in 2025 by Weiser Books, an imprint of
Red Wheel/Weiser, LLC
With offices at:
65 Parker Street, Suite 7
Newburyport, MA 01950
www.redwheelweiser.com

ISBN: 978-1-57863-846-8

Library of Congress Cataloging-in-Publication Data

Names: Farrington, Laurie, 1955- author. Title: How to read and interpret a birth chart : guideposts
for understanding natal astrology / Laurie Farrington ; Foreword by Theresa Reed.
Description: Newburyport, MA : Weiser Books, 2025. | Includes bibliographical references and
index. | Summary: "Each of us possesses an individual astrology chart, cast for the moment of
our first breath. Understanding the basics of signs, planets, houses, and aspects is the first step for
anyone interested in this topic. It must then be determined what is most important and how to merge
the many astrological patterns into a coherent whole. This book is for those who have mastered the
basics and are ready for more"-- Provided by publisher.
Identifiers: LCCN 2024039628 | ISBN 9781578638468 (trade paperback) | ISBN 9781633413467
(ebook) Subjects: LCSH: Natal astrology. | BISAC: BODY, MIND & SPIRIT / Astrology /
General | BODY, MIND & SPIRIT / Divination / General Classification: LCC BF1719 .F377 2025
| DDC 133.5--dc23/eng/20240924 LC record available at https://lccn.loc.gov/2024039628.

Cover and interior design by Sky Peck Design
Interior images by Laurie Farrington
Typeset in Times New Roman

Printed in the United States of America
IBI
10 9 8 7 6 5 4 3 2 1

To my granddaughter, Eleanor Gale Pheiffer.
With our nodal axes exactly aligned, we each travel a path
from intellectual curiosity to the development of expansive wisdom.
This is our hidden bond. I am proud to be aligned
with such a strong and confident spirit.

Contents

Where Do I Start?

Interpreting a natal chart is not just a skill; it's an art. It's also a journey that can be filled with anxiety and uncertainty, a path many of us have walked.

Picture this: After years of study, you've finally mastered the astrology basics. You understand the zodiac signs, planets, houses, and aspects. Friends and family think you have serious chops. You might think so, too. Now, you're ready to read astrological charts for the masses! Yay, you!

Yet, you find yourself breaking into a cold sweat the first time someone commissions you to read a natal chart. Suddenly, all that information you have gleaned over the years goes swirling down your brain drain, leaving you blanker than an empty astrological house.

You spend too many hours in prep work, reviewing every detail, panicking over what you might miss. Eventually, you have a small novel filled with notes, numbers, and glyphs. You're ready. But now you're bombarding the other person with a nonstop stream of astro-speak, without taking a breath. Worse yet, you don't even bother to look up to see if any of this resonates. Instead, you keep going, anxious about getting every single detail fleshed out.

The truth is, you're too terrified to look up or breathe, because you don't want to be wrong. Nor do you want to underdeliver. You want to do a good job and prove that all those years of study haven't gone to waste.

After hours of intense babbling, you finally finish your first consultation, feeling both relieved and anxious. The client's polite thank you and shell-shocked look leave you with mixed emotions. You survived, but it wasn't the smooth start you had hoped for. The fear of this becoming a recurring pattern in your astrological career lingers long after that session.

Sound familiar?

I've been there more times than I can count, especially in the early days of my professional career. I didn't have the advantage of a teacher or mentor, so much of my knowledge came from personal exploration and the goodwill of a few willing participants who thought I was decent enough to begin interpreting charts professionally.

It took a lot of nerve to jump into a full-time practice. But that's not a surprise, considering that I have six Mercury-ruled planets in my own natal chart. I thrive on mental challenges. But this Mercury overload also meant that my early consultations were scattered, anxiety-ridden, white-knuckled, joyless rides in which I sweated over the details like an over-worked miner sifting through dirt for gold.

When I began consulting, I relied on astro-babble too much because I was fearful I wouldn't sound as if I knew what I was doing. So my poor clients were deluged with a relentless ticker-tape of stuff that didn't matter or make sense. These sessions felt less like astrological consultations and more like astrological assaults.

But over time, I developed a structure for interpreting natal charts. I still use that checklist to this day. It covers all the details that I think are important, but leaves enough room for clients to ask questions. As a result, my readings got much better and more efficient. Even so, I still wondered if there were a better way. What was I missing? How could I deliver a meaningful consultation that made sense to my clients?

Ultimately, this all boiled down to one big question: Where do I start?

My guess is that most astrologers ask that same question. It doesn't matter whether you're a beginner or a seasoned pro. You want to do a thorough job without overwhelming your client. Knowing where to begin and what to cover can take a lifetime to figure out. But in the end, you don't have to dive in without a life preserver.

How to Read and Interpret a Birth Chart is a game-changer in the world of astrology literature. In this insightful book, Laurie Farrington presents a comprehensive list of "guideposts" that will empower every astrologer to deliver confident and meaningful chart interpretations. She also demonstrates how these guideposts can serve as springboards for asking insightful questions, leading to deeper insights for both astrologers and clients. This book can give you a solid framework on which to build engaging, profound astrological discussions, rather than fumbling through your consultations.

How I wish I had had this book at the beginning of my career! I made so many mistakes and wasted so many hours. Instead, I could have had a road map to help me navigate the difficult terrain of astrology. I wouldn't have had to figure it out the hard way. I could have avoided the typical errors that so many budding (and seasoned) astrologers make.

Even though I've been a working astrologer and tarot reader for over three decades, there is always room to learn—and to grow. This book has not only given me a whole new set of "guideposts" to steer me; it has also ignited a renewed sense of inspiration and motivation in my practice.

Whether you have a long-standing relationship with astrology or are just beginning your journey, this book is a valuable addition to your shelf. It provides a solid foundation for beginners, and offers new insights and perspectives to seasoned professionals.

Laurie Farrington has delivered the book we've all needed and been waiting for—even though we may not have realized it.

—Theresa Reed,
author of *Astrology for Real Life*

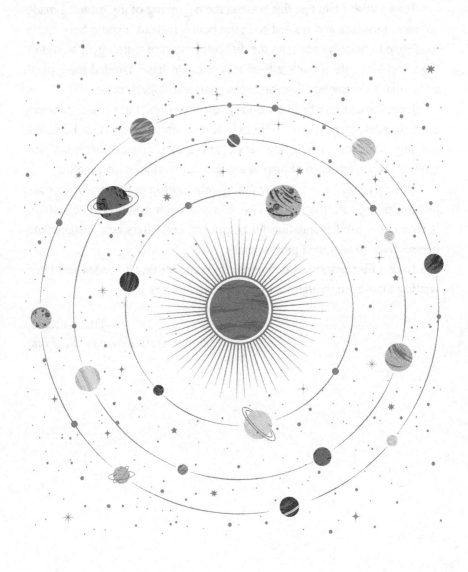

Introduction

I began teaching astrology at my dining room table in Vermont in the 1990s. I taught the basics of signs, planets, and houses, and the aspects between the planets. As my students and I looked down at the charts in front of us, I taught them to memorize symbols and keywords. We studied our own charts and the charts of famous people. We looked inward to understand how our charts matched our understanding of ourselves and reflected our lives.

It is shocking to think of now, but it took years before I realized the importance of looking to the sky to better understand the charts I studied so diligently. I hadn't made a clear connection to the planets in the cosmos, or even to the seasons as they played out and shifted in the world beyond my small apartment.

When I read *The Lunation Cycle: A Key to the Understanding of Personality* by author, composer, and pioneer of modern transpersonal astrology Dane Rudhyar, that all changed. As I came to understand the lunar cycle and the relationship between the Sun and the Moon, my entire perception of astrology shifted, surging into new terrain. My attention was riveted as I turned my eyes upward to the night sky. This began my study of the cycles and patterns in the cosmos. Making the connection between the birth chart and the interplay of the planets above was a mind-altering experience.

It was then that I began to study the ephemeris—a book of tables that gives the position of the planets over time. This led me to actively consider the movement of the planets before and after the moment in time depicted on a birth chart. I taught myself to see and understand the cycles unfolding between each pair of planets. As those same cycles came into view on a natal chart, I learned to appreciate and understand their importance. Today, you can access ephemerides online, but I recommend that you acquire a printed version and learn to use it.

Thirty to fifty years ago, the pathway into the world of astrology began with a focus on birth charts. Aspiring astrology students read books and attended in-person classes and conferences. Twenty-five years ago, I began encouraging my students to look up from the two-dimensional chart into the night sky to understand the cycles playing out there. To understand a birth chart, you have to become intimately aquainted with the dance of the cosmos. It is important for aspiring astrologers to learn the speed of the planets and clearly envision them in motion, day to day, year to year.

In the early years of my own studies, I learned the language of astrology by studying the signs, the planets, the houses, the aspects, and any horoscopes I could get my hands on. Like so many others, I took it for granted that, other than slight variations, this was how astrology was taught and how we learned.

For me, this changed in 2017, when a young woman approached me in search of an astrology teacher. During our initial conversation, it became evident that she had a solid grasp of the planets and signs, and of the planetary cycles. But she lacked any understanding of the houses or the fundamental structure of the birth chart itself. Initially, I was confused by what seemed to me to be an unusual imbalance in her astrological knowledge. With a bit of contemplation and several conversations, however, I suddenly understood. All that she knew she had learned from the Internet. Nowadays, prospective astrology students have access to a vast sea of information online. But what they find there is not presented in the traditional predictable order. Instead, they are introduced to an entirely different branch of Western astrology distinct from the study of individual horoscopes and natal charts.

This is easy to understand when we realize that astrologers, like all of us, need to make a living. So when they seek clients, they turn to social media. But, because each individual's birth chart is entirely unique and astrologers need to market to the masses, relevent information about natal astrology can not be easily or effectively presented through social media.

In order to become relevant and gain engagement and recognition, many of today's astrologers craft and disseminate content designed to reach a broad audience, emphasizing general information about prevalent cosmic patterns that impact everyone. As this branch of astrology has proliferated online, it has become the starting point for new students of the art. These new students enter directly into the world of planetary cycles and their impact on countries, cultures, and the populace at large. This is mundane astrology, something we will discuss further in part 1.

Astrology, in all its forms, is the study of time. What people are learning online today consists of observing and understanding the moving patterns of time that impact us all. But when we work with natal astrology, we contemplate one moment in time as a reflection of one individual life. And although understanding a natal chart is entirely different from understanding cosmic cycles, grasping their connection is essential.

To work with an individual horoscope, we separate the moment an infant takes its first breath from all other moments in time. We bring the pattern of the cosmos in that moment onto a static page where we can study the patterns and significance of that one moment, that one life. When an infant takes its first breath, the motion of the heavens pauses. In that moment, the pattern of the life is established and the stage is set for the life ahead.

We will discuss the four branches of Western astrology in more detail in part 1. For now, understand that, if your studies have come primarily from the Internet, you may know how to read the patterns of the cosmos more than you know how to read an individual's horoscope. You probably have a deep understanding of the current placement of the planets and their cycles, as well as ingresses, the phases of the Moon, and eclipses. You know when Mercury is retrograde and when the next eclipse will occur. You know when any major outer-planet conjunction is forecast to upend our society and our personal lives. But now it is time to dig deeper into the natal chart and learn to understand more deeply how a single life reflects the patterns we observe in the sky.

Although in the past I have encouraged my students to look up into the heavens for deeper understanding, I now encourage them to refocus their attention on the chart of one individual moment, one life, rather than concentrating solely on cosmic cycles. As a student of astrology, you must come to understand your own natal chart and those of the people you love. We each hold within us the singular moment of our first breath, taken in the midst of the larger cycles swirling above—the moment that began our particular human life.

I present this book as a bridge to guide you from a knowledge of planets, signs, aspects, and cycles to an understanding of and ability to work with an individual natal chart. I hope these pages give you a deep understanding of the natal chart and the person whose life it represents. My goal is to help you cross the bridge from mundane astrology to natal astrology.

If you are reading this book, you probably have a fair grasp of the basics of signs, planets, houses, and aspects. My hope is that what you find here will help you use this basic information to master the deeper layers within each natal chart you encounter. There is much to learn and there are many great books available to guide you in the basics of astrology. Here are just a few:

- *Astrology for Real Life: A Workbook for Beginners* by Theresa Reed (Weiser Books, 2019).

- *Astrology: Using the Wisdom of the Stars in Your Everyday Life* by Carole Taylor (DK Publishing, 2018).

- *The Inner Sky: How to Make Wiser Choices for a More Fulfilling Life* by Steven Forrest (Bantam Books, 1984).

- *The Complete Guide to Astrology: Understanding Yourself, Your Signs, and Your Birth Chart* by Louise Edington (Rockridge Press, 2020).

Welcome to the adventure. I hope you enjoy your journey.

PART I

Reading the Heavens

The Emergence of
Astrological Thought

For far longer than humans have inhabited the Earth, the planets have traveled around the ecliptic—from our perspective, moving forward and backward, coming together, moving apart, and creating cyclical patterns that early humans could not help but notice. The monthly dance between the Sun and Moon was easily observed by them, as were the more dramatic solar and lunar eclipse cycles. In their wonder at the beauty of the night sky and their fear at the vanishing of the light during the eclipses, they quite naturally began to attach stories, myths, and legends to these occurrences. In his book *The Practice of Astrology as a Technique in Human Understanding*, Dane Rudhyar describes this as the result of humanity's attempt to understand the apparent chaos of life through the ordered patterns observed in the sky.

Imagine for a moment that you are living some three million years ago in the early Stone Age, seated around a fire with your family and tribe. From the time you were a child, you have been drawn to the intensity and beauty of the heavens. On a particularly dark night, as you walk a distance from the light of the fire, you look up and see a falling star. You become mesmerized and overwhelmed by the drama unfolding overhead. From that moment on, you are never again quite satisfied to sit by the fire with your attention focused downward into the flames, or even gazing into the eyes of your companions. Once your attention is drawn upward, it remains riveted on the spendor and mystery of what you have seen in the heavens above.

Each night, you head off to watch the drama play out. In these solitary observations, you are mystified to observe that, at regular intervals, certain stationary stars (as you believe the planets to be) turn and move in the "wrong" direction. Imagine how frightened you and your entire tribe are when the Sun is blotted out by a lunar eclipse. Imagine if, at the time that the Sun disappears or a celestial body appears to turn backward, a loved one dies, a child is born, or an earthquake occurs.

You begin to make connections and anticipate events before they occur. New stories are told around the campfire. As your observations become more subtle and pronounced, your imagination is sparked by what you experience and you make more connections. You watch and observe deeply. As you track the patterns, you begin to offer suggestions to the elders of your tribe about the best time to hunt or harvest.

As the observer of the skies, the interpreter, and the storyteller, you come to hold an elevated position among those around you. You gain great respect for your knowledge and understanding of the heavenly world above. You are highly esteemed in your new role as the first astrologer in your tribe.

Indeed, this informal observation of planets, retrograde movement, eclipses, and patterns in the sky is as old as humanity itself. And this is the seed from which the history of astrology was born.

Four Branches of Western Astrology

There are various traditions in astrology—Western astrology, Indian astrology, and Chinese astrology to name a few. In this book, we will work exclusively with Western astrology. If you choose to explore the world of astrology online, make sure you are cognizant of whether you are looking at information about Western astrology or about a different tradition. It is not always clear initially, and I have seen a great deal of confusion among students and even newly practicing astrologers that could be cleared up with a simple basic understanding of these distinctions.

Western astrology is made up of four branches—natal astrology, mundane astrology, electional astrology, and horary astrology. Everything that you encounter when studying Western astrology will fall into one of these categories. When reading a book, a blog post, or a meme, it's important that you know which tradition and which branch of astrology is being presented. So let's take a brief look at each of the four branches of the Western astrological tradition.

Natal Astrology

Natal astrology begins and ends with the natal chart. If what you are reading or studying involves working with the birth chart of a living entity, human or otherwise, it will fall into this category. When you hear folks talk about astrology in the context of their personal charts or horoscopes, this is the branch to which they are referring.

Natal astrology is based on the concept that our character and life path are determined by the patterns and placement of the planets as seen from the location of our birth, at the exact date and time of our birth. When you consult an astrologer to examine your chart, you are appealing to natal astrology. Transits, progressions, solar arcs, midpoints, locational astrology, solar returns, chart comparisons, synastry, and composite charts are all techniques used in natal astrology.

Mundane Astrology

Mundane astrology is considered to be the oldest form of Western astrology, as it is based solely on the observable patterns of the planets and their correlation with events on Earth.

Mundane astrology tracks the planetary cycles and relates them to the rise and fall of nations, to the development of cities, to politics, to world events, and even to weather patterns. Most of what you see on social media is a form of mundane astrology. When astrologers work with lunar cycles, track the eclipses, consider the implications of Mercury retrograde, or watch a pandemic occur as Pluto and Saturn conjunct, they are practicing mundane astrology.

Electional Astrology

Electional astrology is sometimes called "event astrology." When astrologers choose an auspicious date and time to begin a particular endeavor, they are using electional astrology. Historically, this was used to schedule times to go to battle and to crown kings. It is now most commonly used to determine when to begin a trip, start a business, or commit to a marriage.

There are four types of electional astrology:

- **Ephemeral elections:** These are what most of us think of when we speak of electional astrology. They involve choosing a date and time for an event based on the positions of the planets at that time.

- **Radical elections:** These take into consideration the natal chart of the person for whom the election is being determined.

- **Mundane elections:** These consider the natal chart of the city or state of the occurrence as part of the choice.

- **Magical elections:** These use talismans and charms that are imbued with the qualities of the auspicious date and time they were created.

Horary Astrology

Horary astrology is the branch least used today. It involves the divination or fortune-telling side of astrology. The simple idea behind it is that the answer to any question is apparent in the moment that the question is asked. Therefore, horary astrologers cast a chart for the moment a question is asked, and the answer is determined through an understanding and reading of the patterns contained in the chart of that moment. At certain historical times, this was the most common form of astrology. In recent times, it has fallen out of use due, in part, to its complex and rather archaic rules.

Western Humanistic Astrology

Within the four branches of Western astrology, individual practitioners develop their own personal approaches. I have hesitated over the years to put a label on the type of astrology I practice. Yet, I am aware that all that I have read and studied over the years has come together into an amalgamation of thoughts, ideas, and techniques that comprise my own unique personal approach. Over time, I have come to identify that approach most closely with psychological and humanistic astrology.

The term "humanistic astrology" was first introduced by Dane Rudhyar in the 1930s and later developed in Michael Meyer's *Handbook for the Humanistic Astrologer*. Rudhyar was powerfully influenced by Marc Edmund Jones, who brought an understanding of psychology to the more predictive traditional astrological thought. Rudhyar's work marked a major shift in the Western astrological perspective of the time. Rather than seeing various factors in the birth chart as "good" or "evil," he saw the potential within the chart for learning, self-development, and growth. He understood, and showed us, the connection between the immense complexity within each human being and the equally immense complexity within the patterns of the cosmos. He saw the potential for Western astrology to be, in itself, a symbolic language based on the experiences that are common to living life as a human on planet Earth.

Humanistic astrology is not a separate branch of Western astrology, but rather an approach within the Western tradition that emphasizes a person's potential for self-realization, self-understanding, and psychological development. It focuses on astrology as a tool for personal growth and self-actualization, rather than as a method of predicting events and determining fate.

11

Humanistic astrologers believe that the chart reveals the full potential of the life of the native (owner) of the chart. I view humanistic astrology as a spiritual discipline that emphasizes an individual's potential for growth and development, and even offers a path of alchemy by facilitating transformative change. Using astrology in this manner provides a path to the soul's evolution. It links us with the cosmos, highlighting and illuminating the connections between us. Looking into the mirror of the cosmos, we see ourselves, our beauty, our warts, our struggles, and our potential.

Thinking Humanistically

Consider your own natal chart, printed out on a two-dimensional sheet of paper. As you read this book, I recommend having it (along with the natal charts of your loved ones) in front of you. Slow your mind and your breathing as you deeply consider the moment in time that your chart represents. How does the image, with its complex network of symbols, represent the immense complexity of your inner nature and your outer life?

Imagine the scene of your birth as it played out in a hospital or perhaps a quiet room in the home dedicated to the event at hand. Your mother has just given birth. Ideally, another loving parent is standing by her side in profound awe at the wonder of the event. Perhaps your grandparents, aunts, uncles, or family friends are nearby or at home waiting by the phone for the call announcing your arrival. Perhaps you have siblings who hear the news when they wake in the morning, knowing instinctively that their lives will never be the same. Neighbors and friends text and call each other with the news: "The child has arrived; mama is doing well; the baby is healthy."

As you take your first breath, air enters your lungs and your first cry announces your arrival. Imagine a tiny sliver of time—one instant removed from the entire river of time—given to you, the newborn. That moment is yours to decipher, to grapple with, and to understand. You will receive the gifts of that moment, as well as the wounds that need to be healed. The occasion of your first breath is indelibly imprinted upon your heart, your mind, and your soul. In that moment, you are given full responsibility to love, honor, and respect the unfolding of this one precious human life.

Your mother, father, siblings, extended family, neighbors, and friends all hold a place in your chart, represented by the Sun, the Moon, and the inner or personal planets—Mercury, Venus, and Mars. This first level of influence derives from the intimate world of those who immediately surround you.

Beyond this tight circle of family and friends, your growth is supported or thwarted in the coming years by the community, the religious or spiritual organizations, and the municipality into which you are born. This second level of influence is represented by the social planets, Jupiter and Saturn.

The outer planets represent the forces beyond your perception that will ultimately impact you in ways that are far-reaching and profound. These planets—Uranus, Neptune, and Pluto—move very slowly and represent generational cycles, the rise and fall of governments and cultures. They reflect the differences between generations that are inherent in large planetary and cultural shifts. Because they are so far removed from Earth, these planets are invisible to the naked eye.

Discovering the Natal Chart

For most of us, the zodiacal signs are the initial hook that draws us into the study of natal astrology. It is easy to see why. If your new friend's birthday is in early January, you know that person is a Capricorn. If someone's birthday is in mid-April, you know that person is an Aries. This in itself gives you tantalizing information. Your curiosity about the people who populate your life is instrumental in drawing you inexorably toward astrology.

If this interest persists and you don't get stuck within the intrigue of cycles, eclipses, and all things mundane, the next thing you reach out to understand is the horoscope—the birth chart itself. The first time you see a birth chart, you discover that you have stepped into something mysterious and unknown. A secret language calls you forward, leading you to understand your horoscope as a map of the heavens at the moment of your first breath. As your focus turns to the planets, you see that each one speaks through the sign it is in, providing deeper understanding. It is a fun and exciting process to put these two pieces of the puzzle together, and you can engage in all kinds of interesting considerations. What would it be like to have Mars in Cancer or Mercury in Scorpio? In which sign was your mother's Moon, and how was that reflected in her abilities or challenges in mothering?

It is fascinating to reflect on what you see in the personalities of those around you. Your sister, born in the Sun-ruled sign of Leo, is loud and brash and always finds herself in the spotlight. No wonder you, without a single planet in water signs, never understood your mother, who was born in deep winter, with the Sun and Mercury in the sign of Pisces and her Moon in Cancer. She was sweet and kind, as well as a bit spacey. She doesn't quite seem to belong on this rough and tumble planet. What would that combination feel like? It is hard to imagine, and yet the consideration helps you to understand your mother in a way that you have never been able to in the past. Through this process, you realize the power of astrological understanding to help us develop compassion and understanding toward others. This is one of the great superpowers we receive through the understanding of natal astrology.

As you continue observing your circle of family and friends, it all seems to make sense—until you run into someone new. When you meet new people, before you know the date of their birth, you may watch them and try to think it through. It's not really that you are trying to guess, so much as that you are testing your skills of perception and understanding. This new friend is loud, direct, self-confident, and dynamic. Imagine your surprise to discover that person was born in early March when the Sun was in Pisces! What went wrong?

Nothing went wrong. It's just that you lack the full picture. Underneath an exterior that does not show the core Pisces self is the sensitive mystical nature of the two fishes. Knowledge of the full chart will fill in the picture and provide the necessary information and understanding.

Reading a Natal Chart

Every natal chart you encounter merits careful and meticulous consideration. It's essential to recognize that each one serves as both a reflection of an individual and a moment frozen in celestial time. Imagine it as a snapshot of the universe's grand dance, in which the moving planets come to a standstill and imprint themselves onto, not only the heart and mind of a person, but also onto a two-dimensional chart.

When you hear discussions about challenging eclipses or dramatic planetary aspects happening in the current week or month, remember that these celestial events become ingrained in the birth charts of those born during the time frame in question. Reflect on significant historical moments, like the tragic assassination of Martin Luther King on April 4, 1968, or the fateful day when the Twin Towers fell in New York City. Babies were welcomed into the world on these days, and they each carry the resonance of those historical moments within their very DNA. Whenever astrological events like a Full Moon, an eclipse, or a potent outer-planet transit appear, keep in mind that the children born at these times will carry the impact of those powerful moments into the future.

Regardless of how many natal charts you work with, make a conscious effort to approach each one with fresh eyes and a beginner's mind. Be clear about what you are seeing. A natal chart encapsulates an exact moment in time at an exact location. It shows you a symbolic representation of the positions of planets and significant celestial points at that very moment of birth. It depicts the full potential that began at the moment the chart was cast. It captures a single instant in the ceaseless flow of time.

With each chart you look at, stop and take the time to visualize the one moment—the moment of birth—as a tangible entity detached from the ever-moving river of time, entrusted to the person whose chart it represents. The purpose of each individual's life is to decipher the challenges and potentials encoded within that specific moment, and to accept the associated work, rewards, suffering, and healing inherent in the chart.

Consider the substantial motion depicted in each chart. Picture the planets in motion both before and after birth. Start with the horizon and contemplate the day in question. From our vantage point on Earth, the Sun seemingly rises over the horizon in the morning and sets in the evening. Simultaneously, the actual movement of the planets moves them counterclockwise through the zodiac wheel. Understanding these simultaneous yet distinct movements is essential to avoid confusion and gain deeper insights into the chart's narrative.

The Importance of
Having a System

As with anything that you do over and over that you want to do well, it is important to develop a system when practicing natal astrology. A system is an organized or established step-by-step procedure that follows a fixed plan or set of rules. Reading charts without a well-established system is like randomly throwing spaghetti against the wall. The more often you do a particular thing in a particular manner, the better the results. Eventually, you will hardly have to think about it, and it will become second nature. Your mind learns to operate within the stable system that you have learned to trust over time.

In fact, your overall understanding of natal charts and your confidence in working with them will only be as good as the system you develop to support your confidence and understanding. After all, throwing spaghetti against the wall may be fun, and may even occasionally produce results, but is not a very effective way to get a job done.

Another advantage of having a solid system is that, if you lose your way or fall down a rabbit hole, it is much easier to catch yourself and regain your footing so you can get yourself back on track. If you've ever talked to friends or family members about their charts, you know how easy it is to fall into this trap. There is so much information in each chart that you may find it difficult to identify and address the most important parts. This is not always a bad thing, because you can learn a great deal at the bottom of a rabbit hole. But that is best done on your own, not when you are preparing for a conversation with others about their charts.

Having a clear system in place also ensures the quality of your work. When you enter into a conversation with a friend, family member, or client, it will show you exactly what you need to discuss. This will build your confidence and free your heart and mind to connect deeply with the native of the chart. With your mind free of anxiety and clutter, you can enhance your understanding and tap into your intuition.

Your system for reading a birth chart need not be anything elaborate. It can simply be a list of the steps that you follow as you prepare for the conversations you want to have with those whose charts you are reading. The guideposts given in part 2 comprise the system (the list) that I use with every chart as I prepare for consultation or contemplation. You may find that some of these guideposts resonate with you, while others may not. And that's fine. Just discard the ones that don't work for you, and perhaps add some of your own. The goal is to develop a system that works for you—a system that will support your understanding of each and every chart you encounter. When talking with others about their charts, you want to get to the heart of what is most important. Keep this in mind as you develop a personalized system that works for you.

As you develop your system, remember to keep it simple. Streamline your process in order to focus on what is really important. When you talk to friends, coworkers, family members, or clients about their charts, the less you say, the greater the impact you will have. In fact, I believe that astrologers do their best work when they know a great deal and say very little. When you work with the charts of others, your purpose is to help them understand and see themselves in a more empowered light. Your purpose is never to show how clever you are or how much you know!

Now let's look at some of the factors that can contribute to your understanding a natal chart—houses and house systems, planetary classifications, aspects and orbs, elements, modalities, and orientation.

Houses

This is where things begin to get complicated, so hang on for the ride. If your learning has occurred mostly online and you have immersed yourself in mundane astrology, you may not be very familiar with houses. But houses bring you face to face with the depth and complexity of the art of natal astrology. This is also where it gets more interesting and where your understanding of human nature grows beyond anything you could have imagined.

In Western natal astrology, it is the houses that bring the patterns, eclipses, lunar phases, and cycles of mundane astrology down to Earth. They are the form and structure of the horoscope (chart), displayed on the flat screen or the two-dimensional sheet of paper in front of you.

The signs of the zodiac are set counterclockwise around the circle of the natal chart. Envision the zodiac as a band that wraps around the Earth, following the Sun's (apparent) annual rotation around it. This path is called the "ecliptic." All of the planets travel this path as they circle the Sun. As you look at any horoscope, think of the planets as moving counterclockwise through the chart.

Now imagine the planets in the heavens retaining their positions relative to each other as they drop onto the printed chart in front of you. In fact, there are no "houses" in the cosmos. They have been developed in order to give the horoscope an essential structure that brings the meaning of the planets to our everyday lives.

If the planets moving counterclockwise around the chart were the only movement you had to consider, it would be easy. But as the planets travel through the signs along the path of the ecliptic, the Earth itself is spinning on its axis, and its twenty-four-hour rotation is the movement that determines the placement of the houses. Imagine the Sun's (apparent) movement as it rises over the horizon as day begins. Rather than the counterclockwise motion of the planets moving from sign to sign around the ecliptic, this is seen as a clockwise movement around the chart. The orientation of the houses shifts hour to hour as the Sun rises toward noon at the top of the chart, falls below the horizon at sunset, travels toward the nadir in the middle of the night and rises again at dawn.

It is tricky, but essential, to grasp this dual motion. Don't worry if it doesn't come easily at first or if you sometimes get confused and have to review it. There is a lot of motion going on in the heavens that must be accounted for when conceptualizing a chart. When looking at a horoscope, picture the signs of the zodiac as the backdrop of that motion. The planets move counterclockwise as they traverse the pathway around the Sun. At the same time, they appear to move clockwise in their daily (apparent) movement as they rise over the horizon each morning and fall below it each evening.

The astrological houses divide this path into twelve segments that represent the areas of human life, and this is the structure that grounds the chart to earthly matters. Each house represents a particular area of practical real life. Reading from the first to the twelfth house, the identified areas of life are: self, resources, communication, home, creativity, lifestyle routines, relationships, other people's values, higher understanding, career, community, and the deep unconscious.

Consider your new friend with the hidden Pisces nature. Why is your experience on meeting her not what you would expect of a Pisces? Let's say that Sagittarius was rising in the east at the time of her birth. This places her Pisces Sun in the 4th house (home and family). With Sagittarius rising (see Guidepost 7), Jupiter "rules" the chart (see Guidepost 2). Because Jupiter rules, not only her Sagittarius rising, but also her Pisces Sun, Jupiter is a key player in this chart. And if Jupiter is in the 9th house (higher understanding) in Leo, it is this expansive Leo exuberance that you encounter when you meet this person. Nonetheless, regardless of your experience or the personality she projects, the sensitive imaginative nature of Pisces is hidden deep in her core. With her Pisces Sun in the 4th house (home), her family will certainly see it.

House Systems

House systems are a complex topic among astrologers. Because they are a structure imposed by humans, everyone has an opinion on how the divisions should be created and conceptualized, and how they should be organized. Keep in mind, however, that there are no dividing lines in the cosmos. The most important thing to understand is that whatever house system you choose will work for you.

In my early thirties, I hit a metaphorical wall in my astrology studies. At the time, the Placidus house system was the one generally agreed upon and the one I encountered in my studies. (I won't explain this system in more detail here, but you can find information about it online if you are curious.) I had not initially known there were any other house systems, much less many others. I could not get my mind beyond the duality of "right" and "wrong." In my limited way of thinking at the time, if one house system was right—well, the others had to be wrong. And if, despite the long history of this art, astrologers themselves couldn't settle on one correct house system, I wasn't having any of this crazy study!

In retrospect, that was when I should have searched for a teacher. A teacher would have been a godsend. Instead, my (Aries Moon) quick-triggered frustration prompted me to pack up all my astrology books and store them in the basement. The topic of house systems frustrated and confused me so much that I planned to sell them and never look back.

I am grateful there was not, in those days before the Internet, an easy way to sell those books. For several years, I remained stuck in my confusion, but the call to the charts was strong and, eventually, I brought them up from the basement. When I did so, I promised myself that I was going to choose a house system and never look back.

Since I had begun with the Placidus system and it was the one most commonly used at the time, I settled on that. I successfully ignored thinking about other house systems for many, many years. This was a good strategy for me in the short run, but not in the long term. Ultimately, all astrologers must grapple with the topic of house systems.

And sure enough, in 2014 or 2015, my unwillingneess to consider other house systems caught up with me. As more and more people began questioning the Placidus system, I began hearing conversations about another house system called the Whole Sign system, one in which the sign boundaries also create the boundaries of the houses so the signs line up perfectly with them. And the more I heard and read about it, the more intrigued I became. I read everything that I could regarding houses and house systems. Eventually, I started working with client charts in both the Placidus and Whole Sign systems while considering the differences.

But first, I had to accept that choosing one system did not make other systems wrong. Once I understood that each house system was simply a different filter through which to examine individual human lives, I could take a more balanced view. In fact, accepting my own chart as presented in the Whole Sign system helped me to get over a personal hurdle and led me into deep waters where I experienced profound emotional healing, growth, and self-understanding. Over the next few years, I came to embrace this system and have found it to be highly reliable and deeply satsifying. As a bonus, it is far easier to learn and to teach.

Planetary Classifications

In modern Western astrology, there are two luminaries and eight planets. If you like, or feel the need to, you can add asteroids, fixed stars, the Part of Fortune, Black Moon Lilith, the vertex, Arabic parts, and even the kitchen sink. But I recommend sticking with the eight planets and two luminaries, at least for now. As you deepen your understanding, you may want to bring more into the picture, but do so sparingly and begin with Chiron. You already have plenty to manage, and it's important not to take on more information than you can absorb without becoming overwhelmed and frustrated, or losing focus on what is most important.

The planets are generally divided into four classifications—the lights or luminaries, the personal planets, the social planets, and the transpersonal planets.

- *The lights or luminaries*—the Sun and the Moon—are the heart and soul of every chart.

- *The personal planets*—Mercury, Venus, and Mars—are, along with the Earth, relatively close to the Sun and represent the most personal expression and characteristics of the native.

- *The social planets*—Jupiter and Saturn—are farther away from the Sun, but still visible to the naked eye. They act as a bridge between the inner (personal) and outer (transpersonal) planets, and represent social structures and dynamics.

- *The transpersonal planets*—Uranus, Neptune, and Pluto—are not visible to the naked eye and are far distant from the Sun. They are associated with collective and transpersonal influences that extend far beyond the individual.

Although you may encounter different classifications in other sources, what I use here is a commonly accepted and useful system.

One way to envision the role of these four classifications is to view the Sun and Moon as the heart and soul of the individual, and also representing the parents in early childhood. The personal planets can be viewed as sisters, brothers, cousins, and close friends. The social planets extend beyond the family unit and involve relationships in the community, local government, religious organizations, and social circles. The transpersonal planets extend to the larger forces of governments, and international and global concerns. The importance of these classifications on the natal chart, particularly as it relates to retrograde motion, will become abundantly apparent as we explore the guideposts in part 2.

For now, let's just take a brief look at how each of these classifications influences the chart.

Lights or Luminaries

The combination of the Sun and the Moon in the natal chart forms the initial and most distinct statement of the personality. In astrology, we treat these as if they were planets, even though they are not. A planet is defined as a celestial body that orbits a star. The Sun, on the other hand, is called a star because it produces its own energy through the fusion of gasses. In a sense, however, the Sun is our personal star, because the Earth and all the other planets are held in place by its gravitational pull. Because the Moon orbits the Earth rather than a star, it is a satellite. In astrology, we simply call the Sun and the Moon the lights or luminaries. The combination of these two bodies and the relationship between them are the first and most personal statement that any chart makes. With the Moon covering approximately 12° to 13° each day, the span between the Sun and the Moon changes constantly and rapidly. Because the lights are not planets, they are never in retrograde motion (see Guidepost 11).

Personal Planets

The personal planets are Mercury, Venus, and Mars. Even those born within weeks or months of each other will have very different sign placements and aspects to these relatively fast-moving planets.

Mercury's egg-shaped orbit is quick and erratic. It travels the ecliptic in eighty-eight days and, as we will see in Guidepost 11, appears to reverse direction (moves retrograde) three or four times each year, with each retrograde period lasting approximately three weeks. So clearly a lot of babies are born each year with Mercury retrograde. Because Mercury's orbit is closer to the Sun than our own, it is never more than 28° from the Sun in a natal chart.

Venus travels the ecliptic in 225 days. It too is closer to the Sun than we are, and will never be found more than 48° from the Sun in a natal chart. Every eighteen months, Venus appears to pause (stations) and reverse direction (moves retrograde) for approximately six weeks, so this planet appears retrograde much less often than Mercury in a natal chart.

Mars travels the ecliptic in 687 days. This is the first planet outside Earth's orbit around the Sun. For approximately nine weeks every two years, Mars appears to move in retrograde motion.

Social Planets

Jupiter and Saturn hold the space between the personal and transpersonal planets. Because they occupy this middle space, they are also referred to as the "bridge" planets.

Jupiter takes nearly twelve years to traverse the ecliptic—11.86 years to be exact. It moves in retrograde motion for approximately four months each year. Saturn takes nearly twenty-nine years to cover the distance of the ecliptic, and appears to move in retrograde motion for approximately four and a half months each year (see Guidepost 4).

Transpersonal Planets

The transpersonal planets are Uranus, Neptune, and Pluto. Because they are very far away from us here on Earth, these planets are seen as remote, abstract, and impersonal. They are called the "generational planets" because they travel so slowly through the zodiac that even those born years apart can have the same sign placements. The slow movement of these outer planets produces similarities within generations rather than between individuals. For instance, you can likely assume that everyone in a high school graduating class will have Pluto, Neptune, and Uranus in the same sign. The personal significance of these planets comes through the aspects they make to the personal and social planets, and to other sensitive points in the natal chart, rather than the sign they are in.

Uranus takes eighty-four years to travel the entire distance of the ecliptic and appears in retrograde motion for approximately five months each year. Neptune takes 165 years to orbit the Sun and remains in retrograde motion between five and six months each year. Pluto takes 248 years to travel the full distance of the ecliptic and moves in retrograde motion for approximately six months each year.

Aspects and Orbs

Aspects are the angles that planets make to each other in a chart. They indicate the relationships formed between planets or specific points in a natal chart, based on the relative distances between them. I recommend sticking with the five major aspects, also known as the Ptolemaic aspects—conjunctions (0° separation), sextiles (60° separation), squares (90° separation), trines (120° separation), and oppositions (180° separation). Sextiles and trines are considered "aspects of ease," which facilitate a smooth flow of energy. Squares and oppositions are considered "aspects of challenge," which can inhibit or restrict energy flow. Conjunctions are relationships that allow the specific energies of two or more planets to blend and merge.

There are many minor aspects—for instance, semi-sextile, quincunx, quintile, bi-quintile, semi-square, sesqui-square, semi-quintile, and septile—and you can certainly add these for more information. But ask yourself first if it will add anything important to your understanding. Bringing in more aspects often simply muddies the water and distracts from the most important information in a chart, which likely is perfectly clear when using the major aspects.

I recommend that you set the preferences of your astrology program so that charts are printed with an aspect grid, but without aspect lines drawn between the planets. Use colored pens and a straight edge to draw these aspects by hand. This will connect your mind to the movement of energy between the planets. Use a red pen to draw the lines for squares and oppositions and a blue pen for sextile and trines. As you draw in the aspects, the relationships at play will be clearly displayed on the page, and you can almost feel the incredibly powerful dynamic they represent.

The term "orb" refers to the allowable distance between two celestial bodies or points in a horoscope that still permits their aspect to be effective. The orb essentially provides a margin of flexibility, acknowledging that the effects of planetary interactions are not confined to exact angles, but extend within a certain range.

For example, a square aspect is typically 90°. But with an orb of 6°, the square's influence could be felt anywhere from 84° to 96°. The orbs used by various astrologers can vary widely, but it is generally understood that the closer the aspect is to being exact, the stronger its influence.

I recommend not allowing your orbs to become too broad—limiting them to between 6° and 8°. Over time, you will learn what works best for you. If there are very few aspects in a chart, extending the orbs can provide more information.

Elements

The twelve signs are divided into four elements consisting of three signs each, and each element indicates a distinct method of response that will be characteristic of the native of a chart. We'll return to elements and the role they play in balancing the various influences found in a chart in Guidepost 10. Here, we'll just look at their general characteristics and their impact on the individuals involved.

Fire signifies a fast, automatic response. Earth suggests a consistent, unwavering response. Air signifies an intellectual response. Water suggests an emotional response. The balance of elements within a natal chart exerts its influence on the way an individual reacts to different situations, other people, and environments.

An absence of one element in a chart can result in an increased emphasis or reliance on one of the other elements. This can create imbalances in an individual personality and affect the ability of that person to respond to situations in an appropriate manner.

Fire—Aries, Leo, Sagittarius

Fire is a potent force and one that must be handled with care. It ignites creativity, inspires spontaneity, encourages boundless enthusiasm, and prompts an unwavering passion for life. It serves as the wellspring of creativity, initiative, and unyielding courage. Fire embodies idealism, visionary thinking, assertiveness, motivation, dynamism, and inspiration, but it can also result in irritability and a quick temper.

Individuals with a heavy focus on the fire element respond physically and quickly to stress or stimulation. They often act on impulse, prioritizing action over the assessment of its practical or emotional consequences. To maintain stability, they require physical outlets like intense exercise, structured disciplines like martial arts, and competitive activities. Providing a means for them to release their abundant energy is crucial. In order for fire to thrive, it must express itself freely and receive recognition for achievements, but this can mask a debilitating fear of being overlooked.

An immature expression or an overabundance of this element can lead to egotism, selfishness, self-indulgence, fanaticism, unnecessary risk-taking, or impulsiveness. When very little or no fire is present in a chart, the person is likely to struggle with lack of initiative, passion, and enthusiasm.

Earth—Taurus, Virgo, Capricorn

Earth possesses a deep understanding of the essential requirements for living in a physical body. It holds qualities of grounding, stability, unwavering determination, and a steadfast commitment to practical objectives. This element's nature is characterized by practicality, composure, tenacity, stubbornness, and a resistance to change. It focuses on producing tangible, real-world results.

Individuals with a prominent earth influence are marked by their remarkable persistence and enduring patience. They evaluate circumstances through a practical lens and anticipate tangible acknowledgment for their efforts. They approach life with logic, and reject sentimentality or even excessive passion or excitement. Regardless of the time it takes, they persistently pursue their goals with unwavering patience and determination. To thrive, they must establish a connection with the tangibility of the

Earth itself through activities like gardening, pottery, massage, cooking, or time spent in nature.

An immature expression or an overabundance of this element can manifest as materialism, excess caution, and fearfulness. Issues related to control, resource hoarding, and possessiveness can be a problem. A chart with little or no earth may suggest struggles to feel embodied. Caring for the physical body and successfully engaging with the practical realities of life can be difficult to achieve.

Air—Gemini, Libra, Aquarius

Air is the element of the mind and intellect, making it the most human of the four elements. It embodies objectivity, perceptiveness, a focus on ideas and concepts, and the ability to observe external events from a neutral point of view.

Individuals with a strong presence of the air element in their charts tend to have an intellectual orientation and a natural inclination toward education and communication. They naturally gather information in order to form concepts, ideas, and opinions. To thrive, they must actively work on developing their capacity for objectivity, rational thinking, and effective communication. In practical matters, they will do well to recognize that what works in theory may not always work in practice.

An immature expression or an overabundance of this element can result in detachment, superficiality, aloofness, coldness, and/or anxiety. Those whose charts have little or no air may find it challenging to articulate their thoughts, maintain objectivity, or come up with innovative solutions.

Water—Cancer, Scorpio, Pisces

Water represents emotion, depth, and sensitivity. Those with strong water energy are highly attuned to emotion and naturally grasp the motives and feelings of others. They are guided by feelings, react and respond emotionally, and allow intuitions and impressions to guide their choices. They can follow their emotions to great heights of inspiration or into deep wells of loneliness or despair. The emotional environment of childhood significantly impacts their well-being as adults. It's important that they learn healthy methods of self-care. Water thrives on forming strong emotional connections and finds solace and comfort in music, poetry, and introspection.

An immature expression or an overabundance of this element can result in the tendency to absorb negativity from others and a struggle to establish healthy boundaries in relationships. They may also tend toward emotional dependence, and may hinder growth and happiness by holding on to sentimentality or nostalgia. Charts lacking in water energy suggest struggles with feeling, understanding, or expressing empathy and love.

Modalities

The twelve signs are further broken down into three modalities consisting of four signs each—cardinal, fixed, and mutable. We will discuss them in more detail in Guidepost 10. For now, let's just consider how they help to define the different ways in which individuals approach the circumstances and people they encounter in their environment. The cardinal signs are Aries, Cancer, Libra, and Capricorn. The fixed signs are Taurus, Leo, Scorpio, and Aquarius. The mutable signs are Gemini, Virgo, Sagittarius, and Pisces.

The cardinal modality suggests a very direct approach of beginning a process and pushing it forward. The fixed modality suggests a focus on maintaining and keeping things as they are. The mutable modality suggests a more flexible and adaptable approach with an eye toward modification and change.

Cardinal Signs—Aries, Cancer, Libra, Capricorn

The cardinal signs must get things started, create, and make things happen. Each cardinal sign occurs as each new season begins. These signs are active, ambitious, forceful, assertive, independent, and self-motivated. They are strong-willed and contain what is necessary to initiate something new, to give birth, and to generate momentum. Each cardinal sign is assertive within its own element. Aries brings enthusiasm and passion to the table (fire). Cancer brings emotional awareness (water). Libra makes social connections occur (air). Capricorn makes practical tangible things happen (earth).

Fixed Signs—Taurus, Leo, Scorpio, Aquarius

The fixed signs are responsible for preserving and maintaining. They are consistent, purposeful, patient, willful, powerful, and persistent. They bring forth what is needed to maintain what the cardinal signs begin. They come at the midpoint of each season. Each fixed sign maintains and holds steady, with sheer force of will, what is embodied by its element. Taurus maintains the structures that Capricorn builds (earth). Leo maintains the passion and enthusiasm that Aries begins (fire). Scorpio maintains the emotional awareness that Cancer initiates (water). Aquarius is tasked with maintaining the intellectual and social conversations that Libra introduces (air).

Mutable Signs—Gemini, Virgo, Sagittarius, Pisces

The mutable signs must release, change, and adapt in preparation for letting go or changing direction. These signs are flexible, adaptable, and able to change tactics. They are quick on their feet and can see many sides to an issue. The mutable signs come at the end of the season and are necessary for releasing what is no longer needed in preparation for what is to come.

Each mutable sign changes something that is fundamentally related to the element of that sign. Gemini gathers more information, releasing the intellectual hold of Aquarius (air). Virgo analyzes details in order to understand what needs to be reconfigured in Capricorn's structures (earth). Sagittarius seeks out new experiences, thereby breaking down the hold of Leo's passion (fire). Pisces's imagination and dreams allow the powerful emotions of Scorpio to adapt and release (water).

Orientation

The twelve signs are broken down into two orientations consisting of six signs each. In the past, the orientations of the signs were referred to as "genders," symbolizing the yin and yang of the universe. The orientations represent fundamentally distinct perspectives on circumstances and people. We'll talk more about them in Guidepost 10 when we consider signature signs.

Signs with outward (yang) orientation—Aries, Gemini, Leo, Libra, Sagittarius, and Aquarius—are active expressions. They are assertive, outgoing, and expressive. This is the centrifugal force of the universe, which includes the fire and air signs.

Signs with inward (yin) orientation—Taurus, Cancer, Virgo, Scorpio, Capricorn, and Pisces—are passive, receptive, reflective, inward, and yielding. This is the centripetal force of the universe, which includes the earth and water signs.

Preparing for a Reading

When you schedule a time to talk with someone about their chart, set aside the time you need to prepare. With practice, you will be able to prepare a chart in twenty to thirty minutes. And if you use the same system each time, you will train your mind and create a simple and highly efficient process. While you are learning, give yourself as much time as you need. I'd be embarrassed to admit the amount of time I spent preparing for readings in my early days of working with clients!

You have already done the most important preparation of all by devoting hours of study to the craft of astrology. Moreover, all the life experiences you have gathered over the years will be central to your success—including all your efforts at self-development, as well as all that you have lived, felt, experienced, and suffered. The internal job of living is the most important thing you can bring to all your relationships and to every conversation you have about astrology.

When you speak with another about their chart, you act as an interpreter of the cosmos. You become a link between universal wisdom and the very real human before you. Don't underestimate the responsibility of your task or the power of your words. Never take them lightly. Bring all of yourself unreservedly to the table with deep compassion, full acceptance, and endless kindness.

Consider your own responses to different signs or planet combinations. Know yourself. Perhaps every time you see the Moon conjunct Uranus you think of your first girlfriend who brutally broke your heart. If the thought of Pisces brings your mother to mind or the thought of Sagittarius brings up images of your problematic brother, consciously set those judgments aside.

Remember that what you experienced with your Moon-conjunct-Uranus girlfriend involved much more than that one aspect in her chart. The problems likely concerned aspects between your two charts, or transits (ongoing planetary movements) that one or both of you were going through at the time of the break-up. Do what you need to in order to remove the judgment of any particular aspect, sign, or house placement from your mind.

It is very common to equate signs with certain people that you know, and gleaning colorful stories from those relationships can be a helpful tool. These stories can bring the qualities of the signs to light in powerful ways and become the most memorable parts of your conversations with others as you work with their charts. Stories are important tools in your toolbox. Develop them and toss away personal judgments about any signs, placements, or aspects. In order to do justice to any natal chart or to the native of the chart, you must approach it with an open mind that is clear of judgment.

Implementing Your System

When it comes time to prepare for a reading, settle your mind. Get to know what works best for you to create a flow state. Maybe twenty minutes of meditation or a twenty-minute walk gets you there. Maybe burning a bit of sage or listening to chant-like music does the trick. Everyone is different and there is no "right" or "wrong" way to go about this. Once you find your mind in flow, it will be easy to absorb what you need from the chart.

Gather pens and paper for taking notes, as well as the natal chart you are considering. Prepare a cup of tea, a glass of kombucha, or a glass of wine. If silence doesn't work for you, try playing some inobtrusive background music—1990s ambient space music is oddly delightful for studying the planets! Set aside all judgments of yourself and the person whose chart you are exploring.

Remember the *Choose Your Own Adventure* children's books that were popular in the 1980s? Think of the seventeen guideposts in part 2 as one of them. Your job is to decide which of the steps you want to include in your system of preparation and presentation. As you are learning, I recommend that you use them all as many times as you need to in order to get a clear idea of which ones work best for you and which ones you want to set aside. Over time, you will likely add some that are not included here as well. The important thing is to have a clear and specific system that you go through each time with each chart. The more times you work with charts in the very same manner, the more proficient you will become.

Comments and Caveats

Before moving on to part 2 of this book, there are two important things you need to know.

In my descriptions of the guideposts that follow, I use the charts of a number of individuals to illustrate the points under discussion. I derived the birth information given for those individuals from either the professional astrology software *IO Series* or from the astro-databank found at *astro.com*. In all cases, it is the most accurate information available at the time of this writing. Be aware, however, that new information surfaces all the time, and that updated birth information can radically affect the interpretation of a given chart.

Many practicing astrologers today feel the need to make clear distinctions between different schools of study. If you prefer psychological astrology, you may struggle to bring in more traditional ideas, and vice versa. For myself, I am a big proponent of using techniques that work. Where they come from is of secondary importance. I encourage you to explore both traditional and modern techniques, and to experiment with ways to make your readings deeper and more meaningful for both you and your clients. Take the time to read a variety of authors and examine many perspectives. This will give you a wide range of knowledge and a variety of ideas you can bring to your craft.

In 1993, an initiative called Project Hindsight began under the direction of Robert Schmidt, Ellen Black, Robert Zoller, and Robert Hand. This project was dedicated to making the primary source texts of Western astrology accessible in modern English translations, an effort that has added a vital dimension to the art and profoundly changed the landscape of today's practice.

Today, thanks to this initiative, students new to astrology can choose to focus their studies on either modern or traditional techniques. My personal journey with astrology predated Project Hindsight, so I did not have access to primary sources on traditional astrology for many years. Consequently, my foundational knowledge and understanding stem from modern, more psychological, astrological techniques. Nonetheless, it's essential to recognize that a mutual exchange of insight and understanding between psychological and traditional astrology can deeply enrich both approaches. By blending components of the two, you can expand and optimize your understanding of the natal horoscope. This is particularly true when considering the first two guideposts.

Traditional and modern astrology offer distinct approaches to understanding and interpreting the influence of celestial bodies on human life. Traditional astrology is rooted in historical practices and emphasizes a more deterministic, event-oriented perspective. Modern astrology, on the other hand, embraces a more psychological and humanistic approach and focuses on personal growth and self-awareness. Both branches provide valuable insights. I firmly believe in blurring the lines between these approaches in order to find what works best, as you will see as you move on to part 2 of this book.

PART II

Guideposts for Understanding

Sect—Diurnal and Nocturnal Charts

Traditional astrology draws a distinction between diurnal (daytime) and nocturnal (nighttime) charts. This distinction is called "sect" (see Figure 1). I have found that even a very simplistic use of sect is helpful in understanding the individual whose chart is under consideration. For an in-depth discussion of how to work with sect when reading a chart, I recommend Demetra George's excellent book *Ancient Astrology in Theory and Practice*. For our purposes here, we'll keep it very simple.

Sect	Power Luminary	Most Beneficial	Most Challenged
Day Chart	Sun	Jupiter	Mars
Night Chart	Moon	Venus	Saturn

Figure 1. Diurnal and nocturnal signs by sect.

Daytime vs. Nighttime Charts

The discovery of the simple difference between daytime and nighttime charts came as a surprise and a delight to me after many years of study. Because this distinction is such a powerful and important one, I feel I must include it here as the very first guidepost. I encourage you to train yourself to recognize this in your first glimpse of any chart.

Choose one of the many charts you have examined over your years of study—preferably one with which you are not terribly familiar—and pay attention to the first thing that draws your eye. Consider the child who was born at the moment represented by the chart. Imagine that someone who has been waiting for the birth wraps that baby in a receiving blanket and quickly carries it outside, laying it on a blanket in an open field facing the dome of the heavens. What does the infant see? Although you may be aware of many things, from the perspective of the child, there are probably only one or two things that are clear.

The first thing the newborn sees is darkness or light, and the quality of that darkness or light. Did the birth occur at sunrise? High noon? Sunset? Or has the infant come forth in the dark of night? If the birth took place at night, are the heavens illuminated by a bright Full Moon? A quarter Moon? A tiny sliver of a crescent Moon? Or did it occur in the inky darkness of a New Moon? Will the infant see a glow in the western sky as a remnant of the previous day? Or will it see a glow in the eastern sky as a preview of the dawn ahead?

Now imagine the impact of the time of birth on the personality. If newborns open their eyes to radiant daylight, they tend to exhibit more extroverted traits and a stronger connection to their Sun sign. Conversely, if their first glimpse is of the night's darkness or the ethereal moonlight casting shadows against a blanket of stars that stretches to infinity, they are likely to display more introverted qualities and resonate more strongly with their Moon sign. To assess the influence of the quality of light in a nocturnal chart, observe the relationship between the Sun and the Moon within the chart.

In essence, individuals born during the day—those with diurnal charts— tend to express themselves outwardly and align with their Sun, its sign, its placement, and its conditions. Conversely, those born at night—those with nocturnal charts—lean toward inner contemplation and emotional receptivity, reflecting their deep connection to their Moon, its sign, its placement, and its conditions. This is a simple and powerful first observation. Don't neglect it and don't complicate it. Record it in your notes and move on.

For those born with diurnal charts, the Sun holds the distinction of the "power luminary," Jupiter is the most beneficial, and Mars is the most challenged. For those born with nocturnal charts, the Moon holds the distinction of the "power luminary," Venus is the most beneficial, and Saturn is the most challenged.

GUIDEPOST 2

Planetary Rulers

It is important to understand that astrology, in one form or another, has been around for as long as there have been humans to watch the heavens. Long before the discovery of the outer planets (Uranus, Neptune, Pluto), astrologers had developed an elegant system of planetary rulerships using the planets that were observable from Earth at the time. Therefore, in traditional astrology, the system of rulership involves the luminaries (the Sun and the Moon) and the five planets visible from Earth (Mars, Venus, Mercury, Saturn, and Jupiter) before the discovery of the outer planets.

But before talking about the differences between modern and traditional rulers, let's be clear about what rulership means. Rulership refers to the association between a planet and a sign with which it has a particular affinity. In traditional rulership, the Sun and the Moon rule one sign each, and the visible planets each rule two signs. For example, Mars, as the ruler of both Aries and Scorpio, has qualities that deeply connect with these signs, and individuals with these signs prominent in their charts will exhibit Martian traits more prominently.

Uranus was discovered in 1781, Neptune in 1847, and Pluto in 1930. With these discoveries, astrologers scrambled to reassign and re-envision the traditional system of rulership. By adding the three outer planets, the original symmetry of the system was disrupted. In the intervening centuries, the very meaning of the signs shifted in significant ways due to this change in understanding.

In the traditional system of rulership, the Sun and the Moon rule Leo and Cancer respectively. These signs were considered to be of a very pure expression, given that they were ruled by one of the all-important "lights" and did not share rulership of another sign. Leo holds the pure light of the "luminary of the day"; Cancer holds the pure light of the "luminary of the night." This leaves very little ambiguity as to the meaning of these two signs. On an intuitive level, we understand them as we understand the heavenly lights that pass overhead each day and each night.

Leo and Cancer stand side by side in the zodiac. Moving outward from the Sun and Moon, Mercury is the first planet and it holds rulership of the next two signs, Virgo and Gemini. The next planet, Venus, holds rulership of the two following signs, Libra and Taurus. Mars holds rulership of the two signs that follow it on the zodiac wheel, Scorpio and Aries. Jupiter holds rulership of Pisces and Sagittarius, while Saturn holds rulership of the last two signs, Aquarius and Capricorn. Visualizing this within the zodiac wheel illuminates the simplicity and elegance of this system (see Figure 2).

Figure 2. Planetary rulership on the zodiac wheel.

The key to understanding the differences between the two signs that are ruled by one planet is found in the element of the signs involved. Mercury rules one air sign (Gemini) and one earth sign (Virgo). In both cases, Mercury provides us with a view into how the mind functions. In its rulership of Gemini, the mind is quick and flighty, skimming along the surface

How to Read and Interpret a Birth Chart

with the silvery lightning speed of air. In its rulership of Virgo, the mind slows down. It becomes more practical and analytical, and is tied to the steadfast pragmatic purpose of earth.

Venus also rules one earth sign (Taurus) and one air sign (Libra). In a natal chart, Venus provides an understanding of the native's values regarding love, resources, and beauty. In its rulership of the earth sign Taurus, it conveys values that are concerned with the physical senses, the body, and the sensual and natural world—all very much earth-based. In its rulership of the air sign Libra, it represents values that are aesthetic and ephemeral. Here we encounter the beauty and charm that develop within the mind rather than the body.

Mars rules one fire sign (Aries) and one water sign (Scorpio), providing an understanding of the native's drive, passion, and ability to take direct action in life. In the fire sign of Aries, that drive is simple, direct, hot, and fast. In the water sign of Scorpio, it is complex, emotional, deep, and private.

Jupiter also rules one fire sign (Sagittarius) and one water sign (Pisces), and indicates the native's philosophical bent as well as the call toward growth and expansion. In the fire sign of Sagittarius, the native embraces broad experience and exploration as a way to grow and understand the world. In the water sign of Pisces, the native dreams, aspires, and absorbs awareness in a deeply imaginative manner.

Like Mercury and Venus, Saturn rules one earth sign (Capricorn) and one air sign (Aquarius). Saturn requires that we pay attention to reality, face responsibilities, and work hard. In its rulership of Capricorn, Saturn emphasizes practical responsibility, serious ambition, and hard tangible work. In its rulership of Aquarius, it focuses on the intellectual responsibility and discipline required to support humanitarian freedom.

Of course, the discovery of the outer planets turned this system on its ear as astrologers grappled to incorporate Uranus, Neptune, and Pluto into its elegant framework. For now, it is enough to know that the addition of these planets created a sea-change in the understanding of the signs themselves, and your overall astrological studies are not complete without a basic understanding of these changes. If you have only studied modern psychological astrology, it will take time, study, and an open mind to understand Saturn as the ruler of Aquarius, Jupiter as the ruler of Pisces, and Mars as the ruler of Scorpio. But this understanding is well worth the time and attention you give it.

Because the outer planets (Uranus, Neptune, Pluto) move so slowly, their impact is felt by entire generations. This is why they are called collective or generational planets. People in your aproximate age range or generation will share the same sign placement of these three outer planets. Their personal impact is experienced through the aspects they make to personal planets or points in the horoscope. For example, Pluto in a particular sign identifies the generation to which individuals belong, but says nothing about the individuals themselves. If, however, Pluto forms a powerful aspect to a personal planet or point in their chart, their generation will have an outsized impact on them—or, conversely, they may have an outsized impact on their generation.

Knowing the planet that rules a sign is essential in understanding the relationship of the native to any planet in that sign or the house that holds that sign. If we use only modern rulers, any planets in Scorpio or the house that holds Scorpio will be ruled by Pluto; the house that holds any planets in Aquarius or the house that holds Aquarius will be ruled by Uranus; any planets in Pisces or the house that holds Pisces will be ruled by Neptune. Without using the traditional rulers, the planets and houses involved will be experienced as detached from the native of the chart, as they will be ruled by a generational, not a personal, planet. Consider those with Pisces in the 7th house or Venus in Pisces. This would effectively remove anything personal from their experience of relationship or personal values.

When you use only the modern rulers, the simplicity and elegance of the system break down. But when you focus on the traditional rulers and add the modern rulers as co-rulers, this effectively solves the problem. Combining modern and traditional rulerships yields an entirely different picture. Scorpio is ruled by Mars with Pluto as the co-ruler; the rulership of Aquarius remains with the traditional ruler Saturn, to which we add Uranus as the co-ruler; Pisces is ruled by Jupiter with Neptune as the co-ruler. Blending the traditional and modern systems of rulership enriches them both and provides a more nuanced understanding of the respective zodiac signs.

Essential Dignity

Two foundational pillars of traditional astrology are the principles of sect (see Guidepost 1) and a framework known as "essential dignity," which defines the ability of each planet to function well or poorly in a person's life as determined by its placement within a specific zodiac sign. The classifications known as essential dignities help you determine how well a planet is able to express itself in the sign it inhabits. The four categories of essential dignities are: domicile/ruler, exalted/crowned, detriment/exile, and fall/adversity (see Figure 3).

Planet	Rulership/ Domicile	Exaltation/ Crowned	Detriment/ Exile	Fall/ Adversity
Sun	Leo	Aries	Aquarius	Libra
Moon	Cancer	Taurus	Capricorn	Scorpio
Mercury	Gemini/ Virgo	Virgo	Sagittarius/ Pisces	Pisces
Venus	Taurus/ Libra	Pisces	Aries/ Scorpio	Virgo
Mars	Aries/ Scorpio	Capricorn	Taurus/ Libra	Cancer
Jupiter	Sagittarius/ Pisces	Cancer	Gemini/ Virgo	Capricorn
Saturn	Capricorn/ Aquarius	Libra	Cancer/ Leo	Aries
Uranus	Co-ruler: Aquarius			
Neptune	Co-ruler: Pisces			
Pluto	Co-ruler: Scorpio			

Figure 3. Essential dignity by planet, showing rulership.

A planet is most powerful when positioned in its domicile—the sign it is said to "rule." This planet is said to be "in its dignity." When a planet is in the sign opposite its rulership, it is said to be in "detriment" or "exile." I think of a planet in its detriment as someone whose shoes are too tight, unable to function with any sort of ease or comfort.

The next classification is that of "exaltation," where a planet is also said to be "crowned." This is the sign in which the planet in question functions with an added dose of awareness. Although this condition is not quite as strong as rulership, a planet is delighted to be in its exaltation. The sign opposite the sign of exaltation is the one in which the planet is said to be in its "fall." This is an area of adversity and weakness for the planet.

Having planets in domicile or exaltation certainly gives individuals an advantage in the areas of life that are ruled by these planets. Things simply work out more easily in these areas of life. But when planets are in detriment or fall, this does not mean that they are doomed in the area involved. It just means that they are likely to face more frustration and be required to put more effort into those areas of life.

Rulership of Houses

The concept and implementation of house rulership may initially seem elusive, but it will propel your understanding forward and open an entirely new dimension in each horoscope you consider. The concept itself is very simple.

In the natal chart, there are twelve houses. In the Whole Sign system, one full zodiac sign is held within the borders of each house. Regardless of whether a house has planets in it or not, you must consider the sign and the ruling planet of that sign when seeking to understand the house in question. Although the sign contained within the house has a powerful impact on the matters that the house represents, the planet that rules that sign extends the story and provides important information about the issues of that house.

For example, if Capricorn is held within the 7th house, intimate partnerships will be approached with caution and seriousness. The native's one-on-one relationships will have a distinctly Saturnian feel to them and that person is unlikely to be interested in casual, easy-going, or light-hearted connections, but will seek and attract partners who are ambitious, responsible, traditional, and/or reserved.

In order to gain more information about these individuals' approach and experience in close partnerships, look for the placement of Saturn, the ruler of Capricorn. If you find Saturn in Leo in the 2nd house, consider how that relates to Capricorn in the 7th house. We have already determined that those with this placement will seek responsible, traditional, and serious partners. With the ruler of the 7th in the 2nd house, what constitutes stability in a partnership will certainly include finances and resources. They will likely desire, attract, and be attracted to partnerships with those who are generous (Saturn is in Leo) regarding finances within the relationship.

These individuals will not be satisfied in an intimate partnership with a brilliant but starving artist. They will be attracted to those who appear to be ambitious, self-sufficient, generous, and playful with their resources. But since Saturn is in its detriment in Leo (see Figure 3), it will be difficult for them to find partners who are as generous and playful as desired, while at the same time being serious, traditional, and responsible. You can easily imagine how the desire for a serious responsible partner can clash with someone who is also generous and magnanimous with their money and resources. Due to this conflict, partnerships may require additional effort and be a source of challenge and growth.

On the other hand, individuals with Capricorn in the 7th house and Saturn in Taurus in the 11th may be attracted to partners they meet through organizations, to those who hold leadership positions in their community, or to those who provide them with access to a particular community.

Let's consider the hypothetical chart of an individual with Cancer in the 10th house. The 10th house brings us to issues of career, vocation, and/or social reputation. This person's career will deeply engage the emotions. You can expect to find this person caring for, nurturing, and/or protecting others. Because Cancer is ruled by the Moon, in order to gain additional information, locate the Moon in the chart. If you find the Moon in Taurus in the 8th house, you can anticipate the person's career or reputation involves a practical and tangible manner of navigating "other people's values," "other people's baggage," or "other people's money" (8th house). Because the Moon is exalted in Taurus, you can expect that he or she will receive practical benefits from other people's money or resources.

Learning to incorporate rulership in this way will expand your understanding exponentially. Over time, your mind will follow rulership pathways automatically. As you get comfortable with this process, you can begin to incorporate the aspects other planets make to the ruling planet for more information and even deeper understanding.

Empty Houses

Identifying and working with the planets that rule the houses also answers a common question about empty houses. I can't tell you how often I have heard clients bemoan their empty houses. If they have an empty 7th house, they worry that it means they will never have an intimate partner, or that they are doomed in relationships. If they have an empty 5th house, they worry that they will never have children or have no creative potential. Understanding and working with the planet that rules the house in question fills in the blanks of those empty houses, giving you plenty of information that can soothe these anxieties.

The chart of Monica Lewinsky, born July 23, 1973, at 12:22 PM PDT in San Francisco, California, is a good illustration of the issue of empty houses.

Because Lewinsky's 2nd house is empty, I imagine her looking at her astrologer and asking: "Does this mean I'll never have money?" Looking at her 2nd house of money, resources, and self-worth, you find Scorpio. This immediately cues you to the fact that both finances and self-worth will be issues of deep intensity for her, as well as an area of major change and transformation over the course of her life.

Next, notice that the traditional ruler of Scorpio, Mars, is strongly positioned in Aries, one of the signs that it rules, in the 7th house of partnership. The co-ruler, Pluto, is in Libra in Lewinsky's 1st house. This suggests that intense transformation of her finances and self-worth will come through the polarity of the 1st and 7th angular houses. Intense power dynamics between self and other, as well as the strength to face them clearly—opposition between Mars and Uranus suggesting courage, clarity, and vision—are at the core of her developing self-worth and her ability to create the life she wants with regard to money and resources.

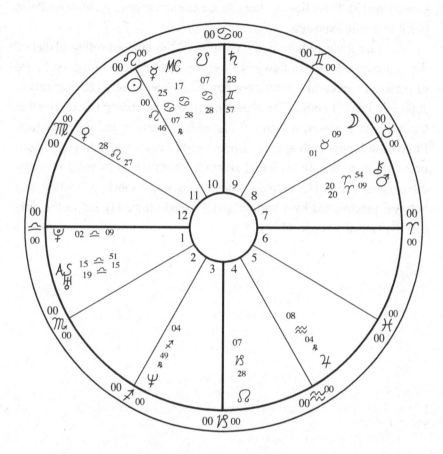

Figure 4: Chart of Monica Lewinsky, born July 23, 1973, at 12:22 PM PDT in San Francisco, California.

Going a bit deeper, note that her Mars, in the 7th house conjunct Chiron, is involved in a T-square (a very tense and challenging aspect pattern that suggests a series of crises, tests, or challenges), opposed by Uranus and square Mercury, which is the closest planet to the Midheaven. Thus you can anticipate that there will be a sudden, unexpected, and very public betrayal by a partner or close friend. Simply noting this and asking pertinent questions would certainly lead to a significant conversation with this woman. The incredibly public cultural impact of her story is further suggested by Pluto square Saturn, each conjunct the Aries Point (see

Guidepost 13). Pluto ties her story to the cultural moment; the Aries Point ties it to public exposure.

Another thing to note is the co-ruler or the modern ruling planet of the 2nd house, Pluto. In Lewinsky's chart, Pluto resides in the 1st house of personal expression, forming a powerful trine aspect (120° aspect) to Jupiter in her 5th house. The abandonment and wounding she received at the hands of a powerful man left her with a dramatic and moving story. Pluto trine Jupiter (ruling the 3rd house of her voice and communication) opens a gift of deeply profound creativity from which to build her self-esteem and wealth. Her dramatic tale of unexpected shock, wounding, and betrayal precipitated by a partner and a friend ultimately led to the gifts that dynamically support her life.

Hemispheres, Quadrants, and Houses

The positioning of the planets within the hemispheres, quadrants, and houses of a natal chart provides valuable information about the way in which we experience the world and express ourselves in it. These positions also provide information about the relative balance or imbalance of our lives. You will often see planets clustered in one hemisphere, one quadrant, or even one house. Understanding the significance of this emphasis offers a gratifying, accurate, and rapid impression of the energies that are operating in the chart.

First, let's examine how these divisions are drawn in the chart.

Drawing the Map

It is important to understand that a horoscope is a map. When you look at a regular map, you get a bird's-eye view of a particular place or region as seen from above. But when you look at a horoscope, you see a depiction of the heavens from *below*. Think again of that baby placed on the blanket moments after birth, looking up into the sky. The map of a horoscope can be loosely thought of as being a view from that perspective.

Because of this, the directions on a birth chart are the opposite of those on an Earth-centered map. When you examine a natal chart, east is on the left, west is on the right, north is at the bottom, and south is at the top. The horizon cuts from left to right, from the Ascendant to the Descendant (see Guidepost 7), through the center of the circle. This is the line that divides day from night.

Houses 1 through 6 represent the northern hemisphere—the hemisphere that falls below the horizon and reflects the inner life of the native. This is what the baby on the blanket cannot see. Houses 7 through 12 represent the southern hemisphere—the hemisphere that is above the horizon and reflects the public life of the native. This is the bowl of the heavens that the baby on the blanket is able to see with its eyes wide open (see Figure 5).

Southern Hemisphere

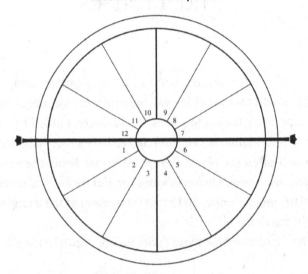

Northern Hemisphere

Figure 5. The horizon, the division between the northern and southern hemispheres.

The meridian cuts through the chart perpendicular to the horizon. This line divides the chart between east (to the left of this axis) and west (to the right of this axis). It separates morning from afternoon above the horizon, and makes a division of the night at midnight below the horizon. The meridian is the symbolic line that separates the individual self from relationships with others.

Houses 10 through 3 represent the eastern hemisphere—the hemisphere to the east of the meridian (seen on the left side of Figure 6) and reflects the personal self of the native. Houses 4 through 9 represent the western hemisphere—the hemisphere that is to the west of the meridian (seen on the right side of Figure 6) and reflects the relationships the native has with others.

How to Read and Interpret a Birth Chart

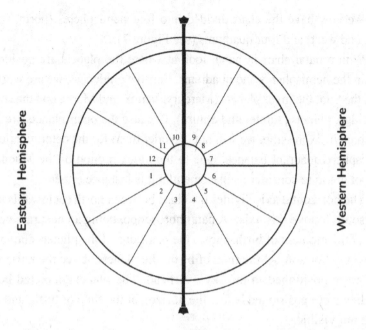

Figure 6. The meridian, the division between the eastern and western hemispheres.

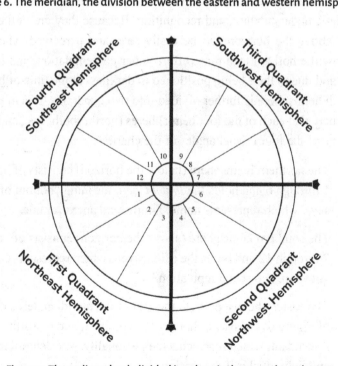

Figure 7. The zodiac wheel, divided into hemispheres and quadrants.

We now have the chart divided into four hemispheres (north, south, east, and west) and four quadrants (see Figure 7).

With a natal chart in hand, look at where the planets are positioned within the hemispheres and quadrants. For this guidepost, we are working with the Sun, the inner planets (Mercury, Venus, and Mars), and the social, or bridge, planets (Jupiter and Saturn). Because the outer planets are generational in expression, we will not consider them for the determination of hemisphere/quadrant balance. Due to the quick motion of the Moon, we are not going to consider its placement in this instance either.

The horizontal axis divides the chart between north (below this axis) and south (above this axis). A natal horoscope, being an accurate depiction of the moment of birth, shows the positions of the planets above and below the horizon. At the time of birth, the planets above the horizontal axis were positioned in the sky overhead. The planets depicted below this line were positioned below the horizon at the time of birth, and thus were not visible.

The horizontal axis separates day from night. Think of it as a line of awareness, understanding, and recognition. Because they are in the light, planets above the horizon can be easily seen and perceived. The planets below the horizon take more effort, inner contemplation, and time to understand due to their being positioned in darkness at the time of birth.

Each hemisphere is further divided into two quadrants. It is important to note here that each of the four hemispheres (north, south, east, and west) holds one of the four crucial angles of the chart.

- The northern hemisphere (below the horizon) consists of houses 1 through 6 and holds the *Imum Coeli*, meaning "bottom of the sky," which represents home, family, and ancestral line.

- The southern hemisphere (above the horizon) consists of houses 7 through 12 and holds the Midheaven, which represents career, vocation, and social reputation.

- The eastern hemisphere (to the east of the meridian, left side of Figure 6) consists of houses 10 through 3, and holds the Ascendant, which represents the personality, self-determination, and individual self-expression.

How to Read and Interpret a Birth Chart

- The western hemisphere (to the west of the meridian, right side of Figure 6) consists of houses 4 through 9, and holds the Descendant, which represents contractual relationships and partnerships.

As you consider a natal chart, envision the planets on the left side of the meridian rising in the eastern sky. Similarly, envision the planets on the right side of the meridian setting in the western sky. Make it a habit to envision this daily movement clearly. Doing so will enhance your understanding by connecting your thought process to the constantly moving planetary cycles.

Emphasis and Life Balance

The determination of hemisphere and quadrant emphasis builds nicely on the immediate impression gained from the analysis of the diurnal and nocturnal planets outlined in Guidepost 1. After all, it makes sense that, if one hemisphere holds all the cards, the angle (or aspect) at its center is going to be a major focal point of the life.

When a chart shows an imbalance in one hemisphere, it can be extremely helpful for the life of the native to bring more attention to the opposite angle. In other words, if too many planets are gathered in the southern hemisphere, encourage the native to focus on developing a connection to the issues of the northern hemisphere.

Let's take a brief look at the respective emphasis and focus of each of the four hemispheres.

Northern Hemisphere

When the northern hemisphere (houses 1 through 6) is emphasized, you can anticipate unfinished business from the early home life. The angle at the center of this hemisphere puts the focus on the family of origin and how the patterns within that family have impacted the life of the native. Much of the adult life may be spent untangling the destructive circumstances of childhood.

Once again, this observation will prompt important questions. Why is this so? What was the issue within the family that has kept so much attention focused on this area? Was there no social safety net? Is this focused attention still needed in the adult life?

Those with the northern hemisphere highlighted tend to focus a good deal of their lives and attention on internal issues and old stories of childhood and family. Turning their attention toward the outer world of the southern hemisphere can yield many benefits. Involving themselves in a new career path, travel, education, or community will go a long way toward bringing more harmony to their lives. Pay special attention to transits that support building a career, a vocation, or a healthy reputation.

Southern Hemisphere

The Midheaven is the focus of the southern hemisphere (houses 7 through 12), which places the emphasis squarely on the outside world, far away from the grounding presence of family and the ancestral home. It is likely that the early lives of those with this placement were somehow unhinged from a solid foundation. As children, they may have been swept away and left to the mercy of the outside world without necessary preparation. They may have been victimized by the outer world—a strong way of putting it, but perhaps appropriate.

Allow this observation to color your questions. Why is this so? How was the native swept away into the outer world? Why was a firm grounding of protection absent in the early life?

Those with a highlighted southern hemisphere tend to be overly focused on career and other accomplishments in the outer world. Supporting and encouraging their deepening involvement with their current experience of home and family—as well as with their family of origin, their ancestral line, and their deep interior life (northern hemisphere)—can bring more balance into their lives. Pay special attention to transits that support inner work, family, and home connections.

Eastern Hemisphere

With an eastern hemisphere emphasis, the planets are gathered in houses 10 through 3, and the Ascendant, as the angle in that hemisphere, is a strong point of focus. Those with this emphasis feel a great need to protect the Self. They often express defensiveness and self-protective behaviors. Think of the planets that are gathered around the Ascendant as doing what they can to bind, sustain, and protect the personality.

This initial observation will generate certain questions. Why is this so? Why do these individuals feel this strong need to protect the Self? From whom (or what) are they protecting themselves? Perhaps this pattern was needed early in this life, but is it needed now?

Encourage these people to develop deeper intimacy and connections with others in order to harmonize their lives. As they shift their focus toward the western hemisphere, their defensiveness will lessen. Pay special attention to and utilize any transits that support healthy relationship-building.

Western Hemisphere

With a western hemisphere emphasis (houses 4 through 9), the planets are gathered around the Descendant, putting the native's focus on others. Those with this emphasis may feel the need to give themselves away in relationships. But with so much attention given to the development of relationships, the Self can be left behind.

This observation brings certain questions to mind. Why is this so? Why do these individuals feel such a powerful need to uplift others rather than themselves? Does this suggest that the Self is being neglected in service to others? Perhaps this was needed early in life, but is it needed now?

Encourage those with the western hemisphere highlighted to bring more attention to themselves. Turning their attention to the eastern hemisphere can help them understand and respond to their own needs, develop deep personal values, and build strong individual personalities. Pay particular attention to transits that support the building of a strong individual identity.

Combinations

The distribution of planets in a chart can sometimes dominate two hemispheres, bringing the focus to one of the four quadrants. Let's take a brief look at the consequences of these combinations.

Northeast Quadrant

With a northeast focus, the majority of planets fall in houses 1 through 3. This suggests that unfinished business from the early home life (northern focus) has resulted in the need to protect the ego and the personality (eastern focus).

Those with a highlighted northeast quadrant place their attention on their inner world, their personality, their personal values, and their own thought patterns. Encourage them to focus on the southwest quadrant through a deep understanding of various worldviews or religions, an appreciation of different values, and a respect for the beliefs of others. Travel, higher education, and the exploration of other cultures will do much to help bring balance to the life.

Northwest Quadrant

In charts focused on the northwest quadrant, the majority of planets fall in houses 4 through 6, suggesting that unfinished business from the early home life (northern focus) has resulted in giving the Self away (western focus). By caring for the needs of others, these individuals may have relinquished the responsibility of caring for the Self.

Those with a highlighted northwest quadrant turn their attention to deeply offering themselves to family and others. Encourage them to develop the southeast quadrant by giving more attention to their careers, their ability to receive support from community, and their understanding of their individual unconscious processes.

Southwest Quadrant

In charts with a southwest quadrant focus, the planets reside predominantly in houses 7 through 9, suggesting that a lack of grounding in early life has resulted in a personal vulnerability to being victimized in the outer world (southern focus). The resulting need to give too much to others leaves these individuals bereft of energy or inclination to care for the Self (western focus).

Those with a highlighted southwest quadrant are naturally focused on loving, supporting, and understanding others through various relationship dynamics. They need encouragement to develop a connection to the northeast quadrant (houses 1 through 3). They will learn a great deal and balance their life directions by developing a stronger understanding of themselves and their personal values, and learning to recognize how they think about and process personal information. Relationships with siblings or neighbors will also help bring balance.

Southeast Quadrant

In a chart with a southeast focus. the planets are gathered in houses 10 through 12, suggesting that these individuals are vulnerable to forces of the outside world (southern focus) due to a lack of grounding in the early home life, resulting in the need for self-protection (eastern focus).

Those with a highlighted southeast quadrant focus their attention on their reputations and careers, on those who support them, and on unconscious forces. Encouraging them to develop the northwest quadrant (houses 4 through 6) by supporting close family connections, personal creativity, and organizational routines can help them build a more balanced life.

Balance and Self-Understanding

We all struggle with the need to create balance in our lives and personalities. When you see one hemisphere or quadrant highly tenanted in a natal chart, you can deduce where an imbalance resides. In order to support those with imbalances, bring their attention to the opposite hemisphere or quadrant. But make your suggestions gently. After all, there will always be things you cannot know. Perhaps personal imbalances help to balance families, communities, or even humanity at large.

Be sure to exercise sensitivity in your choice of words when discussing other people's charts. Avoid making absolute, unyielding statements.

Always ensure that they have room to either embrace or question your observations. Adopt an approach of inquiry and recommendation. The importance of this cannot be overstated.

Ultimately, the responsibility for making definitive statements about themselves or their lives rests solely with the individuals concerned. Try replacing the word "means" with "suggests." This simple change in phrasing can encourage a more open and suggestive dialog rather than asserting absolutes. No matter how much astrology you know, your understanding can never overshadow that of the person whose life you are investigating.

Ask questions and do not make assumptions. Whatever someone's hemisphere emphasis is—and regardless of the suggestion it prompts—remember to step back after making that statement and ask yourself why that is so. What created the circumstances that led to the imbalance you see in the chart?

Every chart you look at belongs to an infant who grew into a child and then an adult. And during the intervening years, that person has encountered many challenges and difficulties. Those challenges and difficulties are simply part of the individual and the human story. The hemisphere emphasis can provide a clear idea of where the core challenges originated—perhaps from unresolved issues in the early home or from being swept unprepared into an unmanageable situation. Either way, there was a problem and a deep difficulty in the early life. Once you see where that problem was initiated, you can begin to question what lies at the root of the imbalance.

It is in the parental relationships that we find the root issues beneath these initial imbalances and difficulties. We can explore them in a chart by working with the condition of Saturn, which represents the paternal role, and the Moon, which represents the maternal role. In Guidepost 4, we will examine some issues tied to paternal role models; in Guidepost 5, we will explore issues tied to maternal role models.

Ideally most of us come into the world with two parents who fulfill the roles of mother and father in our early years. Even if one parent is absent, their ghost remains. To be clear, these roles may not be held by the actual biological mother or father. They may be held by an aunt, an uncle, a grandparent, a step-parent, a family friend—or an invisible ghost.

When you identify the parent or parental figure who may be responsible for an imbalance, discuss it only briefly. Don't get stuck in these problems. Rather bring the attention and responsibility back to the native. For example, let's say you have identified a northern hemisphere focus in your friend's chart. You know that she has deep childhood traumas that she is working with to this day. You see that Pluto is conjunct her Moon. You may briefly ask her about her relationship with her mother or a mother figure in her life, and she may respond with a story of power dynamics. Perhaps she had a deeply damaged or heavily controlling mother. Don't get stuck in the details of the story. Instead, ask her to identify her own internal emotional power issues. Point out that you are not looking at her mother's chart, only hers. It is *her* Moon, *her* Pluto. Her mother is a mirror of her own internal landscape.

How does that change the conversation? How can this observation change your friend's perspective and even her relationship with her mother? Was it that very dynamic that supported her in becoming the incredibly powerful woman she is, perhaps able to work with the deep emotional issues of others?

As humans, we tend to see our mental and emotional landscapes reflected in the mirror of relationships more easily than we see them directly within ourselves. Our inner troubles and strengths are reflected in the outer world; we see them in the eyes of others—our parents, our lovers, our friends. When we come to accept the strengths and demons that reside within us, we have a great opportunity for growth—and often this can be the beginning of powerful inner work.

Now that you understand the importance of hemisphere and quadrant emphasis, it is time to look at the individual houses. The natal chart is divided into twelve houses, each of which represents a different area of life. Each hemisphere holds six houses; each quadrant holds three. These are divided into various classifications. We'll look at these next.

House Classifications

The houses of a natal chart represent specific areas of life. Although it is helpful to memorize keywords and lists of associations for each house, in order to grasp the deeper meaning of the houses, you must understand how they relate to one another. A deep understanding of these classifications can be more helpful to your work than any number of memorized keywords. Here we will look at the complex relationships between the various houses in a natal chart and the classifications into which they fall—including opposition and polarity, the grand cross system, and the functional system.

Opposition and Polarity

Houses that are in opposition to each other are connected much like two sides of the same coin—they reflect polarity, or juxtaposition. The 1st and 7th houses reflect self vs. other. The 2nd and 8th houses denote mine vs. yours. The 3rd and 9th houses represent communication vs. understanding. The 4th and 10th houses reflect home and family vs. career and reputation. The 5th and 11th houses indicate giving love vs. receiving it. The 6th and 12th houses juxtapose the care of the physical body with the care of the mental, emotional, and spiritual body.

These polarities are important in understanding a chart, because they help to explain tensions and issues in the lives of the individuals concerned.

The Grand Cross

This house classification divides the houses into three classifications—the angular houses, the succedent houses, and the cadent houses. Each consists of four houses, two oppositions at a 90° angle to each other. There is a great deal of tension and stress within each of these classifications.

The angular grand cross consists of the 1st, 4th, 7th, and 10th houses. These are the houses positioned at the start of each of the four quadrants. They are the most powerful houses, offering strength and prominence to any planets positioned in them. Always envision them as a cross within the circle of the chart. These houses relate to the four most significant points of the individual's identity—self, home, partner, and social status. They are highly supportive of identity and are areas of action and initiation. Tension in any of them will invariably impact all of them. The angular houses bring together two polarities: self and other (1st and 7th), and home/family and career/public reputation (4th and 10th).

The succedent grand cross consists of the 2nd, 5th, 8th, and 11th houses. These are the houses positioned at the center of each quadrant. Again, visualize them as a cross, understanding that any distress experienced in one will impact them all. The succedent houses relate to the stabilization of resources. They bring together two polarities—personal values vs. other people's values (2nd and 8th), and giving love and creativity vs. receiving love from the community of others (5th and 11th).

The cadent grand cross consists of the 3rd, 6th, 9th, and 12th houses. These are the houses that are positioned at the end of each quadrant. They relate to learning and information. As with the other grand crosses, understand that challenges in any of them will cause ripple effects throughout the others. These houses bring together two polarities—learning and communication vs. worldview and higher education (3rd and 9th), and practical routines and lifestyle that support physical health vs. psychological and spiritual understanding that supports mental, spiritual, and emotional health (6th and 12th).

Functional Houses

The functional houses appear in four groups of three houses that are called "trinities"—the trinity of life, the trinity of substance, the trinity of association, and the trinity of endings. The houses in each of these trinities work together in the chart to define the individual.

The trinity of life consists of houses 1, 5, and 9. Known as the "individual houses," they are concerned with the most personal areas of life. These houses focus on self-development, personal creativity, and the growth of understanding, perspective, and wisdom. In these areas of our lives, we encounter enthusiasm, drive, and inspiration.

The trinity of substance is made up of houses 2, 6, and 10. Called the "houses of wealth," they are concerned with the material realities of life. These houses focus on what is of practical use and the achievement of tangible results. In these areas of our lives, we encounter the use and stabilization of our efforts and resources.

Houses 3, 7, and 11 form the trinity of association, also known as the "relationship houses." These houses are concerned with our ability to communicate, our partnerships, and our social relationships. In these areas of our lives, we learn cooperation and encounter powerful connections to others beyond our immediate family.

The last group is made up of houses 4, 8, and 12. This has been called the trinity of endings, or the "terminal houses." These houses are concerned with issues that pertain to the intense emotional undercurrents of our lives. In them, we encounter our deepest ancestral roots, the need for boundaries between ourselves and others, and the hidden patterns within our hearts and minds.

GUIDEPOST 4

Saturn Retrograde

When we say a planet is retrograde, we mean simply that it appears to be moving backward from our perspective here on Earth. The consequence of this is that the expression of the planet is turned inward. It is in a state of rumination and is unable to function as socially, culturally, or personally expected.

From our perspective on Earth, Saturn appears to be retrograde for approximately four and a half months of each year, so you will find this placement in many of the natal charts you encounter. In fact, the difficulties implicit in this placement are all too common. Therefore, getting comfortable talking about Saturn retrograde can open the door to many rich and meaningful conversations. Humanistic astrologer Noel Tyl has done extensive research on Saturn retrograde—research that brought him to a powerful understanding of how the retrograde motion of this planet manifests in the lives of those who have it in their natal chart.

The Father and Inner Authority

Saturn itself represents necessary controls, authority, leadership, and responsibility. For most of us who grew up in a Western culture, this signifies, among other things, the role of the paternal parent. We encounter Saturn in our relationship with our fathers or other father figures. When Saturn is retrograde in the natal chart, however, it suggests that the paternal figure was absent, or overly passive, or tyrannical, or a combination of these. In one manner or another, the father or father figure was not available, or was inadequate—either incapable or unwilling to provide the steadfast authoritative love, protection, and care children need.

When you come upon Saturn retrograde in a chart, the words you use to discuss it matter. This is one of the most powerful lessons that Noel Tyl taught me. Instead of using words like "tyrannical," or "inadequate," or "unavailable," try using words that are less confrontational and more reassuring: "There is a suggestion in your chart that, when you were a child, your father or father figure was absent, unwilling, or unable to give you the steadfast authoritative love, protection, and care you needed. Let's be clear that this, in itself, does not indicate that he was a bad person or even a bad parent. It simply suggests that you did not receive from him what would have best supported your growth to maturity." This is a powerful statement that you can make with confidence. Then listen carefully to the response you get from the native of the chart.

Be prepared to reiterate that Saturn being retrograde does not mean that the father was a bad person or lacked love for the child. That is something entirely different. Nor does it necessarily mean that the father was not present, was passive, or tyrannical. What it does mean is that the child perceived him in this manner. Remember, you are looking at the chart of the child, not the father. This alone should give you cause to pause and think about issues regarding fate, free will, and personal responsibility.

The house placement of Saturn tells you the area of life in which the child grew up feeling a lack of parental authority. The houses that Saturn rules—those that hold Capricorn and Aquarius—are the areas of life where this lack will leave its stamp and long-term impact. The aspects between Saturn and other planets in the chart offer deeper understanding of the gifts and challenges encountered through the relationship with the father. If the Sun is conjunct, square, or opposing Saturn, you may encounter a similar dynamic. When you find Saturn in challenging aspect to the Sun, you can safely use similar wording and ask similar questions.

In Louis Armstrong's natal chart, Saturn falls in the 10th house, ruling the 10th and 11th (see Figure 8). Saturn is also in its home sign of Capricorn. This is a powerful consideration, indeed. Armstrong's mom was little more than a child when she gave birth to him, and his father left the family shortly afterward. With this Saturn placement, it is likely that his focus on career and reputation (10th house), along with his need to be loved by a community (11th house), were due, in large part, to the lack of paternal involvement. Perhaps he felt the need to prove himself to a father he never knew.

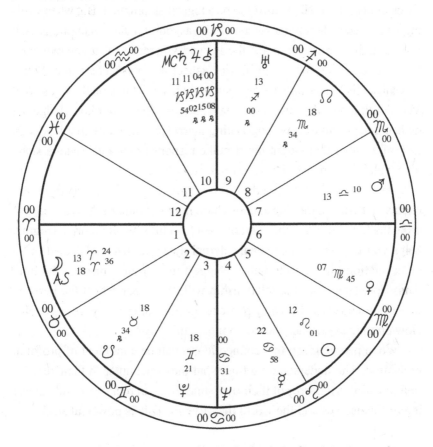

Figure 8. Example of Saturn retrograde, seen in the chart of Louis Armstrong, born August 4, 1901, at 10:00 PM CST in New Orleans, Louisiana.

So how would you speak with Armstrong about his chart? You could ask about his father and follow up with a question about the connection between his missing father and his career, his public reputation, and his connection to his community. Looking at the aspects that Saturn makes in this chart gives you lots of pathways for conjecture, contemplation, and questions. Jupiter is conjunct Saturn in Capricorn at the Midheaven. Did Louis have an over-inflated belief about his missing father that pushed him to success? Saturn is square both the Moon and Mars, being the center point of a T-square.

What questions could you ask regarding the impotent anger he felt toward his father in support or protection of his mother? Did he feel that it was his job to support his mother because the father was not present? Given the times Louis grew up in, that would be a logical assumption. But when working with friends, family members, or clients, don't make assumptions. Ask. It is through your questions and the answers you receive that you will learn.

Notice as well the beautiful trine aspect in Louis's chart from Saturn to Venus. His "inner father story" supports his most personal values. With Venus ruling his 7th house of intimate partnership and our knowledge that he had a supportive, very long-lasting marriage, it is likely that it was the lack of a father that taught him to take responsibility and create a stable love match. Again, ask. There is a rich story here.

Once you have explored the Saturn retrograde story in a chart, remind clients that you are looking at *their* chart, not their father's. You are considering the father through the chart of the adult child. What Saturn retrograde helps you uncover is a personal internal dynamic that is reflected in the outer relationship with the father. Suggest turning the mirror to the inner landscape. How does the relationship with the father reflect the personal inner landscape? How do they relate to outside authority figures as adults? How do they experience their own inner authority?

When people grasp this connection, it can be a moment of profound revelation. The understanding that what they encounter in their real-life relationships is a mirror of their own inner life can rock their understanding of themselves and the world they live in. This is powerful stuff.

Questions, Questions, Questions

As you work with each chart, remember that the person whose life you are exploring has lived the life represented by that chart for many years. There are many ways that a single chart and a single life can be expressed. Bring your understanding of the person to the chart, rather than the other way around. You may have a general understanding of an aspect or a placement, but you never have a clear view of how it has been experienced by the person living that chart without asking questions. The questions you ask may be the most important part of your conversation.

The chart provides the questions. Only the person living the life can provide the answers. The reality is that there is nothing you can tell individuals by looking at their charts that they don't already know. What you bring to light is a cosmic perspective, a reflection that offers confirmation and profound reassurance. Our deepest understanding of the Self is often hidden under layers of denial, confusion, and self-doubt. When you are able to speak clearly and directly to someone's inner "knowing," recognition is close at hand. The sense of being clearly seen by another is a profound experience.

We have all lived with the patterns in our charts throughout our lives. We wake with them each morning and fall asleep with them each night. How arrogant it would be to think that we know more about people than they know about themselves! Clearly, we do not. However, we have powerful tools at our disposal. Our understanding of astrological patterns, our natural curiosity, our ability to ask pertinent questions, and our willingness to listen with an open heart are quite powerful. With these tools, we can hold a mirror up to our friends, our family members, and our clients. Each time we speak to others about their horoscope, this is what we are doing— holding up a mirror and allowing them to see themselves from a perspective that can clear away years of denial, confusion, and misunderstanding.

Approach each chart with curiosity, and use that curiosity to craft your questions. Each question helps to polish the mirror you are holding up. Those you are speaking with will see themselves more clearly with each question you ask. Trust your curiosity. When you ask questions, you shine a light on areas they may have kept hidden from themselves or denied for many years. No matter how powerful their denial, they have known all along that something was there under the surface. The questions you ask will help them open the door to remembering and recognizing it. Don't be surprised when what has been denied and hidden is actually the most powerful and beautiful part of the person in question. It is not always the darkness that we hide; but it is always the darkness that hides our light.

Don't spend too much time looking for answers in the chart. Look instead for questions. If you come up against serious resistance, don't push. If there are particularly frightening skeletons in the closet, the person may not be ready to open that door. Be respectful and move on. When you determine the hemisphere emphasis in a chart, you discover whether the core early challenges were based within the early home or in the outer world, and you are able to see the results of those challenges as a tendency to be defensive or overly passive. When Saturn is retrograde or in challenging aspect to the Sun, it opens the door to exploring the father's role in the pattern of life development.

The influence of parents in early development cannot be overestimated. It is the soil, the sunshine, and the sustenance through which the child grows. To understand the native of a chart, you must explore these conditions. The soil may have been lacking in vital nutrients, too wet or too dry. Or perhaps it was paved over, so to speak, years ago. On the other hand, the person may have been lucky enough to have grown in rich dark soil fully capable of supporting and upholding the developing life.

When Saturn is retrograde, indicating that the relationship with a father figure was weak, damaged, or nonexistent, it often turns out that the relationship with the mother, symbolized by the Moon, increases in strength or significance. The next guidepost explores the impact of the mother or mother figure, as shown by the role of the Moon in the chart. As with paternal figures, the challenges within this relationship will be seen most clearly during childhood, but will continue to be reflected in the emotional life of the native through the lifetime.

GUIDEPOST 5

The Nurturing Moon

Every symbol in astrology has many layers of meaning. The Moon in the horoscope represents the primary need of our lives—our emotional nature, our deepest inner need and struggle, and our experience of the mother figure or primary caregiver. In the symbolic language of astrology, the conditions of the Moon describe how we experience being nurtured and cared for. As adults, we instinctively style our emotional lives and our own parenting along these lines.

This guidepost focuses on our experience of the mother, or mother figure. We'll look at other issues regarding the Moon in Guidepost 6 when we discuss the blending of solar and lunar energies. To understand the role the mother plays in our lives, we look to the conditions of the Moon—its sign, its house placement, its aspects to the Sun and planets, and the house that is ruled by it (the house holding the sign of Cancer). We'll discuss the significance of the planet that rules the sign of the Moon in Guidepost 17 when we explore dispositors.

The Mother and Inner Security

As we saw in Guidepost 2, the Sun and the Moon each rule one sign—unlike the planets, which each rule two. A luminary is said to be "in detriment" in the sign that opposes the sign it rules (see Figure 3). Because the Moon rules the sign of Cancer, it is in detriment in the sign of Capricorn. In Cancer, the Moon feels very much at home and the emotions are closely connected to the mother figure. In the opposing sign of Capricorn, the relationship to the mother and the native's own emotional nature are experienced as adversarial. In Taurus, the Moon is exalted and the native connects well with his or her own emotions and the mother. In the opposing sign of Scorpio, the Moon is considered to be "in its fall," placing both the mother and the emotional nature in a somewhat depressed light.

The first thing to notice about the Moon in a natal chart is its sign and house placement. The sign indicates how individuals experience the mother's nature and the mother's ability to care for and nurture them. The house in which the Moon resides suggests the area of life where the mother had a particularly strong influence. This is the area of life in which the mother taught through instruction or example. The house that the Moon rules (the house that holds Cancer) suggests an area where these lessons are expressed in individuals' lives. The aspects the Moon makes to other planets will color the experience individuals have of the mother and the area of life suggested by the house that holds Cancer. This information brings depth and texture to our understanding of the relationship with the mother as well as an individual's emotional nature.

Before we delve deeper into the sign, house placement, and aspects of the Moon, let me remind you that you are not looking at the mother's chart. What you are actually seeing is the reflection of the mother through the eyes of the native of the chart. Within the Moon, you encounter the deep emotional life and needs of the native—not the mother. For a person born at night, the Moon will be the more powerful of the luminaries, suggesting that the relationship with the mother has a heightened impact, while the father's importance retreats. If Saturn is retrograde, this is often the case as well.

Let's look briefly at the impact that each of the signs has on the role of the Moon in a chart. Then we'll look at house placement and rulership. I have provided the name and birth information for a well-known individual with each of the Moon signs and its house placements. Although you may not know much about the relationship that these individuals had with their mothers, this will give you an opportunity to consider how the relationship with that particular mother/Moon left its stamp on the person's life.

The Moon by Sign

The sign of the Moon indicates how people experience the mother or mother figure, and their emotional nature. This can have both positive and negative impacts.

Moon in Aries

- These individuals experience the mother or mother figure as independent, courageous, assertive, and dynamic.

- On a more challenging level, they likely recognize her selfish, argumentative, and impatient side as well.

- *Example:* Louis Armstrong, born August 4, 1901, at 10:00 PM CST in New Orleans, Louisiana (see Figure 8).

Moon in Taurus

- These individuals experience the mother or mother figure as patient, dependable, loyal, and comforting.

- On a more challenging level, they likely recognize her as stubborn, inflexible, and overly materialistic as well.

- *Example:* Pina Bausch, born July 27, 1940, at 6:45 AM CED in Solingen, Germany.

Moon in Gemini

- These individuals experience the mother or mother figure as enthusiastic, clever, talkative, and friendly.

- On a more challenging level, they likely see her anxious, superficial, and gossipy side as well.

- *Example:* Simone Biles, born March 14, 1997, at 6:02 AM EST in Columbus, Ohio.

Moon in Cancer

- These individuals experience the mother or mother figure as sensitive, protective, emotional, and nurturing.

- On a more challenging level, they likely struggle with her moody, clingy, and defensive side.

- *Example:* Willie Nelson, born April 30, 1933, at 12:30 AM CST in Abbott, Texas.

Moon in Leo

- These individuals experience the mother or mother figure as playful, exuberant, and generously affectionate.

- On a more challenging level, they likely see her overbearing, self-centered, and arrogant side as well.

- *Example:* Chelsea Clinton, born February 27, 1980, at 11:24 PM CST in Little Rock, Arkansas.

Moon in Virgo

- These individuals experience the mother or mother figure as kind, practical, insightful, and detail-oriented.

- On a more challenging level, they likely deal with her critical, worry-prone, and compulsive side.

- *Example:* Chaz Bono, born March 4, 1969, at 12:55 AM PST in Los Angeles, California (see Figure 20).

Moon in Libra

- These individuals experience the mother or mother figure as charming, fair, social, and popular.

- On a more challenging level, they likely realize her dependent, people-pleasing, and indecisive tendencies.

- *Example:* Julian Lennon, born April 8, 1963, at 7:45 AM GMT in Liverpool, England.

Moon in Scorpio

- These individuals experience the mother or mother figure as powerful, intense, and passionate.

- On a more challenging level, they are likely influenced by her manipulative, jealous, and secretive characteristics.

- *Example:* Prince Andrew, born February 19, 1960, at 3:30 PM GMT in London, England.

Moon in Sagittarius

- These individuals experience the mother or mother figure as optimistic, philosophical, and fun-loving or funny.

- On a more challenging level, they are likely victims of her opinionated, tactless, and overconfident behaviors.

- *Example:* Rosemary Kennedy, born September 13, 1918, at 7 PM EWT (war time) in Brookline, Massachusetts.

Moon in Capricorn

- These individuals experience the mother or mother figure as responsible, realistic, and ambitious.

- On a more challenging level, they likely recognize her pessimistic, distrustful, and fearful qualities.

- *Example:* Betty Friedan, born February 4, 1921, at 4:00 AM CST in Peoria, Illinois.

Moon in Aquarius

- These individuals experience the mother or mother figure as intellectual, open-minded, and avant-garde.

- On a more challenging level, they likely see her as unpredictable, eccentric, and detached as well.

- **Example:** Quentin Crisp, born December 25, 1908, at 12:30 PM GMT in Surrey, England.

Moon in Pisces

- These individuals experience the mother or mother figure as sensitive, empathetic, and imaginative.

- On a more challenging level, they likely struggle with her passive, spacey, and confused nature.

- **Example:** Lisa Marie Presley, born February 1, 1968, at 5:01 PM CST in Memphis, Tennessee.

Practice turning each of the statements above into questions. Let's say you find the Moon in Aquarius in someone's chart. Rather than making a statement about the quirky nature of that mother or mother figure, ask a few simple questions and listen to the native's perspective: "What was unusual or unique about your mom?" Listen to how the person describes Aquarius. When you hear things that are decidedly not Aquarian, notice how they match up with the aspects to the Moon. They always will.

The Moon by House Placement and Rulership

The house in which a planet resides is always linked with the house that is ruled by it. The house placement of the Moon signifies the specific area of life where the influence of the mother is of particular significance. You will find a powerful emotional vulnerability in the house that holds the Moon and the house that holds the sign of Cancer (the house ruled by the Moon). The sign in which the Moon is positioned also tells you how people perceived their mothers and how they model and experience their emotions in relation to them.

When you consider someone's relationship with the mother or mother figure, it is important to include both the sign and house placement of the Moon, as well as the house that holds Cancer. These are the areas of life to consider as you formulate your questions and interpret the answers you receive. Asking these questions will help support deep conversations with the native of the chart. The house in which the Moon resides indicates a particular area of the native's life that is charged with emotion. The relationship with the mother has a particularly strong influence in this area of life. For good or ill, through instruction or by example, the mother's influence regarding the concerns of this house prevail.

While the house that holds the Moon is profoundly influenced by the maternal role model or mother, the house ruled by the Moon (the house holding Cancer) is where the mother's influence leaves the native deeply emotional and potentially vulnerable. Always keep in mind that the Moon's importance extends beyond the maternal figure or mother proxy. It serves as a gateway into the deeply personal realms of the native's emotional essence. The Moon in the chart acts as a symbolic key, granting access to the intimate core of our emotional needs, deepest struggles, and innermost instinctual nature.

Just as our exploration of Saturn led us to understand our relationship to authority and the paternal role model, our exploration of the Moon brings our understanding to our internal emotional landscape and our maternal role models. The insights provided by the Moon about the mother reveal a deeply personal and internal narrative—a profound emotional story that initially manifests through the bond with the maternal figure and is later discovered to be a reflection of our own personal emotional nature. When we study the Moon, we delve into the deep emotional dynamics imprinted on our souls and expressed through our personalities. Through the Moon's dynamics in the chart, we gain a deep understanding of our internal landscape as we experience it as a reflection of our relationship with our mothers.

When discussing the Moon and the mother connection with others, encourage them to reflect upon their own inner world. How does their relationship with the maternal role model or mother mirror their emotional nature, their deepest needs, and the struggles of their personality? Recognizing that their understanding of their mothers serves as a reflection of their own inner lives and deep emotional yearnings can be a profound revelation. It can significantly shake their self-perception, as well as change their relationship to the actual mother figure.

Approach this exploration with care and reverence. Each chart you work with provides a profound opportunity to learn. The people whose charts you examine have lived their entire lives with this dynamic. Ask questions! I have included questions for each of the house placements below. Come up with more and develop questions for the house that holds Cancer as well. Combining these will facilitate a deep understanding of an individual's sensitivities as well as the mother's impact and influence.

1st House

Those with the Moon in the 1st house identify personally, emotionally, and strongly with the mother figure. Their self-expression is shaped as a direct response to the mother's example or teaching. The mother's emotional nature is intricately woven into the expression of their personality. The house that is ruled by this Moon (the house that holds Cancer) is an area of life where they are emotionally susceptible to how they feel about their personality as well as how it is experienced and received.

Example:

- Dolly Parton, born January 19, 1946, at 8:25 PM CST in Sevierville, Tennessee. Dolly is one of the best-selling singers and songwriters of all time, as well as an actress, a philanthropist, and a businesswoman. She has a 1st-house Virgo Moon with the sign of Cancer in her 11th house. Her Moon rules the area of life relating to the need to be received and supported within community (11th house). She is sensitive and responsive to the needs of her community and fans. The love she receives from them is a direct result of the very personal service she offers to others (1st-house Virgo Moon). You can anticipate that the lessons she learned from her mother regarding how she expresses her personality left her susceptible to a deep need for love and support from her community.

Questions:

- How has your mother influenced your sense of self-expression and personal identity?

- How has this left you open or vulnerable in the house that holds Cancer?

- How do you respond if you feel unseen or your personal self-expression is misunderstood?

The answers to these questions will reflect the best and worst expressions of the sign the Moon is in.

2nd House

The emotional well-being of those with the Moon in the 2nd house is intimately tied to the lessons they learned from their mothers concerning money, resources, and self-worth. Through her example or teachings, they have learned the emotional importance of financial security as a way to manage self-esteem. Their emotional well-being and sense of security are deeply intertwined with material possessions, financial stability, and personal values. The house that is ruled by this Moon (the house that holds Cancer) is an area of life where they are emotionally susceptible to how they utilize, make, and/or spend money and resources, as well as how that is perceived by others.

Example:

- Martha Stewart, born August 3, 1941, at 1:30 PM EDT in Jersey City, New Jersey, is a businesswoman, television personality, and writer known for her expertise in homemaking, cooking, and entertaining. As of this writing, her estimated net worth is approximately $400 million. She has a 2nd-house Sagittarius Moon with Cancer in her 9th house—the area of life relating to higher understanding and worldview. Her mother's teachings greatly influenced her values on resourcefulness and frugality, shaping her successful entrepreneurial ventures. Stewart's broad cultural understanding and strong work ethic have been crucial in building her empire. However, this placement also makes her emotionally susceptible to challenges and criticisms related to her beliefs and public image.

Questions:

- How has your mother shaped your relationship with money and self-worth?

- How has this left you open or vulnerable in the house that holds Cancer?

- How do you respond if your personal resources or financial security are threatened?

The answers to these questions will reflect the best and worst expressions of the sign the Moon is in.

3rd House

The emotional well-being of those with the Moon in the 3rd house is intimately tied to communications, the activities of the mind, and the daily environment. This area of life has been powerfully influenced, directly or indirectly, by lessons learned at the mother's knee. Their relationship with the mother has also fostered an emotional connection, for good or for ill, in their relationships to siblings, cousins, and neighbors. Emotional well-being, communication style, and environment are closely intertwined. The house that is ruled by this Moon (the house that holds Cancer) is an area of life where they are emotionally susceptible to their siblings and neighborhood, and their ability to communicate, as well as to how their communications are experienced and received.

Example:

- Temple Grandin, born August 29, 1947, at 2:30 PM EDT in Boston, Massachusetts. Grandin is a scientist, an animal behaviorist, and a prominent advocate for the humane treatment of livestock raised for slaughter. She is also an outspoken champion of autism rights and acceptance of neuro-diversity. She has a 3rd-house Aquarius Moon with the sign of Cancer in her 8th house. You can anticipate that the lessons she learned from her mother regarding communication have left her very sensitive to other people's values and her need to reinforce her personal boundaries.

Questions:

- How has your mother's influence impacted your communication style and your relationship with those in your immediate environment?

- Do you see how this has this left you open or vulnerable in the house that holds Cancer?

- How do you respond if your communications are disregarded or misunderstood?

The answers to these questions will reflect the best and worst expressions of the sign the Moon is in.

4th House

The emotional well-being of those with the Moon in the 4th house is intimately tied to their understanding of home, family, roots, and ancestry—an understanding that has been shaped by the example or teaching of the mother or maternal role model. They are motivated by a powerful need to establish a nurturing home environment that embodies family traditions and preserves their bonds with their ancestral heritage. The house that is ruled by this Moon (the house that holds Cancer) is an area of life where they are emotionally susceptible—their family and ancestry.

Example:

- Meghan Markle, born August 4, 1981, at 4:46 AM PDT in Canoga Park, California. This actress and popular blogger became Duchess of Sussex when she married Prince Harry in 2018. As a biracial woman with a diverse cultural background, her heritage and lineage have brought a unique perspective and challenges to the traditional notions of royalty and aristocracy. She has a 4th-house Libra Moon with the sign of Cancer in her 1st house. You can anticipate that the lessons she learned from her mother regarding the need to be diplomatic and pleasing within the home and toward family members have left her vulnerable in a very personal way, feeling that her very "self" is at stake.

Questions:

- How has your maternal role model shaped your understanding of and relationship to home, family, and ancestral roots?

- How has this left you open or vulnerable in the house that holds Cancer?

- How do you respond if your home, family, or ancestral origins are disregarded or disdained?

The answers to these questions will reflect the best and worst expressions of the sign the Moon is in.

5th House

The emotional well-being of those with the Moon in the 5th house is intimately tied to creative pursuits, the ability to give love wholeheartedly, and the capacity to play and to take risks. This area of life has been greatly influenced by the mother through teaching or example. These individuals seek emotional fulfillment through artistic endeavors, play, and self-expression. The house that is ruled by this Moon (the house that holds Cancer) is an area of life where they are emotionally susceptible to their creative endeavors, their children, and their ability to play.

Example:

- Robert Mapplethorpe, born November 4, 1946, at 5:45 AM EST in New York, New York. This American photographer is known for his starkly beautiful black-and-white photographs. His work created great controversy when he documented the NYC subculture of gay male BDSM. He has a 5th-house Pisces Moon with the sign of Cancer in his 9th house. You can anticipate that the lessons he learned at his mother's knee regarding risk-taking and creativity left him vulnerable in the area of higher education, engagement with the law, publishing endeavors, and overall worldview. The connection here is clear. The 1990 obscenity trial concerning the Constitutional limits of free speech as it related to Mapplethorpe's art serves as a relevant example.

Questions:

- How did your mother influence your creative expression and your ability to give love, raise children, and take risks?

- How has this left you open or vulnerable in the house that holds Cancer?

- How do you respond if your creativity or offer of love is dismissed or rejected?

The answers to these questions will reflect the best and worst expressions of the sign the Moon is in.

6th House

The emotional well-being of those with the Moon in the 6th house is intimately tied to their work habits, and their self-care practices are deeply influenced by their relationship with the mother. The mother's impact, whether through direct instruction or by example, has significantly shaped their approach to habits, routines, self-care, and lifestyle. Their ability to manage order, structure, and the patterns of everyday life becomes a crucial factor in determining their emotional fulfillment and overall well-being. The house that is ruled by this Moon (the house that holds Cancer) is an area of life where they are emotionally susceptible to the patterns of their life, their health, and their lifestyle.

Example:

- Stefani Joanne Angelina Germanotta, known as Lady Gaga, born March 28, 1986, at 9:53 AM EST in Manhattan, New York. This American singer, songwriter, actress, philanthropist, dancer, and fashion designer is known for her musical versatility and her ability to change her public image and presentation. She was diagnosed with fibromyalgia in 2017 and has a history of eating disorders. She has a 6th-house Scorpio Moon with the sign of Cancer in her 2nd house. You can anticipate that the lessons she learned from her mother regarding dietary, exercise, and healthcare routines have left her emotionally vulnerable to issues of money and resources. Her ability to make money, acquire resources, and feel good about herself is a direct result of the power and control with which she manages her day-to-day routines.

- How has your mother's impact shaped your approach to work, daily routines, lifestyle, and self-care practices?

- How has this influence left you open or vulnerable in the house that holds Cancer?

- How do you respond if your routines are disrupted or your dietary needs disrespected?

The answers to these questions will reflect the best and worst expressions of the sign the Moon is in.

7th House

The emotional well-being of those with the Moon in the 7th house is intimately tied to close relationships and their choice of intimate partners. This area of life is profoundly influenced by the mother through teaching or example. The mother's impact has shaped their approach to establishing, maintaining, and managing intimate connections, one-on-one relationships, and equal or contractual partnerships. An emotional connection within partnership is of paramount importance to them and this connection is immediately and strongly felt by others. The house that is ruled by this Moon (the house that holds Cancer) is an area of life where they are emotionally susceptible to their partners and relationship dynamics.

Example:

- Leonard Cohen, born September 21, 1934, at 6:45 AM EDT in Montreal, Canada. The songs of this Canadian poet and singer-songwriter focused on romance, love, sex, isolation, depression, and loss. He was known for his charisma, his passion, and his deep love of women. He has a 7th-house Pisces Moon with the sign of Cancer in his 11th house. You can anticipate that the lessons learned at his mother's knee regarding intimate relationships are directly connected to his sensitivity and responsiveness to the community of fans who support and love him. His ability to build and create this supportive community is a direct result of his expression of transcendence through love and relationship. As he sings to one woman (7th house), he sings to all women (11th house).

Questions:

- How did your mother influence your approach to relationships and your choice of intimate partners?

- How has this influence and your subsequent choice of partners left you open or vulnerable in the house that holds Cancer?

- How do you respond if you are rejected or dismissed by your closest intimate partners?

The answers to these questions will reflect the best and worst expressions of the sign the Moon is in.

8th House

The emotional well-being of those with the Moon in the 8th house is intimately connected to experiences of other people's values, shared intimacies, and profound emotional connections. By example or design, the mother's influence has played a significant role in shaping their ability to navigate differences in values and establish personal boundaries within powerful relationship dynamics. They will encounter intense emotional experiences as they seek to forge deep ties and set boundaries with others. The house that is ruled by this Moon (the house that holds Cancer) is an area of life where they are emotionally susceptible as they learn to navigate other people's values and set personal boundaries.

Example:

- Amy Winehouse, born September 14, 1983, at 10:25 PM GMT in Enfield, England. This English singer and songwriter is known for her deep, expressive voice and her amazing range of musical genres. She struggled with substances, and her husband, her father, and the paparazzi were well documented as being contributing factors in her death at age twenty-seven. She has an 8th-house Capricorn Moon with the sign of Cancer in her 2nd house. You can surmise that lessons learned from her mother included the ability, or lack thereof, to navigate the demands and expectations of others, and the ability to set boundaries. Her Moon ruling her 2nd house suggests a great vulnerability regarding money, as well as her own self-worth. Her ability to set and hold personal boundaries had a direct relationship to her personal resources, money, and beliefs regarding her worth.

Questions:

- How has your mother's teaching or example influenced your ability to navigate issues of trust and power, as well as your ability to establish personal boundaries in intimate relationships?

- How has this influence left you open or vulnerable in the house that holds Cancer?

- How do you respond if your boundaries are crossed or disdained by others?

The answers to these questions will reflect the best and worst expressions of the sign the Moon is in.

9th House

The emotional well-being and worldview of those with the Moon in the 9th house are profoundly connected to and shaped by the mother's direct or indirect influence. Their beliefs, philosophies, and spiritual pursuits are deeply connected to their emotional fulfillment. The mother's impact will extend into their education, their travel experiences, their religious and political beliefs, their cultural understandings, and all that expands their worldview. The house that is ruled by this Moon (the house that holds Cancer) is an area of life where their worldview leaves them emotionally susceptible.

Example:

- Andy Warhol, born August 8, 1928, at 6:30 AM EDT in Pittsburgh, Pennsylvania. Warhol's worldview was profoundly connected to and shaped by his mother, who was a devout

Catholic. The themes of ritual, religious iconography, and the concept of sainthood are evident in many of his works. Her direct influence played a significant role in his beliefs, philosophies, and artistic pursuits, and were deeply tied to his emotional fulfillment. Her impact extended into his education, his cultural experiences, his religious beliefs, and his understanding of diversity, all of which expanded his worldview.

Questions:

- How has your mother's influence shaped your higher understanding of the world around you and your worldview?

- How has this understanding left you open or vulnerable in the house that holds Cancer?

- How do you respond if your worldview is rejected, dismissed, or disrespected? This may include educational, religious, political, or cultural understanding.

The answers to these questions will reflect the best and worst expressions of the sign the Moon is in.

10th House

The public image, social reputation, and career achievements of those with the Moon in the 10th house hold significant emotional weight. Their choice and management of career and reputation are strongly influenced, directly or indirectly, by the mother. The mother's influence on their career and public image may not be obvious, but it is a pivotal factor in understanding their professional aspirations or lack of them. The house that is ruled by this Moon (the house that holds Cancer) is an area of life where their career or social reputation may leave them emotionally susceptible.

Example:

- Billie Jean King, born November 22, 1943, at 11:45 AM PWT (war time) in Long Beach, California. This legendary tennis champion was an advocate for gender equality. Her 10th-house Libra Moon rules Cancer, which is in her 7th house. The lessons learned from her mother involved building a strong public image and pursuing a career with a significant social impact. Her mother's influence was instrumental in shaping her professional ambitions and her determination to succeed in a male-dominated sport. With the Moon ruling her 7th house, her emotional vulnerability in relationships was linked to her deep commitment to her social and public reputation.

Questions:

- How did your mother influence your career choices, and your public image and reputation?

- How have these choices left you open or vulnerable in the house that holds Cancer?

- How do you respond if your reputation or career is threatened?

The answers to these questions will reflect the best and worst expression of the sign the Moon is in.

11th House

The emotional well-being of those with the Moon in the 11th house is powerfully connected to their ability to receive support and love through a community of like-minded individuals or organizations. The mother, through teaching or example, has had a strong influence on this area of their life. Their social networks and community involvement are deeply intertwined with their ability to accept and receive love from a community of "like-minded others." The house that is ruled by this Moon (the house that holds Cancer) is an area of life where they are emotionally susceptible to acceptance, or lack of it, from their community.

Example:

- Quentin Crisp, born December 25, 1908, at 12:30 PM GMT in Surrey, England. This English writer and actor lived flamboyantly and without compromise. Unable to blend into the culture of the times, he chose to be himself—a defiantly effeminate exhibitionist. He has an 11th-house Aquarius Moon with the sign of Cancer in his 4th house. By example, influence, or teaching, he learned about his need for community support and understanding of social networks from his mother. Within an unusual and avant-garde community, he was able to express his most authentic nature. This emotional need for community support resulted in a sensitive vulnerability regarding home and family.

Questions:

- How did your mother influence your interest, ability, and need to receive love, support, and acceptance from a social network or community?

- How have these choices left you open or vulnerable in the house that holds Cancer?

- How do you respond if you are rejected, dismissed, or unloved by your community?

The answers to these questions will reflect the best and worst expressions of the sign the Moon is in.

12th House

The spiritual beliefs and deeply unconscious psychological patterns of those with the Moon in the 12th house are profoundly influenced by the mother through teaching or example. They may possess heightened emotional sensitivity and seek solace and emotional fulfillment through introspection, solitude, or spiritual practices. The mother plays a significant role in shaping their hidden beliefs, unacknowledged aspects of themselves, and their spiritual journey. The house that is ruled by this Moon (the house that holds Cancer) is an area of life where they are emotionally susceptible to their hidden psychological patterns or spiritual understanding.

Example:

- R. D. Laing, born October 7, 1927, at 5:15 PM GMT in Glasgow, Scotland, was a pioneering Scottish psychiatrist known for his unconventional understanding of mental illness and his belief in the anti-psychiatry movement. His mother, described as "psychologically peculiar," had a significant influence on his understanding of the unconscious, as well as his spiritual understanding. This profound maternal impact shaped Laing's sensitivity and emotional vulnerability, particularly in his creative endeavors and his ability to give of himself. His approach to psychiatry emphasized empathy and understanding in the treatment of patients.

Questions:

- How has your relationship with your mother influenced your deep unconscious or your spiritual connection to unseen realms?

- How have these choices left you open or vulnerable in the house that holds Cancer?

- How do you respond if you are unable, somehow not allowed, or unwilling to explore these inner elusive depths?

The answers to these questions will reflect the best and worst expressions of the sign the Moon is in.

The Influence of Aspects

Examining the aspects that other planets make to the Moon in the natal chart adds depth to your understanding of individuals' personal emotional landscape, as well as their early relationship with the mother. By considering the sign, house, and aspects of the Moon, along with the house that is ruled by it, you can gain a comprehensive understanding of people's relationship with the mother, their emotional vulnerabilities, their self-perception, and their emotional behavior patterns. The aspects offer color, depth, and texture to that understanding. The five major aspects— squares, oppositions, trines, sextiles, and conjunctions—give you plenty to work with; there is no need to consider the minor aspects.

As you learned in part 1, aspects are the relationships formed between planets or specific points in a natal chart, based on the mathamatical distances between them. These include the aspects that bring challenges, the aspects that offer ease, and the conjunction, which is challenging, easy, or neutral, depending on the planet involved. Before considering how each planet exerts its influence on the Moon, let's take a general look at the function of the aspects themselves.

Squares and Oppositions

Squares occur when planets are separated by 90°, plus or minus the orb you allow. Oppositions occur when they are separated by 180°, plus or minus the orb you allow These aspects suggest challenges and difficulties we encounter in our lives. They serve as catalysts for personal growth, as the difficulties involved motivate us to do the necessary work to push our way through the obstacles we encounter.

A square aspect brings two planets into direct conflict. The energies involved are at cross-purposes and can render one part of us, as symbolized by one planet, unable to clearly understand or even see the part of us symbolized by the other planet. An opposition is a dynamic that occurs as the two planets, or parts of ourselves, pull in opposite directions. The important difference here is that, in an opposition, the two are within clear view of each other. Compromise and adjustment come more easily when the opposite position can be seen.

When squares and oppositions involve the Moon, you can expect these difficulties to first surface in childhood, most likely in the relationship with the mother. The challenges represented require great effort to work through. This emotional work may take a lifetime of effort on the part of the native. The same challenges will follow the individual later in life in other relationships until the issue is resolved.

Trines and Sextiles

Trines and sextiles (120° of separation and 60° of separation, respectively— plus or minus the orb you allow) are known as "easy aspects." These are generally fruitful, fortuitous, and beneficial. Trines signify a natural gift, while sextiles present opportunities for growth and development.

When these aspects connect other planets to the Moon, they indicate benefits, favors, rewards, and support that we experience as coming directly from the mother.

Because the mother and the emotional nature reflect each other, these aspects also contribute to the emotional strength, fortitude, and flexibility of our emotional intelligence and depth. Accepting the gift of trine aspects and embracing the opportunities of sextile aspects involving the Moon further develop our emotional resilience and allow for more fulfilling dynamics within all our relationships.

Conjunction

A conjunction, considered a "neutral aspect," occurs with 0° of separation plus or minus the orb you allow. This aspect often creates a blind spot, as the planets understand themselves as a unit rather than as separate internal influences. When a conjunction involves the Moon, the energy of the additional planet becomes fused with the relationship with or understanding of the mother, as well as with the individual's emotional nature.

The relationship with the mother or mother figure cannot be separated from the planet that is conjunct the Moon. The energies and qualities of that planet will impact the dynamics associated with the mother-child relationship, as well as our emotional nature in general. Understanding how this planet impacts the emotional nature enables us to address our emotional blind spots and explore the complexities of our inner nature, as well as our relationship with the mother, with greater clarity and depth.

The Planets in Aspects to the Moon

Understanding the relationship with the mother or mother figure as a reflection of our own emotional nature can be truly transformative. With this understanding comes a unique perspective that allows us to delve deeper into the dynamics of our upbringing and the impact it has had on our life and well-being. Understanding these challenges and actively doing the work necessary can create profound changes in our relationship with our mothers, as well as our understanding of our own parenting style and how we experience, accept, and understand our own emotions. This perspective can unlock new levels of personal growth and allow us to create a more authentic and empowered path forward in life.

Remember: We are not looking here at the chart of the actual mother. Just as Saturn in a natal chart reflects the native's experience of the father or father figure, but not the actual person, the Moon in a chart shows nothing about the actual mother or mother figure, but rather the native's experience and perception of her. The gulf between that perception and reality can be immense. It is the perception of these relationships that we see in the natal chart and it is the perception of these relationships that we respond to in our formative years. And when you are working with an individual's chart, that is all that matters.

Let's look briefly at the impact that each planet can have as it stands in aspect to the Moon.

The Sun

Aspects between the Sun and Moon provide valuable insights into the internal blending of the emotional nature with the ego or will. They also speak to the relationship that we, as children, witnessed between our parents and its impact on our lives and intimate relationships. Those with the Sun and Moon conjunct have their emotional nature blended with their basic character—they become one and the same. "I feel; therefore, I am." Or "I am what I feel." Similarly, they will see their parental figures as being "on the same page," for good or ill, in their parenting attitudes and style.

When the Sun and Moon form harmonious aspects—trines and sextiles—you can expect a supportive and balanced relationship between the inner and outer self, as well as the perception of the relationship between the parents. Cooperation, understanding, and a sense of harmony prevail. What these individuals strive for (Sun) and what they need (Moon) are in agreement. Conversely, challenging aspects between the Sun and Moon—squares and oppositions—indicate tension and conflict between the inner and outer self, between individuals' needs and desires, as well as between the parents in childhood. Their emotional needs are in conflict with their ego and vice versa. As they navigate these complex and challenging dynamics, they grow in emotional maturity.

Exploring and understanding the aspects between the Sun and the Moon provides valuable insight into the dynamics of the parental relationship and its influence on our individual lives. The interplay between the Sun and the Moon opens a window into our emotional landscape, our parental dynamics, and the patterns we carry into our lives and our relationships.

Mercury

Aspects between Mercury and the Moon provide valuable insights into the internal blending of the emotional nature with the mind or thought processes. This suggests that these individuals were keenly observant of their mother or maternal role model in their early years. You can anticipate that the opinions, ideas, vocabulary, communication style, and intellect of the mother have had a great impact on their way of thinking and communicating. As adults, when their emotions are heightened, these communication skills will be rooted in the foundation of their intellectual interactions with the mother or mother figure. Any aspect between Mercury and the Moon will also tell you a great deal about their comfort level in sharing their emotions with others.

Those with Mercury conjunct the Moon may have simply assumed that the mother knew what was right and promptly absorbed her ideas and beliefs as well as her emotional responses to those ideas and beliefs. With more challenging aspects, they may have resisted or even railed against her ideas and way of thinking. If a trine or sextile is present, you can anticipate that they learned effective communication skills through emotionally resonant conversations and intellectual sharing with the mother.

Venus

Aspects between Venus and the Moon provide insight into the internal blending of the emotional nature with personal values, love, and beauty. These indiviuals may perceive the maternal role model as a lover of peace and harmony, someone who is beautiful, and who embodies fairness and social grace. The mother may have strong feelings on the state and impact of women's social issues. The relationship between them and the maternal role model serves as the foundation—as well as a template—for their emotional understanding of value, beauty, and love.

Those with Venus conjunct the Moon absorb the charming, diplomatic, or beautiful qualities exhibited by the mother. Her beauty becomes the very definition of beauty to them. With the challenging aspects—squares and oppositions—they may perceive her as weak, subordinate, or dependent. Those with a square aspect often feel apprehensive about the role of parenting, as it feels at odds with their sensual desire nature. In the case of a trine or sextile between the Moon and Venus, they will see the mother as beautiful, artistic, friendly, and socially at ease. These positive or challenging aspects contribute to their values, their sense of beauty, and their relationships with other women far beyond their relationship with the mother figure.

Mars

Aspects between Mars and the Moon indicate the internal blending of the emotional nature with action, courage, and anger. These individuals may perceive the mother as a passionate, assertive, or possibly angry woman. Somehow issues of assertiveness, aggression, anger, and/or direct action and courage are tied up with their image and idea of the mother or maternal role model. As adults, their ability to assert themselves when their emotions are involved is rooted in their experience of the foundational relationship with the mother.

Those with Mars conjunct the Moon perceive the mother as emotionally direct, passionate, angry, assertive, determined, or aggressive. She suffers no fools. They themselves will express and experience their emotions with those same qualities. Obviously, the sign the conjunction is in will determine much of how this is experienced. The Moon conjunct Mars in Pisces will be quite different from the Moon conjunct in Scorpio or Aries.

With squares and trines, issues of anger become intertwined in the maternal relationship. Those with these placements may feel anger toward the mother. They may see her as an angry woman, or they may feel anger and the need to protect her in response to a perceived wrong. The concepts of motherhood and anger are linked in their experience. On the other hand, if trines and sextiles are present, they will likely perceive the mother as having great willpower and determination, and the ability to get what she needs and do what she wants. And they will live their lives with this same level of determination and willpower.

Jupiter

Aspects between Jupiter and the Moon show how the emotional nature has blended with belief, expansion, and luck. These individuals may experience the mother or mother figure as someone who embodies optimism, wisdom, enthusiasm, or a strong belief system. She may be seen as wise, highly educated, or religious. The connection between the natal Moon and Jupiter will reflect their level of enthusiasm, their expansive beliefs, and their educational pursuits, which are reflected in the foundation established in their relationship with the mother.

Those with Jupiter conjunct the Moon perceive and understand the mother as strongly influenced by her beliefs, educational values, and idealism. As a result, their emotional nature may become infused with her beliefs, her idealism, her education, and her faith. Squares and oppositions between Jupiter and the Moon, however, suggest issues of excessive behaviors in the maternal relationship. Perhaps they see the mother as wasteful, overly indulgent, or overly dependent on religious beliefs. If trines and sextiles are present, they are likely to perceive her as enjoying a high level of enthusiasm and self-confidence, and a willingness to seek deeper emotional understanding through belief, travel, or cultural explorations.

Saturn

When Saturn forms an aspect to the Moon, individuals perceive the mother as authoritative and serious. They experience her as having a strong sense of duty and self-control. Their emotional resilience and integrity are reflected and rooted in the foundation established in their relationship with her. Understanding the dynamics between the Moon and Saturn can provide valuable insights into their emotional development and their sense of personal responsibility.

When Saturn is conjunct the Moon, the perception of the mother is heavily influenced by her serious and responsible nature. Those with this placement will absorb an earnest, no-nonsense attitude toward their own sensitivities and their ability to connect with others emotionally. Squares and oppositions between the Moon and Saturn can introduce feelings of loneliness, restriction, coldness, and difficulty into the maternal relationship, causing them to see the mother as fearful, harsh, and critical. On the other hand, trines and sextiles can cause them to perceive her as a mature, serious, and responsible individual. She may not be warm, but she is likely to be civil, considerate, and respectful.

Uranus

Aspects between Uranus and the Moon provide insight into the blending of the emotional nature with innovation and humanitarian awareness. These individuals may perceive the mother as unique, innovative, highly independent, emotionally cool, and objective. They may experience her as being in some way ahead of her time—without much personal warmth, but with a highly developed humanitarian understanding of the world. As adults, their emotional independence, excitability, and objectivity are rooted in the foundation established in their early relationship with the mother. Exploring the dynamics of the aspects can give you valuable insights into their sense of emotional excitement and their individuality, as well as their alignment with progressive and humanitarian values.

Those with Uranus conjunct the Moon see little of the mother beyond her dedication to her unusual and unique nature. They absorb this level of originality, objectivity, and independence as part of their own emotional make-up. Difficult aspects like squares and oppositions can cause them to experience emotional coldness, detachment, and anxiety from the mother. They may see her as emotionally cut-off, inconsistent, anxious, and unpredictable, leaving them with their own emotional instability and anxiety. On the other hand, trines and sextiles in the chart can indicate that they see the mother as exciting, original, and innovative, with a deep dedication to unusual forward-thinking perspectives.

Neptune

Aspects between Neptune and the Moon offer insights into the blending of the emotional nature with suffering, compassion, or mysticism. These individuals may perceive the mother as dreamy, whimsical, imaginative, and possibly spaced-out. Conversely, they may experience her as someone with deep psychic suffering, someone who struggles with substances, or as a benevolent person with deep compassion for others. As adults, they will view their own imagination, compassion, and mystical nature as deeply connected to their foundational relationship with her. Exploring these dynamics can provide valuable insights into their creative expression, their empathy, and their spiritual understanding.

Those with Neptune conjunct the Moon may see little of the mother beyond her passive, sympathetic, suffering, compassionate, or visionary nature. Challenging aspects like squares or oppositions can introduce emotional confusion, deep suffering, and or struggles with addiction into the maternal relationship. They may see the mother as apathetic, deferential, and compliant. On the other hand, harmonious aspects like trines or sextiles may lead them to see her artistic, mystical, compassionate, and imaginative side.

Pluto

Aspects between Pluto and the Moon show the internal blending of the emotional nature with power, destruction, and transformation. These individuals may experience the mother as powerful, compulsive, and capable of profound change. They may see her as someone with a personal agenda and a remarkable ability to impact and influence the lives of others. As adults, their understanding of and ability to wield power and passion are rooted in the foundation established in their relationship with her. Understanding this dynamic allows them to see and work with their own hidden and potentially dark nature.

Those with Pluto conjunct the Moon may see little of the mother beyond her inherent power and the intensity of her emotions. They absorb this personal emotional power and passion as an integral part of their own emotional make-up. With challenging aspects like squares or oppositions, Pluto can introduce brooding intensity and destructive emotions into the maternal relationship. The mother may be experienced as compulsive, hurtful, and even violent and/or toxic. Harmonious aspects like trines and sextiles can put her in a very powerful light. She may be seen as a formidable woman capable of transforming her own life and catalyzing the lives of others.

However we experience our mothers or mother figures—as suggested by the Moon in the natal chart—that is what we will one day understand to be the sweet or bitter truth of our own hearts.

Union of the Sun and Moon

The relationship between the Sun and the Moon reflects the very essence of life. Most of us know our Sun sign by the time we are five or six years old. We tend to think of ourselves as a Leo, a Capricorn, a Libra, or whatever sign the Sun was in when we were born. This becomes a part of our identity. We say to each other: "I am a Taurus" or "I am a Gemini." But let's be clear. The Sun sign does not represent who we are. We are all so much more than that. I may live with significant Leo energies; you may live with significant Taurus energies. But that does not confine me to a singular box called "Leo," nor you to one called "Taurus."

What the Sun sign represents is our basic *energy*—the core of what is available to us in this lifetime. Noel Tyl described the energy of the Sun as the furnace in the basement that provides the energy for the entire system. Think of the Sun sign as the primary and most readily available energy that you possess. Without the energy of the Sun, the rest of the planets would have no gravitational force to keep them in motion, and we would have no charts to discuss.

After considering the role of the Sun in a natal chart, we usually look next at the Moon. But if the native of the chart is born in the darkness of night, the Moon may actually be considered to be more significant than the Sun. Regardless of the time of day or night we are born, the Moon signifies, among other things, our most pressing *need*. Each step we take in this lifetime is a push toward the fulfillment of the profound need represented by it. The Moon reveals the deep need that drives us forward. The Sun provides the energy to fulfill that need. Throughout our lives, we are learning how to use the energy of the Sun to feed the need of the Moon.

That's why it is important to get in the habit of always considering the Sun and Moon as a unit in the natal chart. In order for life to function smoothly, the core energy available (the Sun) must provide what it takes to support and fulfill the great need of the personality (the Moon). Over the course of our lifetime, we each learn to navigate and work with the specific Sun and Moon combination with which we were born. There are 144 possible combinations, each with its own unique characteristics. Some combinations are inherently easier to manage and understand, while others provide a lifetime of challenges.

Think about the relationship that develops between the Sun and Moon if they are in the same element. For example, imagine an Aries Moon being nourished by the energy of a Leo Sun, or a Capricorn Sun fulfilling the need of a Virgo Moon. This isn't hard to do. Now, compare that to a Leo Sun being asked to feed the need of a Capricorn or a Scorpio Moon, or a Virgo Sun having to feed the need of an Aries Moon. This will certainly take more effort and be reflected in a more challenging life.

It is easy to imagine a fire Sun supporting the needs of a fire or air Moon, or an earth Sun feeding the needs of an earth or water Moon. Think about how the elements work together. Air feeds fire; earth supports water. Fire and air are easily compatible; earth and water are also easily compatible. On the other hand, consider the challenge that arises when a water Sun attempts to fulfill the needs of a fire or air Moon, or when an air Sun must meet the needs of a water or earth Moon. Water puts out fire; air blows away mountains.

This very simple perspective provides a powerful insight and self-understanding to individuals who grapple with a discordant combination.

Blending Sun and Moon Energies

Consider how the powerful and radiant light of the Sun provides luminosity to the Moon in the night sky. This principle holds true within the context of a natal chart as well. The Sun's energy warms, illuminates, and fulfills the Moon's needs. With this fundamental principle in mind, we can establish a straightforward technique for blending the two, like the one presented by Noel Tyl in his book *Synthesis and Counseling in Astrology*. By applying this technique, we can come up with statements that will resonate powerfully with the native of any natal chart.

Let's take a look at just how such a technique might be applied. Then we'll look at some charts that illustrate the results.

The technique itself is very simple. Make a statement for the Sun sign, and have that statement feed and support the statement for the Moon sign. Likewise, the statement for the Moon sign is fed and supported by the statement for the Sun sign. That's really all there is to it.

As an example, let's look at the chart of Brené Brown. She has a Scorpio Sun and a Virgo Moon, and thus enjoys an easy compatibility between a water Sun and an earth Moon. Her energy to explore deep mysteries, gain profound understanding, and transform through intense experiences (Scorpio Sun) supports her great need for accuracy, precision, and insight in order to serve others in practical ways (Virgo Moon). When reading her chart, you can simply say: "I see in your chart the suggestion that you have the energy to explore deep mysteries for profound understanding. This ability feeds and supports your need to be of service to others with practical insights." Or you can make this as simple as: "Your need to be of practical service to others is fed by your exploration of deep mysteries."

As you work with this simple technique, develop your own creative wording to expand on the initial statement. Here are some phrases you can use to describe the energy of each Sun sign to help you get started:

- **Aries**: energy for taking initiative, leading others, and asserting force

- **Taurus**: energy for building and maintaining lasting structures, creating stability, and cultivating material abundance

- **Gemini**: energy for gathering information, communicating, and adapting to diverse situations

- **Cancer**: energy for creating emotional security, nurturing others, and fostering a sense of belonging

- **Leo**: energy for being seen and recognized, and expressing generosity and confidence

- **Virgo**: energy for refining, perfecting, and meticulously serving others with attention to detail

- *Libra*: energy for pleasing others, seeking harmony through diplomacy, and gaining appreciation

- *Scorpio*: energy for exploring deep mysteries, seeking profound understanding, and transforming through intense experiences

- *Sagittarius*: energy for self-assertion, seeking truth, and undertaking philosophical explorations

- *Capricorn*: energy for ambition, organization, and the effective deployment of resources

- *Aquarius*: energy for innovation, engagement in collaborative intellectual pursuits, and championing causes for the benefit of all

- *Pisces*: energy for feeling deeply, cultivating spiritual understanding, and embodying compassion through self-sacrifice

Here are some phrases you can use to describe the need of each Moon sign:

- *Aries:* need for acknowledgment of courage, importance, and leadership

- *Taurus:* need for stability, security, and material comfort

- *Gemini:* need for intellectual stimulation, knowledge, and a clever wit

- *Cancer:* need for emotional security and a sense of belonging within a biological or chosen family

- *Leo:* need for love, admiration, respect, and attention

- *Virgo:* need for accuracy, precision, and insight, to serve others in practical ways

- *Libra:* need for appreciation, fairness, attractiveness, and popularity

- *Scorpio:* need for privacy as well as to be seen as reliable, significant, and self-sufficient

- *Sagittarius:* need for respect and acknowledgment of wide-ranging views and opinions

- *Capricorn:* need for practical accomplishments and progress in the real world

- *Aquarius:* need for making innovative contributions that support communities or social systems

- *Pisces:* need for dreams, to explore the intangible, and to connect with spirit

Remember, the *need* is the Moon; the *energy* is the Sun. The energy feeds the need. The need is fed by the Sun. When you talk with someone about this, take this opportunity to express curiosity about how this works in the native's life. This can open many wonderful conversations that will support your learning. For instance: "I am so curious about how that works in your experience."

Now, let's look at some examples and formulate some statements you can use to describe this dynamic in a chart.

Louis Armstrong (Leo Sun, Aries Moon)

- Notice the ease between the compatible elements of the fire Sun and fire Moon. Armstrong's powerful energy to be seen and recognized, and to express generosity and confidence (Leo) feeds and supports his great need for acknowledgment of courage, importance, and leadership (Aries).

- Statement: "One of the patterns I see in your chart suggests that you have a great need to be in a leadership position, to be recognized for something important. This need is fed by your powerful energy to be recognized and seen for your huge heart, your generosity, and your confidence."

Lizzie Borden (Cancer Sun, Leo Moon)

- Notice the challenge between the incompatible elements of the water (Sun) and fire (Moon). Borden's great need for love, admiration, and respect, and her need for attention are fed and supported by her powerful energy to create emotional security, nurture others, and foster a sense of belonging.

- Statement: "One of the patterns I see in your chart suggests that you have a great need for love, admiration, and respect. Your energy to create emotional security and nurture others must be used to fulfill that need. I am so curious about how that works in your experience."

Yoko Ono (Aquarius Sun, Sagittarius Moon)

- Notice the compatibility of the air Sun and fire Moon. Yoko Ono's powerful energy to innovate, engage in collaborative intellectual pursuits, and champion causes for the benefit of all feeds and supports her great need for respect and acknowledgment of wide-ranging views and opinions.

- Statement: "One of the patterns I see here suggests that you need a good deal of freedom and independence, and you need your opinions to be respected. These needs are fed by the energy you have for collaborative intellectual pursuits, and championing causes for the benefit of all."

Albert Einstein (Pisces Sun, Sagittarius Moon)

- Notice the challenge between the water Sun and fire Moon. Einstein's powerful energy to feel deeply, cultivate spiritual undertanding, and embody compassion through self-sacrifice feeds and supports his great need for respect and acknowledgment of wide-ranging views and opinions.

- Statement: "One of the patterns I see in your chart suggests that your deep sensitivity, compassion, and imagination feed and support your great need to be respected for your wide-ranging views. It is very important to you that you are respected and your opinions valued. You are challenged to find a way to use your imagination and compassion to achieve this end. I am curious about how that works in your experience."

Aspects to the Sun and Moon

Now that you understand how the Sun and Moon work together, it's time to pay attention to the most significant aspect(s) to them. Over time, you will come to identify those that are most important quickly and easily. As part of your analysis, look for the aspect with the closest orb, as well as aspects from Saturn and the outer planets.

We intuitively understand the importance of aspects from Saturn, Uranus, Neptune, or Pluto when they are in aspect to the Sun or Moon. But any aspects to the Sun or Moon are pivotal in understanding the dynamic interplay between the conscious self (the Sun) and the emotional, instinctual nature (the Moon). Don't underestimate the importance of aspects made from the inner planets to one or both of the luminaries.

Sun and Moon in Direct Aspect

- Those with the Sun and Moon in conjunction enjoy a powerful alignment that fuses their core identity with their emotional nature. Their ego needs and emotional needs are one and the same.

- Those with squares between the Sun and the Moon feel a powerful tension between their conscious desires and their emotional needs. Each time they move in the direction of what they most need, contradictory desires pull them in a contrary direction. Their needs and desires work at cross purposes. The native with this aspect must acknowledge and accept that both parts must be honored and a middle path must be found and cultivated. In this way they find a way forward. Square aspects occur between like modalities (cardinal, fixed, or mutable). If, due to degrees and orbs, they are not in the same modality, they lose a good deal of their potency. Because mutable signs are flexible and adaptable, squares between these signs will be the easiest to manage.

- Those with the Sun and Moon in opposition to each other experience a push-pull dynamic, heightening their awareness of differences between their ego and their emotional needs. This is an aspect of stress and a balance point must be found. In their youth, they are likely to project this challenge onto their parents; in adulthood, they may project the struggle onto their intimate partners. In later years, maturity opens the door to clarity and enables them to broaden and adjust their perspective on the stress involved.

- Those with trines and sextiles between the Sun and Moon benefit from a natural flow and harmony between their conscious desires and their emotional needs. This facilitates their ability to balance and navigate these most important parts of the Self. Regardless of other difficulties with which they may have to contend, their core needs and desires are in supportive harmony.

Mercury

- Mercury conjunct the Sun or Moon amplifies the importance of communication skills and the intellect. Due to Mercury's position between the Earth and the Sun, it is often conjunct the Sun. Those with this aspect strongly identify with their thoughts, ideas, and intellect. "I am what I think." However, with Mercury conjunct the Moon, their thoughts and intellect are tied tightly to their emotional needs. They need to understand and express their emotions intellectually.

- Mercury square or opposite the Sun or Moon creates inner tension regarding thought processes or the use of the "voice." Those with this aspect in their charts may struggle to express their emotions (Moon) or their core identity (Sun). Over time, the effort they expend on improving communication and aligning their thoughts with their true authenticity will lead to great personal development and a strengthened ability to use their voice effectively.

How to Read and Interpret a Birth Chart

- Those with Mercury trine or sextile the Sun or Moon enjoy a natural flow and ability to express themselves, and communicate their desires (Sun) or their emotional needs (Moon).

Venus

- Venus conjunct the Sun or Moon emphasizes the connection to values, to love and beauty, and to pleasure and relationships. Those with this placement find their sense of self (Sun) or their emotions (Moon) deeply intertwined with their feelings of love, beauty, and harmony.

- Venus square or opposite the Sun or Moon creates inner tension surrounding matters of love, beauty, and relationships, making it challenging to harmonize or align personal values with egoic desires (Sun) or emotional needs (Moon). Those with these aspects must work to find the balance point between these discordant energies. Through dedicated effort, they can reconcile these issues over time, leaving in their wake a hard-won inner harmony.

- Venus trine or sextile the Sun or Moon indicates a natural flow and ability to express values through emotions (Moon) or the core self (Sun). This is a fortuitous aspect that facilitates authentic self-expression, emotional understanding, and internal harmony, presenting a unique opportunity for life enrichment.

Mars

- Mars conjunct the Sun or Moon amplifies assertiveness and drive. Those with this aspect strongly identify with determination, physical strength, and possibly anger.

- Mars square or opposite the Sun or Moon suggests inner tension and conflicts between an assertive nature and emotional needs (Moon) or the core self (Sun). This aspect demands that individuals resolve this conflict in order to balance assertiveness with their emotions or core identity. Over time, resolution of these conflicts can lead to personal development through the integration of their energy and emotions or self. These aspects raise issues of action, assertiveness, sharpness, or anger. If these go unresolved, they can have a detrimental impact on all relationships. The path to growth and resolution lies in working with courage, determination, and purpose to address and resolve these challenges.

- Mars trine or sextile the Sun or Moon signifies a natural flow of physical drive, opening up opportunities for effortless integration of physical strength and desires with core identity (Sun) or the emotional nature (Moon). This facilitates confident self-expression and effective emotional management, presenting a promising pathway for personal growth through taking constructive action.

It is important to note here that the cultural landscape we live in is always evolving. Not many years ago, expectations of gender norms appeared to be very fixed, at least on the surface. Venus and Mars have traditionally been associated with gender expectations and expression. Because these norms and expectations are rapidly changing, you must approach the influence of Mars and Venus in the natal chart with open-minded curiosity. It is essential to recognize and honor the diversity of experiences and expressions that individuals may embody. Do not make assumptions without asking. By approaching Mars and Venus aspects with an open mind, you will gain insight into how others are navigating the unique journeys reflected in their natal charts.

Jupiter

- Jupiter conjunct the Sun or Moon emphasizes an expansive and optimistic nature, causing those with this placement to identify strongly with their beliefs, their ideals, and their quest for personal growth.

- Jupiter square or opposite the Sun or Moon may create inner tension and challenges regarding beliefs and aspirations,

How to Read and Interpret a Birth Chart

demanding that individuals address these conflicts and reconcile their ideals with their core identity (Sun) or emotional needs (Moon). Over time, they must confront the discord between their ego or emotions and their beliefs and ideals. This will lead to personal development as they strive to integrate their beliefs with their ego (Sun), or their emotional needs (Moon).

- Jupiter trine or sextile the Sun or Moon signifies a natural flow of expansive energy, offering opportunities for effortlessly bringing together personal beliefs with the core identity (Sun) or emotional nature (Moon). This offers a free flow of confidence and well-being. There is little doubt about what these people believe.

Saturn

- Saturn conjunct the Sun or Moon accentuates a sense of responsibility, discipline, and self-control. Those with this aspect strongly identify with their duties and boundaries, and their pursuit of long-term goals.

- Saturn square or opposite the Sun or Moon suggests significant struggles, restrictions, and difficulties in the early life of those with this aspect. These challenges may involve the parents in early life, and their own sense of duty and self-discipline later on. They will need to address these conflicts and reconcile their responsibilities with their ego needs (Sun) or their emotional nature (Moon). Over time, they must confront these issues and work to find balance, leading to personal development as they integrate their obligations with who they are and what they need.

- Saturn trine or sextile the Sun or Moon signifies a natural flow of disciplined energy, offering valuable opportunities for effortlessly bringing together personal responsibilities with the identity (Sun) or emotions and needs (Moon).

- If Saturn is in aspect to one or both of the luminaries, you can anticipate significant core struggles, restrictions, and difficulties in the early life. The childhood itself may have felt bleak, barren, desolate, cold, and stark. Early on, these issues will be manifest in the relationship the native has with the father figure (if the aspect is to the Sun), or with the mother figure (if the aspect is to the Moon). When these individuals have matured, taken responsibility for themselves, and developed their own inner authority over ego (Sun) or emotions (Moon), they will gain mastery over those early difficulties. Their greatest potential comes into focus as they face the reality of the work required and take responsibility for engaging in the effort. The work of Saturn brings them to their full potential.

Uranus

- Uranus conjunct the Sun or Moon emphasizes uniqueness, innovation, and a desire for independence. Those with this placement strongly identify with a need for personal freedom as well as an unconventional approach to life.

- Uranus square or opposite the Sun or Moon suggests a sense of anxiety, restlessness, apprehension, and disquietude in the early home life as those with these aspects push for independence. Over time, they must balance their desire for freedom with their more stable ego (Sun) or emotional needs (Moon). As they work to integrate this conflict, they will find the gift of internal freedom and personal innovation.

- Uranus trine or sextile the Sun or Moon signifies a natural flow of innovative energy, which brings opportunities for a free flow of independence and individuality. This facilitates confident self-expression, emotional freedom, and the potential for personal growth through blending personal uniqueness with ego (Sun) or emotions (Moon).

- Those with one or both of the luminaries in close aspect to Uranus will dance to a tune that others don't hear. The rhythm they respond to is unique, progressive, and unorthodox in some way. Honesty and freedom are important to them and dull routines are intolerable.

Neptune

- Neptune conjunct the Sun or Moon emphasizes deep sensitivity, dreaminess, creativity, and spiritual openness. Those with this placement strongly identify with their dreams and intuition, and with the mystical aspects of life. They may be experienced by others as confused, spacy, or "out of touch."

- Neptune square or opposite the Sun or Moon suggests confusion and escapist tendencies. Those with this aspect must address these conflicts and find a way to balance their spiritual inclinations with the part of themselves that wants to negate such things. Over time, working on this issue will lead to spiritual development, the growth of imagination, and enhanced intuition.

- Neptune trine or sextile the Sun or Moon signifies a natural flow of creative and mystical energy, offering beautiful opportunities for effortlessly tapping into deep levels of sensitivity and intuition. This increases confidence in the intuition or imagination.

- Those with the Sun or Moon in close aspect to Neptune won't be easily pinned down. They have direct contact with dimensions beyond the ordinary. This can manifest as confusion, a lack of boundaries, susceptibility to substances, powerful intuition, or artistic, spiritual, or even mystical inspiration. These are the dreamers and idealists among us, always reaching for something "beyond."

Pluto

- Pluto conjunct the Sun or Moon emphasizes the innate power within. These individuals will strongly identify with a need to regenerate or profoundly alter the Self as they deeply explore the hidden depths of their lives.

- Those with Pluto square or opposite the Sun or Moon are vulnerable to powerful forces working against them, from within or without. They will encounter challenges of great intensity. They must face these challenges head-on and allow their ego (Sun) or emotional needs (Moon) to be transformed to reflect their deepest personal integrity. On the other side of the powerful inner work it takes to confront these issues, they will come to a profound inner development and personal empowerment. This is not for the weak of heart, but what a gift awaits! Tyl describes this challenging aspect as a blanket thrown over a hand grenade, which suggests an immense power being somehow tamped down or held back that is eventually released to realize great empowerment.

- Pluto trine or sextile the Sun or Moon signifies a natural flow of powerful and transformative energy, offering potent opportunities for the development of, or gift of, personal power. Those with these aspects have easier access to the full empowerment of Pluto.

- Individuals with the Sun or Moon in close aspect to Pluto will feel powerful forces at work in their lives. Remember that Pluto has two faces. On the one hand, it represents destruction and annihilation; on the other, it represents transformation and empowerment.

GUIDEPOST 7

Ascendants and Rising Signs

The Ascendant is the eastern-most point on the horizon at the moment of birth. The first breath and the moment of its occurrence determine this point, which further determines the entire orientation of the birth chart and the life. In the Whole Sign house system, the Ascendant defines the rising sign and the first house begins at that sign's 0° position. The Ascendant itself is always contained within the first house.

The terms "Ascendant" and "rising sign" are used interchangeably in many texts. However, they are not the same thing. The Ascendant is the exact degree of the sign that is rising above the horizon at the moment of birth. The rising sign is simply the sign that is on the horizon at the time of birth. Each sign holds 30° on the zodiac wheel. The twelve signs together equal 360°. In the Whole Sign house system, each house holds the full 30° of one full sign.

The rising sign represents our outward presentation or persona—our personality. You can think of this as a mask that we each wear. To be clear, however, it is not a mask behind which to hide. Rather it is a filter through which we express the complexities of our personality. We need this filter between the inner self and the outer world. Consider the result if we were to go out into the world with no filter and simply express all our inner complexities. We would very likely find ourselves in a heap of trouble.

In the Whole Sign house system, 0° of the Ascendant sign begins the first house. If there are no planets in the first house, this sign and the planet that rules it are the main indications of how we present ourselves and are perceived by others. You can simply think of this as the outward, most natural expression of the personality.

We can be surprised when we get to know someone and find that there is much hidden beneath the veneer of personality. The person we initially encountered is not who we find below the surface. Complications of the personality may not be perceived initially, because our awareness is focused on what is presented. This is the filter of the Ascendant at work. And what we encounter differs according to whatever the rising sign is.

It is important to note immediately the modality of the rising sign.

- With a cardinal rising sign (Aries, Cancer, Libra, Capricorn), you can anticipate the personality to be expressed with determination and purpose for the sake of accomplishment. That is the nature of the cardinal signs.

- With a fixed rising sign (Taurus, Leo, Scorpio, Aquarius), you can expect a solid focused personality that changes little over time. Steadfast reliability is the nature of the fixed signs.

- With a mutable rising sign (Gemini, Virgo, Sagittarius, Pisces), you can expect the personality to shift and change as the individual adapts to the changing circumstances of life. This is the nature of mutability.

The Ascendant Ruler

The planet that has rulership of the rising sign is of fundamental importance and can be said to rule the chart (see Guidepost 2). Think of this planet as being sent out into the chart as the ambassador or representative of the personality. This planet plays an influential role in shaping the outward character and expression of the individual. Just as ambassadors represent their country in foreign lands, the ruling planet brings the intent of the personality to the area of life suggested by the house in which it resides.

Like any ambassador, this planet interacts with other planets, thereby influencing how the intentions of the personality are experienced within the whole. The house in which the ruling planet resides will reflect an area of life where the native's personality will be prominently displayed. The sign placement of the ruling planet further influences the personality, adding its unique qualities and characteristics to the mix.

The aspects formed between the ruling planet and other planets and points in the chart provide further insight into how the personality is expressed and best utilized. Harmonious aspects (trines and sextiles) can enhance the expression of the ruling planet and bring out the best qualities of the individual, while challenging aspects (squares and oppositions) may present obstacles that require conscious effort to manage. Thus the planet ruling the Ascendant acts as a representative of the personality, carrying its significance into different areas of life. Its placement and aspects in the chart provide valuable information about how a person's identity is expressed, experienced, and influenced by various factors within the natal chart.

This layering of influences is not unlike the work of Vincent van Gogh, whose paintings were created with thick dense paint that he shaped and layered to create his unique and brilliant style. Imagining the complexity of a multilayered van Gogh painting may help you envision how these layers work together to create the entire picture of a personality and how it is expressed.

The first layer consists of the rising sign itself and any aspects that are made directly to the Ascendant. The second layer is the planet that rules the rising sign and the house in which it resides. The third is the sign that the ruling planet occupies. The fourth is made up of the aspects between that planet and other planets and points.

Personalities can be extremely complex or surprisingly simple. And we each bring various facets of self-expression to the table. Imagine the beauty and simplicity of those with Taurus rising and Venus in the first house making no aspects to other planets or points. What you see is what you get. These people very likely have other complexities, but there will be very few complications in how they express their personality. On the other hand, consider those with the same Taurus Ascendant who have Venus in Aquarius in the 10th house, forming hard aspects to Uranus and Mars, along with a trine aspect to Pluto. With this configuration, you can certainly anticipate a far more complex expression of the personality.

Use your imagination to consider an encounter with the people described above. By fostering curiosity and embracing your intuition, you can gain a deeper understanding of them and their experiences. This will be a great help as you work with charts over the years.

Ascendant Rulership

When developing an understanding of an individual's rising sign, look first at the sign itself and the planet that rules it. Then consider the sign and house that hold the ruling planet and any significant aspects to the ruling planet and to the Ascendant itself. Let's try this with several sample charts to see just how it works.

As you do so, keep in mind that, when looking at people who are famous—either currently or across generations—these charts are likely to be more complex than those of your average friend, family member, or client. Profoundly significant people will have profoundly complex and extraordinary charts.

Aries Rising—Louis Armstrong

Louis Armstrong, born August 4, 1901, at 10:00 PM CST in New Orleans, Louisiana (see Figure 8), was among the most influential figures in American jazz. He was known for his charismatic stage presence, his unique voice, and his powerful trumpet style. He famously stayed out of racial politics and was one of the first Black American entertainers to gain wide popularity with white audiences.

Armstrong's chart shows an Aries Ascendant, which brings to mind certain archetypes—warrior, courageous leader, pioneer, and survivor. Think of the courage it took in the 1920s and 1930s for a Black man to stand on a stage before a white audience and blow a clear tone on a hot trumpet. As a cardinal sign, Aries, ruling the face of the personality, suggests the steady and persistent development of it over time.

This image becomes more individualized when you see that Aries rules Mars in Libra. Now you see that this courageous pioneer understood that, in order to become who he was meant to be, he had to be pleasing and polite to others. He learned to use the determination and courage of his Aries rising to gain the appreciative regard of others. He had great strength of will that was skewed by a clear understanding that diplomacy was the way to reach his goals. Mars is in its fall in Libra, and we can only imagine the frustration Armstrong encountered in his need to please others.

With his Mars in the 7th house, Armstrong used this powerful strength of diplomacy on one individual at a time. He had no choice but to be overtly polite to white people in order to rise to the position he attained in the America of the 1920s. And he was uniquely equipped to do so with the courage of Mars ruling his rising sign. You can develop your understanding of him even further by considering the aspects to his Mars, as well as the aspects to his Ascendant.

Watch a video of Louis Armstrong and observe his impressive ability to step forward courageously in a manner finely calculated to gain the appreciation he needed in order to bring his voice to the masses. How different would his life have been if his Mars had been in Leo, or Scorpio, or Pisces? How different would the world of jazz be today?

Taurus Rising—The Dionne Quintuplets

The Dionne Quintuplets, born May 28, 1934, at 3:55 AM EST in Callander, Canada, were the first quintuplets known to have survived into adulthood. The identical girls were born toward the end of the Great Depression in rural Canada to a farming couple who already had more than enough children—certainly by today's standards. The girls were removed from the family first by the Red Cross and then by the Ontario government, who profited financially by putting them on display and building an entire tourist industry around them.

For our purposes here, let's think of these girls as a unit. We see that they have Taurus rising in their natal chart. Think about what Taurus gave to the personalities of the girls individually and together. First, Taurus rising brings to mind certain archetypes—dressmaker and beauty queen. You may imagine someone arranging a lovely bouquet of flowers, or a teenager dressing for the school dance. And these archetypes translate easily into the way the Dionne sisters were presented to the public, with their ruffly dresses and pink bows. You certainly didn't see them digging in the dirt or rough-housing. With Taurus, a fixed sign, ruling the face of the personality, you can expect little change in the presentation of it over time.

How does the image change when you consider the ruler of the Ascendant? Taurus is ruled by Venus and we find the quintuplets' Venus in the 12th house, in Aries, closely conjunct Uranus, square Pluto and the

Midheaven. How does this change how you see these sisters? You may still see them sitting at a sewing machine or participating in a beauty pageant, but your understanding of that image becomes more contextualized. They may still be pleasant and steadfast, but, in order for them to function in the world into which they were born, they had to learn to survive by managing the unique power (Pluto) of their circumstances. They had to use the strength and courage of Aries in order to manage the expectations and demands of others. They demonstrated steadfast beauty, but that beauty was colored by an intense power and unusual strength, which was sorely needed given the wildly unusual (Uranus) circumstances they experienced.

With Venus in the 12th house, you can also expect that there is an aspect of themselves that they must hide within their rich inner lives. The ruler of their Ascendant is in its fall. Venus does not enjoy being in Mars's sign of Aries. They may appear as lovely and demure, and yet hot blood courses through their imposed self-expression.

In order to make deeper sense of this chart, think about the intensely powerful outer planet transit that was in force between 1932 and 1934. Uranus and Pluto were in a square aspect to each other during these years. Due to the slow movement of these planets, they do not come into direct aspect to each other often. The nearest previous square aspect between them was in the late 1870s, and since then they have formed a square aspect at only one other time—between 2012 and 2015.

This transit is a generational statement that suggests that a great upheaval will occur in the world during this time. In the chart of the Dionne sisters, this powerful transit is tied directly to Venus, the ruler of the chart. This puts them directly in the path of the cultural upheaval forecast. If the culture at large had not been in the dire straits of the Depression, or if Venus had been placed differently, it is unlikely that the world would have become so consumed with the image of these five little girls.

Consider as well the impact on these girls if Venus had been in Capricorn or Pisces at their birth. Videos of the sisters clearly show the inner strength they needed in order to manage life in the crazy fishbowl in which they landed. Theirs was indeed an unusual life tied to the cultural moment of their birth.

Gemini Rising—Dorothy Day

Dorothy Day, born November 8, 1897, at 6:50 PM EST in Bath Beach, New York, was a social activist and journalist who maintained the social and anarchist activism of her Bohemian youth when she became a devout Catholic. She was imprisoned as a suffragette in 1917. In the 1930s, she was instrumental in establishing the Catholic Workers' Movement, which combined direct aid to the homeless poor with nonviolent civil disobedience on their behalf. She herself took a lifelong vow of poverty. Today, the Catholic Church calls her a "Servant of God"—a first step in formally recognizing her as a saint—and is investigating the case for her possible canonization.

Consider the layers of Day's rising sign (see Figure 14). First, her Gemini rising brings to mind certain archetypes—journalist, storyteller, networker, teacher, and witness. All of these certainly fit well with Dorothy's outward personality.

But notice that Day's Gemini Ascendant is ruled by Mercury, which we find in Scorpio conjunct the Sun, Chiron, and Mars. How does this change the image? She will still be sitting at her typewriter, networking and telling stories. But our understanding of the stories she is telling deepens considerably. With Mercury in Scorpio in the 6th house, the intensity of her mind turned to the common plight of daily existence. She focused intently on how to transform the health and everyday lives of others. This depth and intensity of mind were clearly evident through her personality.

But Gemini (a mutable sign) ruling the face of the personality creates the opportunity for significant changes in Day's persona and self-expression over time. This is a woman who can move from being a Bohemian anarchist to the image of a Catholic saint in one lifetime. Consider how different her story would be if her Mercury, as the ruler of the Ascendant, had been in Cancer or Aquarius. On the other hand, what would her story be if she had been born an hour later with a Cancer Ascendant, ruled by her Taurus Moon?

Cancer Rising—Tenzin Gyatso

Tenzin Gyatso, the current (fourteenth) Dalai Lama, was born July 6, 1935, at 6:00 AM LMT in Taktser (Hongya Village), in the traditional Tibetan region of Amdo, Dhomay province (administratively Qinghai, Republic of China). Although he describes himself as a simple Buddhist monk, he is, in fact, the highest spiritual and political leader of Tibet in exile. During the Tibetan uprising of 1959, in fear for their lives, he and his followers fled Tibet and crossed into India, where they set up a government in exile. Today, he continues to fight for the future of Tibet. Clearly, his chart contains many complexities and his life should be explored at length for true understanding. Here we will only look at a few specifics.

Consider the insights we can glean from this chart's rising sign, which resides in Cancer. This brings to mind certain archetypes—protector, defender, advocate, caretaker, and nurturing parent who provides comfort and care. All of these ideas certainly fit well with how the Dalai Lama has conducted his life. We know that he will show up in the world with a veneer of sensitivity, likely expressing his personality in a nurturing and caring manner. Cancer (a cardinal sign) ruling the face of the personality suggests the steady and persistent development of it over time.

Consider how the image of this personality develops as we extend our vision to the ruler of the Ascendant. The Moon rules the Cancer Ascendant and we find his Moon in Virgo in the 3rd house, closely conjunct Neptune. My first thought when I looked at the condition of his ruling planet was: "No wonder he was chosen to be Dalai Lama!" The condition and aspects to the Moon tell a fascinating story. His need to be of practical spiritual service knows no boundaries, and he uses his voice to speak with refinement and eloquence.

Now consider that this need (his Moon) is restricted by a higher authority with the 9th house opposition of Saturn. The ongoing support of others is clear in the trine aspect from Uranus in the 11th house of the community that supports his vision. The Moon being sextile both the Sun and Jupiter puts it at the midpoint between the two, suggesting that his communications are enhanced by optimism, expansive growth, and understanding.

Consider how different this man's life would have been if his Moon, as ruler of the chart, had been in Leo in the 2nd house or in Capricorn in the 7th at the time of his birth. Would he have been chosen as the Dalai Lama at all?

Leo Rising—Tina Turner

Tina Turner, born November 26, 1939, at 10:10 PM CST in Nutbush, Tennessee, is generally regarded as one of the greatest musical artists of the 20th century and is widely referred to as the "Queen of Rock and Roll." She rose to stardom as the lead singer of the Ike and Tina Turner Revue in the 1960s and 1970s. After disentangling herself from a terribly abusive husband, she rallied to achieve what has been considered one of the greatest comebacks in music history. As the recipient of twelve Grammy awards, three Grammy Hall of Fame awards, and a Grammy Lifetime Achievement award—and as a two-time inductee into the Rock and Roll Hall of Fame—she remains one of the top-selling recording artists of all time.

In later years, Turner became a Buddhist and relinquished her American citizenship to become a citizen of Switzerland. After marrying her much younger husband, she suffered a stroke and kidney failure, and received a successful kidney transplant from him.

When you look at Turner's birth chart, the first thing to notice is the shine of her Leo rising. This immediately brings to mind certain archetypes—performer, star of the stage, queen, and heroine. These archetypes fit her like a glove. Without looking any further, you can expect that this person will show up in the world with a warm and generous personality. Leo (a fixed sign) ruling the face of the personality suggests little change in the presentation of it over time.

And this image develops as you extend your vision to the ruler of the Ascendant. We find Turner's Sun, which rules the Leo Ascendant, in Sagittarius in the 5th house. The condition of the Moon and the aspects to it tell the story. The performance of her generous and expressive creativity was unstoppable.

The expansive, expressive Sagittarius Sun in the house of creativity, along with her being born at the Full Moon, suggests that, once Turner was on her path, she didn't question it. With Mercury retrograde conjunct her Sun, her creativity and way of giving love to the world had to involve her voice telling a story that was unlike what was generally told in her time and culture. An 8th-house Mars in a powerful and tight square to this Full Moon tells you that following her path will entail a battle and power struggles with others.

We will revisit Turner's chart in Guidepost 15 when we consider grand trines. For now, let's just say that her life was an amazing example of one lived in full expression of the potential shown in her chart. Consider what her life would have been if her Sun, as ruler of the chart, had been in Pisces in the 8th house or Scorpio in the 4th at the time of her birth? Would her name be a household word?

Virgo Rising—Charles Dickens

Charles Dickens, born February 7, 1812, at 7:50 PM LMT in Portsmouth, England, is widely known as a literary genius who was one of the greatest novelists of the Victorian era. His family dreamed of being rich, but poor decisions and a tendency to live beyond their means landed them in the poor house and debtor's prison. When Charles was twelve years old, he was forced to set aside his schooling to work in a factory—a grim prospect for a child in London in 1824. His experiences certainly colored the depictions of the characters in his novels.

In the winter of 1971—a time when a transiting Saturn was squaring five of my personal planets and opposing my Saturn—I read through almost all of Dickens's novels, taking a deep dive into the depths of human suffering. At the time, I was embroiled in my own struggles and, somehow, his discriptions of suffering soothed my own. They left me feeling connected with the hardships of those beyond my own small world. I think I developed compassion as I read his works by a kerosene lamp, warming myself in a rocking chair by a wood stove. And looking at his chart now, I see how he spoke directly to me through the links between our charts.

The term "Dickensian" evokes a Saturnian ambiance that is reminiscent of the hardships depicted in his writings. It encapsulates the stark realities of social inequities and poverty, drawing on themes of suffering caused by adverse social conditions. Consider the various layers of Dickens's rising sign. Virgo rising brings to mind certain archetypes—perfectionist, craftsperson, analyst, servant, and critic. These archetypes certainly fit well with how he conducted his life and wrote his works. With Virgo rising, you can expect him to show up in the world with a veneer of kindness toward others and a practical earth-based sensitivity, expressing his personality in an analytical, well-crafted manner. With the mutable sign of Virgo ruling the face of the personality, significant changes in the expression of it are likely to occur over time, bringing to mind the message of *A Christmas Carol* and the transformation of Ebenezer Scrooge.

The image of Dickens's personality develops as you extend your vision to Mercury, the ruler of the Ascendant. Mercury in Capricorn in the 5th house points to his disciplined approach to creativity. Mercury forms sextile aspects to Venus, Pluto, and Uranus, as well as a trine aspect to his Ascendant. This underscores his natural talents and unique expression. It's no wonder he became such a prominent voice of his time and social class.

Dickens's ability to blend practical service with serious creative pursuits resonates deeply with the spirit of his era, reflecting his wisdom and his sensitivity to his personal values. Consider how different his life and his novels would have been if Mercury, as ruler of the chart, had been in Pisces in the 7th house or in Leo in the 12th. Would he have created the amazing characters that populate his books?

Libra Rising—Judy Blume

Judy Blume, born February 12, 1938, at 9:59 PM EST in Elizabeth, New Jersey, is a highly acclaimed children's author who has published more than twenty-five novels and won more than ninety literary awards, including three lifetime achievement awards in the United States alone. Blume began writing on topics that other children's authors avoided due to fear of censorship. She was one of the first young-adult authors to write about death, teen sex, menstruation, birth control, and masturbation. Her open, honest management of issues like divorce, sexuality, puberty, and bullying resonated powerfully with young people. She remains passionate about the dangers of censorship.

Blume has Libra rising, which brings to mind certain archetypes— artist, diplomat, charmer, social host, and judge. You can expect that she will show up in the world with a veneer of beauty and social graces. She will likely express her personality in a charming or diplomatic manner. As a cardinal sign, Libra ruling the face of the personality suggests the steady and persistent development of it over time.

Now consider the ruler of the Ascendant. Venus rules the Libra Ascendant, with Venus in Aquarius in the 5th house, closely conjunct the Sun and trine the Ascendant. Through this alone, you see that Blume's personality is going to be bright, shiny, a bit quirky, and highly creative, and that she will have a humanitarian bent. Venus ruling the Ascendant assures that she will be pleasurable to the eyes, and she is, in fact, a lovely woman—albeit with a somewhat unconventional beauty.

Venus is the ruling planet of the chart, being co-present with not only the Sun, but Mercury and Jupiter as well. This tells us that Blume's intellectual creativity is central to her life, and must be innovative and unique. Consider how different her contribution to the world would have been if her Venus, as ruler of the chart, had been in Scorpio in the 2nd house or in Aries in the 7th. Would she have written these priceless pieces of literature that support the growth and understanding of our daughters and granddaughters? We should all be grateful for the birth and life of this wonderful and creative woman.

Scorpio Rising—Sigmund Freud

Sigmund Freud, born May 6, 1856, at 6:30 PM LST in Freiberg/Mähren, Czech Republic, was an Austrian neurologist and the founding father of psychoanalysis. His Scorpio rising suggests archetypes like catalyst, sorcerer, shaman, psychologist, detective, and vampire. These archetypes align well with Freud's intense, probing nature and his inclination to dig beneath the surface while maintaining a cloak of privacy. With Scorpio as his Ascendant, Freud's presentation of personal intensity remained consistent over time, reflecting the fixed nature of this sign.

In modern astrology, Scorpio is governed by Pluto. In ancient systems, however, Scorpio is ruled by Mars, a personal planet. When we blend these two traditions, we see that Mars provides more direct insights into Freud's character, while Pluto represents deeper, transformative forces.

Mars is located in Libra in Freud's 12th house, which relates to hidden knowledge and the subconscious. This placement underscores his fascination with the unconscious mind and his pioneering work in dream analysis and the exploration of repressed thoughts and desires.

Pluto, the modern ruler of his Ascendant, is situated in the 7th house, which pertains to partnerships and public interactions. This indicates that Freud's transformative and intense nature significantly impacted his relationships and how he engaged with others, both personally and professionally. Freud's chart highlights his role as a transformative figure in psychology who delved into the depths of the human psyche to bring hidden aspects of the mind to light—a true embodiment of his Scorpio rising.

Sagittarius Rising—Chaz Bono

Chaz Bono, born Chastity Bono on March 4, 1969, at 12:55 AM PST in Los Angeles, California, is the celebrity child of Cher and Sonny Bono. She was born at the height of her parents' popularity as American entertainers and appeared often with them on their popular television show. In 1995, the tabloid press mistakenly "outed" Chastity as a lesbian and, between 2008 and 2009, she began the physical and social transition from female to male. Today, he is a self-identified trans-man—a writer, a musician, and an actor. He continues his involvement in LGBTQ activism.

Bono's rising sign is the mutable fire sign of Sagittarius (see Figure 20). This suggests an expansive optimistic personality and brings our attention to the archetypes of explorer, student, and philosopher. When a mutable sign rules the face of the personality, you can expect significant change and transformation of the personality over the course of the life. With this simple information, you can expect Bono to show an exterior facade of idealism and develop big opinions that are apt to morph and change over time.

The ruler of the Ascendant develops this image further. Jupiter rules Sagittarius in the 11th house conjunct Uranus and sextile Mars in the 1st house. Despite the fact that, in astrology it is always easy to make things more complex than they need to be, this chart has a certain simple clarity to it. And taking things at face value won't often lead you astray. In fact, the condition of Jupiter and the aspects to it here tell a fascinating and direct story. Uranus conjunct Jupiter demands a very public awakening to an expansion of the presentation of the personality.

Jupiter sextile Mars in the 1st house suggests an opportunity to express Mars fully. Although with Mars itself in the 1st house, you hardly need this confirmation of a direct and assertive (even male) presentation. You can further develop your understanding of the chart by considering the direct aspects to the Ascendant. Consider how differently Bono's life would have played out if his Jupiter had been conjunct the Sun in Pisces in the 4th house or in Cancer in the 8th.

Capricorn Rising—Billie Jean King

Billie Jean King, born November 22, 1943, at 11:45 AM PWT in Long Beach, California, is regarded as one of the greatest women's tennis players of all time. In 1987, she was inducted into the International Tennis Hall of Fame and, over the years, she has won many awards and received much recognition for her skill. Her many accomplishments are impressive. She is also an advocate for the LGBTQ community, as well as an advocate for gender equality and social justice.

King is probably best known for what was popularly dubbed the "Battle of the Sexes" in 1973, in which she went up against her tennis rival, Bobby Riggs. In a chauvinistic public display, Riggs had baited the top women in the sport to compete against him. Earlier in the year, he played Margaret Court and easily defeated her. The match with King was a victory that Riggs certainly believed was his before it began. But King rather easily defeated him before a television audience of an estimated ninety million viewers.

King's chart reveals Capricorn rising, which brings to mind certain archetypes—authority, hermit, strategist, and pragmatist. Capricorn rising always makes me wonder why the child came into the world as such a serious tiny adult. This personality will be expressed in a serious and mature manner. You will find no frivolity here. Moreover, Capricorn (a cardinal sign) ruling the face of the personality suggests its steady and persistent development over time.

Now consider the ruler of the Ascendant. Saturn rules Capricorn and King's retrograde Saturn is conjunct Mars in the 6th house. My first thought when looking at the condition of this ruling planet is: "The physical body must be controlled and conditioned." The Moon in the 10th Whole Sign house square Saturn suggests a need to bring that well-controlled physicality to the public. Mars under the strict control of Saturn is also one of the rulers of the Midheaven. Although this need didn't have to be fulfilled through the sport of tennis, the serious control of her physicality needed to be the vehicle of her career and her work in the world. The difficulty that King encountered in coming out as a lesbian is certainly part of this retrograde Mars conjunction to Saturn as well.

There is much to contemplate in this chart in relation to all that we know of this extraordinary woman's life. Although a great deal of her story can be illuminated by this one guidepost, I know there is a lot more to it than the simple story presented here. Consider how different her life would have been if her Saturn had been in Sagittarius, tucked away in the 12th house conjunct Mercury, or in Cancer in the 7th. Would Riggs's ego have been taken down a notch that day in 1973? Possibly not.

Aquarius Rising—Janis Joplin

Janis Joplin, born Janis Lyn on January 19, 1943, at 9:45 AM CWT, is an iconic figure in rock music, known for her powerful voice and raw emotional delivery. Joplin's chart features Aquarius rising, suggesting a personality marked by eccentricity, innovation, and a forward-thinking approach to life.

Joplin's Aquarius Ascendant is traditionally ruled by Saturn and, in modern astrology, by Uranus. Both of these planets are conjunct in her 5th house of creativity, self-expression, the giving of love, and pleasure. Saturn and Uranus each oppose her Midheaven in the 11th house. This opposition indicates a dynamic and difficult tension between her desire for personal creative freedom and her responsibility to her community. Saturn's trine to her Sun and Mercury in the 1st house further underscores the importance of discipline in expressing her individuality and creativity.

Uranus and Saturn, ruling her personality and conjunct in her 5th house, show both the revolutionary and seriously structured approach to her creative pursuits. This conjunction reflects Joplin's unique style and her ability to break new ground in the music industry while maintaining discipline and structure in her craft. The opposition to her Midheaven suggests that her groundbreaking work was often at odds with conventional expectations, leading to a public persona that was both revered and controversial. Joplin's Sun and Mercury in Aquarius in the 1st house point to a persona that is intellectually vibrant, fiercely independent, and keen on expressing her true self.

This combination of innovation and discipline made Joplin a trailblazer in her field, leaving a lasting legacy in the world of music. The condition and aspects of her Ascendant rulers tell a compelling story of a woman who lived her chart well, embodying the archetypes of the reformer and the innovator. Joplin's ability to channel her intense emotions and rebellious spirit into her music, while maintaining a disciplined approach to her craft, exemplifies the powerful interplay between Uranus and Saturn in her chart.

Joplin's chart reveals a life marked by the struggle to balance personal expression with public expectation. It is a sad fact that she lost this battle, but she certainly left her mark along the way.

Pisces Rising—Elisabeth Kübler-Ross

Born on July 8, 1926, at 10:45 PM CET in Zurich, Switzerland, Elisabeth Kübler-Ross was one of a set of triplets and weighed only two pounds at birth. When she contracted pneumonia at the age of five, she encountered death first-hand when her hospital roommate died peacefully in the bed next to her. Following World War II, still in her teens, she visited the Majdanek extermination camp and was profoundly moved by the images of hundreds of butterflies carved into the walls by those facing death in such dire circumstances. These images drew her attention to what it means to face death.

Kübler-Ross's greatest contributions include her groundbreaking 1969 book *On Death and Dying*, in which she first laid out what is now called the Kübler-Ross model. This model outlined a five-stage process for managing grief—denial, anger, bargaining, depression, and acceptance. I first read this book when I was a teenager, but had no idea at the time of the fascinating life that lay behind it. Kübler-Ross was responsible for founding more than fifty hospices around the world, including the first prison hospice at Vacaville, California. When she tried to start an AIDS hospice for abandoned babies in the mid-1980s, she ran up against the fear and

How to Read and Interpret a Birth Chart

prejudice that were directed toward those with AIDS at the time. An arsonist burned down her home and she lost everything. That event effectively put her into retirement, but she never stopped writing. On her death in 2004 at age seventy-eight, she left behind twenty-four books on death and dying, which are now available in forty-two languages.

Kübler-Ross's chart shows Pisces rising, which brings to mind certain archetypes—dreamer, mystic, poet, and prophet. You can expect that this person will show up in the world with a veneer of tender sensitivity. She will likely express her personality in a mystical or dreamy manner. Pisces, as a mutable sign ruling the face of the personality, allows for significant change and transformation of it throughout the life span.

This image develops more when you consider the ruler of the Ascendant. Both Jupiter and Neptune rule this Pisces Ascendant, with Jupiter in Aquarius in the 12th Whole Sign house opposing Neptune in Leo in the 6th. Think that through carefully.

Jupiter is tucked away in the 12th house, which can represent people who are set aside and away from the culture at large in hospitals, institutions, etc. Her Neptune is in the 6th house of day-to-day routines of healthcare. Her Jupiter forms a powerful flowing trine to her Moon in Cancer in the 5th house, while Neptune forms an equally flowing trine aspect to her Mars in Aries in the 2nd. These trine aspects bring both her emotional sensitivity and her inner strength to take action into full compliance with her overriding desire to make a difference.

Moreover, the powerful Cancer focus in the 5th house indicates the need and insistence to offer love and care to others. Alongside that, the opposition between Jupiter and Neptune is squared by a Saturn powerfully positioned alone at the top of the chart in Scorpio in the 9th house of worldview and teaching. This tells of the hard work this person must do in her life. The conditions and aspects to each of the planets that rule her Ascendant tell us much about her motivations and her life work.

Who would Kübler-Ross have been if Jupiter had been in Capricorn in her 11th house, or if she had been born with Neptune in the 7th? Would she have done the work she did in this world? Would our cultural conversation about issues of grief, death, and dying be as they are today?

GUIDEPOST 8

Idealization

Idealization is the act of believing, considering, or regarding something to be perfect or much better than the reality suggests. To idealize something is to attribute ideal or excessively wonderful characteristics to it. The perception and understanding of idealism varies considerably among individuals, but we can make some generalizations about its effects.

One obvious generalization is that Americans think of idealism as a positive thing. In fact, idealism is a foundational principle in American culture. The concept of the "American Dream," which reflects the idealistic belief that hard work and right attitude will lead to a successful and happy life, is deeply ingrained in our country's ethos. Americans tend to focus on positive thinking and positive self-talk as an antidote to almost everything. But it is also important here to recognize that social values evolve over time, shifting cultural ideals. You can find a useful analysis of this tendency in Noel Tyl's book *Synthesis and Counseling in Astrology* (pages 105–108).

Rose-Colored Glasses

We all know people who dwell exclusively on the positive while ignoring anything in the realm of negativity or even the cold truth of reality. We describe them as "looking at the world through rose-colored glasses." They choose to relate only to the bright shiny view of the world, rather than engaging with the actual realities around them. Idealization requires that we ignore, minimize, or simply don't see weakness, failings, and flaws, while maximizing virtues, merits, and rewards. People can idealize anything. We all know individuals who idealize their past, their children, or their partners.

The planets involved in idealization are our closest neighbors—Mercury and Venus, whose orbits lie between us and the Sun. Because of this positioning, these two planets always appear, from our perspective, to be rather close to the Sun. There will never be more than 28° between Mercury and the Sun in the birth chart, and no more than 48° between Venus and the Sun. As we watch the dance of the planets, these three (Sun, Mercury, and Venus) appear to move as a rather loose unit through the zodiac. It is common to find them gathered together in a horoscope. Although this is not a stellium (see Guidepost 16), it is indeed a gathering with focus and intent.

Think back to Tyl's description of the Sun as the furnace that provides heat and functionality to the entire system. The Sun is the core representation of the Self. Mercury represents the thinking processes, providing the manner and content of thought. Venus represents the most personal values, showing what we cherish and hold in highest regard. When our highest values, the manner and content of our thought, and our deepest core self join together in one sign and one house, it creates a powerful focus. Input from others that contradicts this focus may be perceived as troublesome and unwanted, and disruptive to self-perpetuating assumptions. The sign in which this gathering exists may appear so bright to us that we are led to negate outside ideas or give them little attention. This is how idealism commonly manifests in the natal chart.

Imagine that the Sun, Mercury, and Venus are gathered in Sagittarius in the 4th house. You can anticipate those with this placement will have an overly inflated view of their home as a place where they are able to express themselves fully (Sun), a place of great value (Venus) that holds endless intrigue and interest (Mercury). They are true to themselves within the family. They think about and highly value their home and their ancestry, as well as the members of their biological or chosen family. They will hold on to this view tightly, regardless of the actual reality of that home, family, and ancestry.

But what happens when the idealism held in a particular area of life is unequivocally faced with a very different reality? When we attach high expectations to our identity, our thoughts, and our values, we can expect at some point to be disappointed. Something will inevitably happen to dull the sheen. The family may not comply, or the dark side of an issue or personality may emerge from the shadows. Consider someone with these three primary planets gathered in Pisces in the 7th house and imagine how that person feels when a perfectly idealized and sensitive partner—the musician or poet—falls into a pit of despair or drinks to the point where it can no longer be ignored.

When you find yourself confronted with a chart that has this statement of idealism, look at how the other planets in the chart connect to this gathering. If you find Mars, Saturn, Uranus, or Pluto in a challenging aspect to them, idealism will still exist, but will be tempered with cynicism, skepticism, or possibly denial. These individuals may struggle against all odds to hold on to their idealism and their attachment to it. Eventually, they will learn to question and possibly remove their rose-colored glasses. If Jupiter or Neptune is in the mix or in close aspect to the gathering, however, the issues of excessive idealization may be heightened even further.

The Flip Side

Of course, there are always two sides to every story. Because those with this statement in their charts expect the best in the area involved, they approach this part of life with an unconditional anticipation of positivity. They believe that any problem can be solved and any dream realized. They never see the glass as half empty; they always see it as half full. We all understand that, if we shoot for the Moon, we will get much farther than if we shoot for Detroit.

Nevertheless, being overly idealistic can cause cracks to appear eventually. Sooner or later, the issues within the house involved will fail to meet the ideal. Sometimes this happens in a sudden and overt way; sometimes a series of small events add up to profound disappointment. The Sun's involvement tells us very clearly that there is nothing superficial here. In fact, when this happens, our very identity is at stake. We are profoundly shaken when partnerships (7th house), family (4th house), career (10th house), or the personality itself (1st house) tumble off the pedestal on which we have placed them.

When the ideals that we identify with are defeated, the resulting embarrassment and shame can be a profound challenge. The devastation can result in hurt, conflict, and anger, and we may dig in our heels ever deeper. When this happens, our idealism turns into defensiveness. We may struggle mightily to maintain the blinders that prevent us from seeing what is beyond our ideal belief, even as it stares us in the face.

But just as all bubbles must burst, idealism must fall. The ideals built with dearly held opinions and beliefs can only be upheld for so long. And when the ideals we identify with so strongly crumble, we can hit rock bottom. This can be a dangerous time, as the ego is rocked with a level of shock, embarrassment, and disillusionment that may require a long time to heal. The work that we do to heal this wound, however, can lead to a more practical path of self-expression. The statement of idealism in the chart remains, but when we make the proper effort toward realism and healing, we can learn to approach future endeavors with humility and more realistic expectations. Let's look at how this plays out in a natal chart.

Victoria Woodhull, born September 23, 1838, at 5:45 AM in Homer, Ohio, was a passionate and unconventional reformer who played a leading role in the women's suffrage movement in America. In 1872, she became the first woman to run for president of the United States. She was an activist for labor reform, a spiritualist, a healer, a businesswoman, and an advocate of "free love"—which, in the parlance of the day, referred to the freedom to marry, to divorce, and to produce children without judgment or interference from the government or social pressures. She was passionate about the need for women to enjoy personal agency over their own bodies.

With her Venus, Mercury, Jupiter, and Sun in Virgo gathered within her 1st house, Woodhull's chart tells the story of a person highly invested in developing and perfecting her self-expression and personality. Her view and understanding of herself is intricate, nuanced, and very self-focused. With Mercury retrograde, suggesting an uncommon turn of the mind ruling her 1st and 10th houses and her Midheaven, it is no wonder that she was quite idealistic—and hence not terribly realistic—in her expectations of herself.

We can only imagine her disappointment when she was not able to accomplish the reforms she imagined. As I write this, the shocking reality is that we still have not managed to elect a woman as president of the United States. Clearly, Woodhull's run in 1872 was doomed from the start. And as Tyl points out, it is hard to manage the embarrassment of defeated ideals, and they very often lead to grief.

Idealism in the Chart

When considering idealism in a chart, look for the Sun, Mercury, and Venus gathered together in one sign. If Jupiter and/or Neptune are involved, this can deepen, expand, and complicate the issue. Don't underestimate the importance of this configuration when you see it. A simple question about expectations and disappointments in the area of life where you find it can open the door to an important conversation that can bring about a meaningful shift in how individuals understand their approach to the issues involved. The sign in which the planets reside provides a powerful filter for deeper understanding.

The key to moving beyond this powerful blind spot sounds simple, but is actually very challenging. Within the area that holds the idealism, the native of the chart must learn to face reality and develop humility. Let's look at how that can play out in each of the twelve houses.

1st House

Those with this statement in the 1st house develop grand expectations that are very personal. They have a strong sense of self and a powerful belief in their ability to express themselves in a manner that will be seen as authentic by others. They lean heavily on their personal charisma. Disparagement and disapproval from others can deeply affect their confidence, leading to powerful feelings of personal disillusionment about the Self. When they learn to humbly embrace their imperfections and accept themselves in the light of reality, they can continue growing and developing their high standards and optimism. Watch for the potential of a blind spot here, because they have such certainty about themselves that it is difficult for them to see how they are perceived by others.

2nd House

Those with this statement in the 2nd house approach their financial condition with optimism and assumptions of wealth and personal value. Their self-worth is directly tied to their material wealth, as well as their ability to express their personal values in how they spend and acquire money and resources. Financial setbacks or failure to reach the level of material wealth they desire can result in powerful disillusionment and feelings of personal shame. When they develop humility, generously share their resources, and learn to appreciate inner soul abundance separate from finances, they can develop a healthier sense of self-worth and positivity.

3rd House

Those with this statement in the 3rd house have a strong belief in the power of knowledge and their ability to speak their minds to bring about change. They pursue development of thought, and their focus in this area makes them effective communicators, inspiring others to broaden their horizons. When they encounter lack of interest or skepticism toward their ideas, they can hit a wall of powerful disappointment and dismay that tests their idealism. They are under constant personal pressure to prove themselves intellectually. When they learn to communicate their ideals with humility and an open mind, they can continue growing and developing their mental and communicative skills.

4th House

Those with this statement in the 4th house tend to hold an optimistic vision and beliefs regarding family and home life. Their idealistic focus involves their home environment, their childhood family, and their forbears. They have a powerful connection to their heritage, their ancestry, and their roots. Their deep natural connection to family will be challenged when difficult personal dynamics come into play or skeletons in the closet are revealed. Familial obligations or lack of emotional support can lead to a powerful blow of disillusionment. When they set healthy boundaries with family members and learn to face the reality of the underbelly of the ancestral line with humility, they can continue growing and developing their important ancestral and family connections.

5th House

Those with this statement in the 5th house exude an energy of high creativity. They believe in the power of love, art, and personal self-expression. Their creative self-expression revolves around the act of unself-consciously giving love to children and lovers alike. When they encounter blocks or restrictions on their creativity or disdain from others for their love and creative expressions, they hit a wall of discouragement. When they do not gain validation for their creations, they are disillusioned and disheartened. But when they find intrinsic value as well as humility in their creativity and learn to experience the joy of their creative expression, they can continue growing and developing their creative endeavors.

6th House

Those with this statement in the 6th house enjoy a supportive and service-oriented nature. They believe in the power of helping others and making a positive impact through routine actions. Their focused attention and strong work ethic make them valuable contributors to any endeavor. When they are restricted in their ability to be of help to others through their own health problems or exhaustion, they feel ashamed and betrayed by their bodies. This leads to powerful disillusionment. But when they recognize and internally acknowledge the worth of their efforts, however small, they can learn to maintain their sense of idealism as well as their health.

7th House

Those with this statement in the 7th house have high and often unrealistic expectations regarding their personal relationships. The focused and idealized attention they place on potential partners can be intoxicating indeed. They believe in the power of idealistically connecting with others to build meaningful and lasting intimate partnerships. But when they are challenged by ongoing conflicts, struggles, and unmet expectations, it can result in powerful feelings of betrayal and disillusionment. When they develop a sense of individuality and humility in the face of love and partnership, they can learn to maintain an elevated love relationship, which is really what they were looking for all along.

8th House

Those with this statement in the 8th house experience a high level of confidence in their ability to help others navigate profound loss and deep emotional difficulties. Also at play is their ability to navigate the space between their values and the values of others. They believe in the power of directly confronting the deep emotions that reside beneath their values. When they encounter someone in more pain than they are able to navigate, or when someone's values overpower their own, they feel betrayed, mortified, and disillusioned. But when they learn to embrace and find strength in humility, personal vulnerability, and commitment to setting necessary boundaries, they can continue supporting and navigating the suffering of others.

9th House

Those with this statement in the 9th house tend to hold an idealized philosophical worldview. Their focused attention supports their belief in the power and importance of education, travel, higher understanding, and cultural exchange to expand cultural horizons. The importance in this chart of experiences in the development of understanding can't be overestimated. When these individuals encounter internal challenges to their worldview or are restricted in their pursuit of knowledge, they may be left feeling let down and even mortified. Learning to embrace humility and uncertainty, and to appreciate the journey itself and find understanding in novel places, can support the continuation and growth of their high philosophical ideals.

10th House

Those with this statement in the 10th house approach their careers, vocations, public image, and social reputation with idealism, optimism, and very high expectations. They believe in their ability to create success through their desire to make a positive impact on the world around them;

they embrace the role of leader. This position is challenged when they face setbacks in their careers or must navigate ethical dilemmas in a public or leadership position. The pressure to maintain a flawless public image can lead to burnout, disillusionment, and psychic pain. But when they develop a strong sense of humility within their core values and personal definition of success, they can learn to maintain their sense of idealism as they bring their light to the world.

11th House

Those with this statement in the 11th house enjoy a high level of confidence in their ability to join or develop a community that will support their hopes and dreams for the future. They believe in the power of collective support for social and individual change to create a better world. Their ability to connect with like-minded individuals makes them catalysts for change. But their optimistic expectations are tested when they encounter resistance from members of the community or face the many possible harsh realities of societal structures. Emotions of betrayal and disillusionment leave them feeling unloved and unsupported, without recourse. But when they embrace and find strength in the individual relationships within the group while celebrating small victories of support and change, they discover how to maintain their sense of social optimism.

12th House

Those with this statement in the 12th house possess an optimistic approach as they explore the unconscious mind, the patterns that undergird life, and their spiritual connection with all sentient beings. Their idealized attention is focused on the collective unconscious. This suggests a profound interest in philosophy, psychology, and spirituality. They wholeheartedly embrace intuition and believe in the power of compassion and self-sacrifice to uplift humanity. But this can be a tough place to wear those rose-colored glasses. Compulsions, mental illness, and spiritual distress can overwhelm them, resulting in gut-wrenching depths of psychic anguish and disillusionment. Spending time in solitude and nature, setting boundaries, and prioritizing healthcare practices like sleep and diet can bring them closer to a profound understanding and optimism within the patterns of the unconscious.

Keywords and Personifications

No matter where you are on your journey—from novice to advanced, or even a working professional astrologer—your ability to convey what you see in a chart is highly dependent on your ability to weave together words and stories skillfully. Language and vocabulary always support the development of wisdom.

Very early in my studies, I began what I call my "keyword notebook." Although this is clearly an old-school technique, I encourage all of my students to do the same. Yes, you can create the same thing on an app or in a simple document on your computer or phone, but the benefits of doing it "long-hand" will quickly become apparent.

Using paper and pen rather than a keyboard contributes to, supports, and encourages learning and cognitive engagement. When you write, it engages your fine motor skills, your tactile experience, and even your spatial awareness. Engaging your mind and body in this process enhances your ability to remember and comprehend. The physical act of writing connects your body to your mind and helps you commit the words to memory more easily. Writing by hand is also slower, which gives your brain more time to understand and absorb the information. And when you write on paper, you are not plagued by the distractions that come with using a computer or a phone. This keeps you more focused on your learning.

To create a keyword notebook, you will need a three-ring binder with a minimum of thirty-nine tabs. Label the tabs with the names of the signs, the planets, the houses, and the five major aspects; then place a single sheet of lined paper behind each tab. Beginning with the planets, make a column for keywords and a column for personifications or archetypes. The lists below are meant to help get you started, but you can add to them whenever you come across new keywords in books, online articles, or even memes.

Keep your notebook handy so you can make notes throughout the day of things you see or hear that remind you or connect you to your understanding of the planets, signs, houses, and aspects.

Words for Planets

The keywords assigned to the ten planets encapsulate the fundamental essence of each planet. The personifications attributed to each planet represent different expressions or interpretations of the core character, or archetype, associated with that planet. Here are some examples.

Sun

- *Keywords*: identity, ego, self-expression, vitality, life force, core being
- *Personifications*: self, hero, ruler, leader, king/queen, central character

Moon

- *Keywords*: emotions, instincts, nurturing, receptivity, changeable, core need
- *Personifications*: protector, mother, nurturer, caregiver, emotional guide, comfort seeker

Mercury

- *Keywords*: communication, intellect, learning, curiosity, logic, perception
- *Personifications*: messenger, communicator, student, trickster, storyteller, thinker

Venus

- *Keywords*: personal values, relationships, beauty, harmony, attraction, pleasure

- *Personifications*: lover, artist, diplomat, sensualist, harmony seeker, cupid/eros

Mars

- *Keywords*: action, energy, drive, aggression, passion, assertion

- *Personifications*: warrior, athlete, pioneer, motivator, competitor, defender

Jupiter

- *Keywords*: expansion, abundance, idealism, wisdom, optimism, opportunity

- *Personifications*: teacher, mentor, explorer, philosopher, benefactor, lucky charm

Saturn

- *Keywords:* discipline, responsibility, structure, limitation, life lessons, maturity

- *Personifications:* taskmaster, disciplinarian, authority figure, mentor, timekeeper, wise elder, builder, architect

Uranus

- *Keywords*: innovation, rebellion, defiance, originality, freedom, wake-up call

- *Personifications*: rebel, visionary, revolutionary, inventor, catalyst, disruptor

Neptune

- *Keywords*: spirituality, dreams, illusions, intuition, compassion, transcendence

- *Personifications*: mystic, dreamer, artist, healer, visionary, poet

Pluto

- *Keywords*: transformation, power, regeneration, intensity, rebirth, shadow

- *Personifications*: transformer, detective, shaman, phoenix, alchemist, underworld guide

Words for Signs

The keywords for the twelve signs capture the essential nature of each. When a planet is in a sign, it must adopt the traits of that sign. The personifications for each sign represent humanized versions of the sign's nature. Here are some examples.

Aries—the Ram

- *Keywords:* pioneering, spontaneous, courageous, impulsive, independent, competitive, adventurous, assertive

- *Personifications:* pioneer, warrior, trailblazer, survivor, initiator, risk-taker, leader, champion

Taurus—the Bull

- *Keywords:* patient, reliable, determined, practical, sensual, stubborn, materialistic, traditional

- *Personifications:* steward of the Earth, artisan, provider, gardener, builder, epicurean, preserver of tradition, materialist

Gemini—the Twins

- *Keywords:* curious, adaptable, expressive, witty, social, dualistic, restless, versatile

- *Personifications:* messenger, communicator, journalist, storyteller, scribe, networker, jack of all trades, conversationalist

Cancer—the Crab

- *Keywords:* nurturing, emotional, intuitive, protective, empathetic, moody, sentimental, family-oriented

- *Personifications:* nurturer, caregiver, guardian, homemaker, empath, protector, historian, comforter

Leo—the Lion

- *Keywords:* charismatic, confident, creative, proud, generous, dramatic, attention-seeking, loyal

- *Personifications:* performer, leader, creator, king/queen, entertainer, inspirational figure, charismatic leader, patron of the arts

Virgo—the Maiden

- *Keywords:* analytical, practical, detail-oriented, critical, organized, reserved, perfectionist, helpful

- *Personifications:* analyst, perfectionist, craftsperson, problem-solver, martyr, organizational wizard, healer, servant

Libra—the Scales

- *Keywords:* diplomatic, charming, balanced, social, indecisive, harmonious, relationship-focused, aesthetic

- *Personifications:* diplomat, peacemaker, advocate for justice, partner, artist, social connector, charmer, mediator

Scorpio—the Scorpion

- *Keywords:* intense, mysterious, passionate, determined, powerful, suspicious, resilient, complex
- *Personifications:* catalyst, detective, psychologist, sorcerer, alchemist, keeper of secrets, intense lover, investigator

Sagittarius—the Archer

- *Keywords:* optimistic, adventurous, philosophical, independent, energetic, impatient, freedom-loving, open-minded
- *Personifications:* explorer, philosopher, adventurer, wanderer, seeker of wisdom, student, teacher, optimist

Capricorn—the Mountain Goat

- *Keywords:* ambitious, disciplined, responsible, practical, reserved, authoritative, pessimistic, structured
- *Personifications:* authoritarian, pragmatist, ambitious achiever, disciplinarian, traditionalist, manager, strategist, hermit

Aquarius—the Water Bearer

- *Keywords:* innovative, humanitarian, independent, intellectual, rebellious, detached, eccentric, idealistic
- *Personifications:* innovator, rebel, visionary, humanitarian, futurist, eccentric, community organizer, exile

How to Read and Interpret a Birth Chart

Pisces—the Fishes

- *Keywords:* imaginative, compassionate, intuitive, sensitive, dreamy, elusive, selfless, mystical

- *Personifications:* mystic, dreamer, escapist, empath, spiritual guide, visionary poet, surrealist, romantic

Words for Houses

The surface and deeper-level keywords for the twelve houses capture the essence of the different areas of a person's inner and outer environment. You will generally see the surface level of the houses activated and expressed early in life. Individuals are more apt to be engaged on the deeper levels later in life, after they have developed maturity. Throughout life, you may see them doing a dance between the two.

1st House—Self and Identity

- *Surface level:* appearance, personality, self-presentation, physical body, first impressions, ego

- *Deeper level:* self-awareness, self-development, identity, self-image, personal growth, inner essence

2nd House—Resources and Self-Worth

- *Surface level:* finances, possessions, material values, resources, self-worth, assets

- *Deeper level:* self-esteem, core values, self-assessment, inner resources, sense of value, self-validation

3rd House—Communication and Learning

- *Surface level:* communication, primary learning, siblings and neighbors, short trips, mental activity, immediate environment

- *Deeper level:* thought patterns, mental processes, early education, self-expression, cognitive growth, inner dialog

4th House—Home and Family

- *Surface level:* home, family, emotional foundations, ancestry, sense of belonging, private life

- *Deeper level:* emotional security, family dynamics, psychological roots, inner emotional landscape, ancestral influences, inner sanctuary

5th House—Creativity and Giving Love

- *Surface level:* creativity, self-expression, entertainment, children, love affairs, play

- *Deeper level:* inner child, self-discovery, passion, authentic expression, giving love, joy

6th House—Routines and Health

- *Surface level:* work, health, service, daily tasks, duties, routines, lifestyle

- *Deeper level:* self-care, wellness, personal growth, self-discipline, inner well-being, helping others

7th House—Relationships and Partnerships

- *Surface level:* relationships, partnerships, marriage, others, social connections, one-on-one interactions

- *Deeper level:* projection, interpersonal dynamics, self-discovery through relationships, mirror reflections in partnerships, mutual support

8th House—Intimacy and Boundaries

- *Surface level:* other people's values, shared resources, sexuality, deep connections, shared experiences, boundaries

- *Deeper level:* emotional intimacy, psychological exploration, soul evolution, embracing the shadow, transformation, rebirth

9th House—Worldview and Philosophy

- *Surface level:* higher education, travel, worldview, exploration, beliefs, cultural view

- *Deeper level:* spiritual exploration, personal philosophy, quest for meaning, philosophical pursuits, journey to the divine, higher vision

10th House—Career and Public Life

- *Surface level:* career, public image, reputation, life path, status, achievements

- *Deeper level:* life purpose, public persona, self-realization, soul mission, legacy, achieving recognition

11th House—Community and Receiving Love

- *Surface level:* community, social networks, goals, aspirations, collective ideals, those who support you in your desires

- *Deeper level:* personal aspirations, idealistic visions, humanitarian ideals, collective contribution, collaborative endeavors, receiving love

12th House—Unconscious and Spirituality

- *Surface level:* places of isolation, retreat, privacy, hidden matters, secrets, silence

- *Deeper level:* the unconscious, spiritual/psychological growth, transcendence, surrender, karmic lessons

Words for Aspects

The keywords for the five primary aspects capture the relationships and conversations that planets and points have with each other. Clearly, the ways in which the internal parts of an individual communicate and engage with each other have a profound influence on all areas of the native's life.

Conjunction

- *Keywords:* unity, merging, amalgamation, alignment, cooperation, collaborative necessity

Sextile

- *Keywords:* opportunity, prospect, possibility, chance, options

Square

- *Keywords:* challenge, tension, growth, conflict, motivation

Trine

- *Keywords:* ease, support, talents, harmony, free flow

Opposition

- *Keywords:* awareness, clarity, balance, polarity, vision

Using Keywords

Now that you have created your keyword notebook, let's think about ways you can use this simple but powerful tool. First, let's look at the chart of

Melissa Viviane Jefferson (stage name, Lizzo), born April 27, 1988, at 2:30 PM EDT in Detroit, Michigan (see Figure 9).

Lizzo is a successful rapper, singer, songwriter, actress, and musician. Born in Detroit, she relocated to Houston at a young age and later settled in Minneapolis, where she embarked on a successful hip-hop career that catapulted her to stardom.

Using her Sun in Taurus in the 10th house, make a simple statement with the keywords for Sun, Taurus, and 10th house. Here, we'll use the common convention of the planet representing the "what," the sign representing the "how," and the house representing the "where."

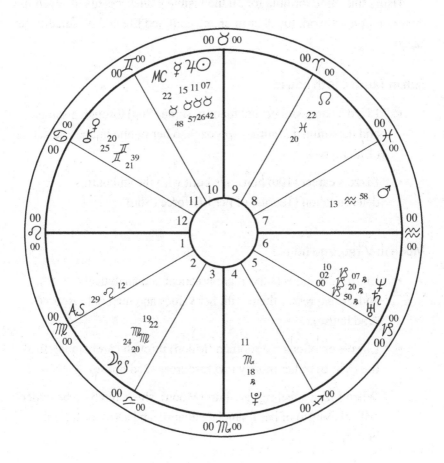

Figure 9. Chart of Melissa Viviane Jefferson (stage name, Lizzo), born April 27, 1988, at 2:30 PM EDT in Detroit, Michigan.

With multiple keywords available, you can make many sentence combinations that will all have the same core theme and feeling. In this example, the "what" is the Sun, so let's choose the keyword "ego." The "how" is Taurus, so let's choose the keyword "sensual," which is always applicable. The "where" is the 10th house, and we'll choose the keyword "career." These three words give you this simple sentence: "Lizzo's ego (Sun) is sensual (Taurus) and is expressed in her career and public image (10th house)." Or you can turn this around and say: "Lizzo uses the sensuality (Taurus) of her vital life force (Sun) in reaching for achievements in her career, public role, and reputation (10th house)."

Using this same formula for all the visible planets results in seven life themes that must work together to create a unified life and personality for Lizzo.

Sun in Taurus, 10th house

- Lizzo's core essence and identity shine (Sun) through a stable and determined (Taurus) approach to her public image and career (10th house).

- Lizzo's career (10th house) is built with the stubborn determination (Taurus) of her life force (Sun).

Moon in Virgo, 2nd house

- Lizzo's emotions (Moon) are practical and analytical (Virgo), and she expresses them with her values and material resources (2nd house).

- Lizzo's emotions are soothed (Moon) through careful analytical use (Virgo) of her money and resources (2nd house).

- When Lizzo's feelings are hurt (Moon), she is likely to be hyper-critical (Virgo) of her financial situation and self-worth (2nd house).

Mercury in Taurus, 10th house

- Lizzo's communication style and thought processes (Mercury) are stubborn and determined (Taurus) with regard to her career and social reputation (10th).

- Lizzo's career and reputation (10th house) are built on the determination and reliability (Taurus) of how she thinks and communicates with others (Mercury).

Venus in Gemini, 11th house

- Lizzo's personal values and approach to love/connection (Venus) are witty and lighthearted (Gemini) and expressed within social circles where she receives the support of others (11th house).

- Lizzo attracts a community that supports her (11th house) by verbally expressing her versatile dualistic approach (Gemini) to love and beauty (Venus).

Mars in Aquarius, 7th house

- Lizzo takes direct action (Mars) in an innovative, objective, or eccentric (Aquarius) manner in her partnerships (7th house).

- Lizzo attracts relationships (7th house) with her rebellious and unusual (Aquarius) passion and drive (Mars).

Jupiter in Taurus, 10th house

- Lizzo's ability to grow in idealism and optimism (Jupiter) come through her stubborn determination (Taurus) in building her career and public image (10th house).

- Lizzo builds a career and public reputation (10th house) by stabilizing and maintaining (Taurus) her expansive idealistic beliefs (Jupiter).

Saturn in Capricorn, 6th house

- Lizzo faces challenges and learns life lessons (Saturn) by working with steadfast discipline, nose to the grindstone (Capricorn), in her day-to-day routine practices (6th house).

- Lizzo encounters obstacles and gains valuable insights (Saturn) by embracing responsibility and structure (Saturn) in her work routines and health habits (6th house).

As you can see, each of these placements combines to create a unique blend of energies that contribute to Lizzo's overall life themes and personality.

Play with the words; move them around; find what resonates with how your mind works. Building and maintaining a keyword notebook will provide you with a never-ending supply of words to support your understanding.

Keywords and Aspects

The next simple and logical way to work with keywords is to use them to help you understand how aspects between planets manifest. Continuing with Lizzo's chart, you see that her Taurus Sun is in a square aspect to Mars. It forms a conjunction with Jupiter, trines Saturn, Uranus, and Neptune, and stands in opposition to Pluto. Let's go through each of these so you will feel confident using this technique with other charts.

Sun in Taurus (10th) square Mars in Aquarius (7th)

- You have already determined that Lizzo's Sun in Taurus represents a steadfast, determined, and traditional core to her personality, and that her Mars in Aquarius represents a rebellious and unusual approach to passion and drive. The square aspect tells you that there is a disagreement or a challenge between the two that will require effort to resolve. Her challenge will be to remain true to her stable traditional core self, while also freely expressing her cool objective and unique approach to sexuality, drive, and passion. Because this square is between the Sun in the 10th and Mars in the 7th, this challenge will play out in how she shows up in her career/reputation and how she manages her intimate and business partnerships.

- Square aspects are never easy to manage, but they do provide the motivation to do so. Over the course of our lives, we learn how to be true to all sides of ourselves, no matter how difficult the challenges may be. There are so many individual stories that could reflect this particular challenge. Because both of these planets are above the horizon and the Sun is in the 10th house in this chart, you can be sure that, for Lizzo, this will play out in the public eye.

Sun in Taurus conjunct Jupiter in Taurus

- Lizzo's Sun in Taurus offers a resolute, sensual, steadfast, and conventional essence at the very heart of her character. Jupiter expands whatever it touches and brings in her beliefs and issues of reward, optimism, and opportunity. The conjunction merges the two. So here you have a huge presence and a woman who is rewarded by the idealism she exudes by this public display of expansion. Taurus represents a feminine sense of embodiment and Lizzo stands as a representative and even an icon of body positivity for large women.

- Now extend your attention to the houses that are ruled by the Sun and Jupiter. This expansive positivity rules the first house (Leo, ruled by the Sun); therefore this is the first thing people see when they meet Lizzo. The 5th and 8th houses are also ruled by this conjunction, so you can surmise that she uses this expansive idealistic view of her body and self in her creativity (5th house) and the way she navigates boundaries between herself and others (8th house). Add Mercury, also in Taurus, to extend the story still further.

Sun in Taurus trine Saturn, Uranus, and Neptune in Capricorn

- Lizzo was born during the gathering of Neptune, Saturn, and Uranus in Capricorn, where the three danced together between 1988 and 1990. Because Saturn is in its domicile, both Neptune and Uranus must answer to Saturn's need to stabilize and build something. This adds a cultural statement of defiance (Uranus) and compassion (Neptune) to Saturn's ability to build and support. Saturn, in this trine aspect to the Sun, offers a flow of strength, determination, and persistence to support what is being built in the career (10th house). Uranus and Neptune both offer their innovative and mystical flow of energy to Lizzo's public expression. Each of these three planets in a trine aspect makes a powerful statement. The combined impact provides Lizzo with a tremendous support for whatever those Taurus planets are building, and building is just what Taurus does! Take note that this gathering is in her 6th house of daily routines, service to others, and health concerns, so you can certainly anticipate that she is a hard worker who will put her shoulder to changing and impacting the culture, even as she is changed by it.

- Whenever you see outer planets interacting in powerful ways with the personal planets, you can anticipate that those individuals will have an outsized influence on the culture of their generation. If that is not the case, you can expect that the culture or generation will have an outsized influence on them. It may be one or the other, or both.

Sun in Taurus opposite Pluto in Scorpio

- The opposition from Pluto to Lizzo's Sun suggests a powerful undercurrent working against her efforts, until she fully recognizes and harnesses the energy for awareness and inner transformation. She will have to do some serious work managing the pain and struggle in the deep roots of her biological or chosen family, her ancestry, or her home. Pluto is the co-ruler of Scorpio, and those born during the years that Pluto resided here (late 1983 through late 1995) collectively have a great deal of painful excavation and inner work to do for the transformation of the culture as a whole. Due to Pluto's position in relation to her personal planets, Lizzo is in a unique position, not only to do this work personally, but to be a catalyst by showing others the way. She may fall down some deep holes along the way, however. Astrology may be a great help to her and the trine aspect from Uranus may open that door.

Take the time to go through all the aspects in Lizzo's chart and then move on to your own chart and those of your family and friends. This is a fun practice that will teach you a great deal about yourself and the people in your life.

Out-of-Sign Aspects

The exercise above works best if you stick with aspects that are in the natural signs that form the aspects involved. But this is complicated by the pesky issue of out-of-sign aspects.

An out-of-sign conjunction occurs when one planet is in the later degrees of a zodiac sign, while the second planet is positioned in the early degrees of the following sign. Similarly, an out-of-sign sextile occurs when two planets are within the appropriate orb for a 60° aspect, but don't share the same receptive-active qualities that are often referred to, annoyingly, as their "gender expression." In the case of an out-of-sign square, two planets appear within the orb you use for a 90° square aspect, yet they don't belong to the same modality. This only occurs when one planet occupies the later degrees of a sign, and the other is found in the early degrees of another. Likewise, an out-of-sign opposition occurs when planets meet the orb requirement for an opposition, but don't share the same modality. As with other out-of-sign aspects, this results when one planet is positioned in the later degrees of a sign, while the other resides in the early degrees of a different sign.

You won't go wrong if you focus on the aspects that are within the appropriate signs for the aspect involved. The best way to understand out-of-sign aspects is to think about any you have in your own chart and ask questions about those you see in other's charts. Your curiosity will support your understanding.

Personifications

Now let's move on to the personifications. Below is a very simple technique adapted from one presented by Steven Forrest in his 1984 book *The Inner Sky*. It uses a formula to create statements by "filling in the blanks" with words from your keyword notebook.

Lizzo's Sun is in Taurus; her Moon is in Virgo; her rising sign is Leo. Choose one personification for each from the lists above and use those words to create a statement by filling in the following blanks:

[Sun sign personification] with a heart of [Moon sign personification], wearing the expression of [rising sign personification].

Here are some resulting statements for Lizzo:

- Lizzo is a *provider* with the heart of a *perfectionist*, wearing the expression of a *performer*.

- Lizzo is a *materialist* with the heart of a *craftsperson*, wearing the expression of a *charismatic leader*.

- Lizzo is an *artisan* with the heart of an *analyst*, wearing the expression of an *inspirational figure*.

Spend some time considering how the different personifications interact as they reside within one person's life and psyche. Imagine them sitting down to a meal together. How well do they get along? Is one feeling frustrated or left out? Do two gang up on the third? Do they like each other and support each other, or bicker endlessly? How does this simple analysis help you understand the person under consideration?

With regard to Lizzo, it is easy to understand that the provider and the perfectionist will be in full support of each other, as will the materialist and craftsperson, and the artisan and analyst. But you can anticipate that those personifications experience a deep awkwardness as they attempt to express themselves through the performer, the charismatic leader, or the inspirational figure.

Creating and working with these simple statements will open your eyes to some of the most basic internal challenges individuals experience. Regardless of how easy or difficult it may be for them, the energy of the Sun and the need of the Moon must both be expressed through the rising sign. How challenging it must be when the essence of the Self isn't able to express itself with ease.

GUIDEPOST 10

Signature Signs

A signature sign is the sign that corresponds to the combination of element, modality, and orientation that is most heavily weighted within the structure of a chart. Quite often, the signature sign is the same as that of the Sun or Moon. But sometimes it is a sign in which the native has no planets whatsoever. Nonetheless, this sign will play a strong role in the presentation or personality of the native.

We discussed the general characteristics of elements, modalities, and orientation in part 1. Here, we'll explore how they can deepen your understanding of a natal chart by helping you determine how the overall balance of these factors will influence the life and experience of the individual involved.

One way to determine a chart's signature sign is to prepare what is called an Element-Modality grid. This grid, which diagrams the planetary elements (E) and modalities (M), will show you where there are imbalances that are very important to your understanding of the native. There are far more complex ways of determining this balance. What I provide here is quick, simple, and efficient.

Creating an Element-Modality Grid

To create an Element-Modality grid, draw a table with five columns and six rows. Starting with the second column and working from left to right, label the next three columns C, F, and M to represent the three modalities—cardinal, fixed, and mutable (see Figure 10). Leave the last column unlabeled. This is where you will record the totals for each element.

Next, starting with the second row and working from top to bottom, label the rows F, E, A, and W to represent the four elements—fire, earth, air, and water (see Figure 10). Leave the last row unlabeled. This is where you will record the totals for each modality. Beneath the grid, leave room for recording the totals for the inward and outward orientations.

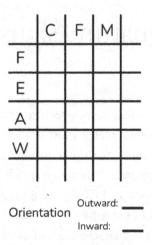

Figure 10. An empty Element-Modality grid ready to be filled in.

Now it's time to fill in the numbers corresponding to the elements and modalities of the signs in the chart. First, find the Sun in the chart and put a score of 2 in the square corresponding to the element and modality of that sign. If the Sun is in Libra, place a 2 in the square corresponding to the cardinal modality and the element of air. Do the same for the Moon, assigning it 2 points as well. Then assign 1 point to the appropriate squares for Mercury, Venus, Mars, Jupiter, and Saturn.

Now, add up the numbers in the columns, working from left to right, to determine the score for each of the elements. Enter that number in the last column. Once you have done this for all four elements, you will clearly see the balance between the elements in the chart.

Next, add up the numbers in the columns to determine the score of each of the modalities. Enter that score in the last row at the bottom of the grid. Once you have done this for all three modalities, you will clearly see the balance between them in the chart.

Finally, add the score for the fire element to the score for the air element to determine the score for the outward orientation and enter that number at the bottom of the grid. Then add the score for the earth element to the

How to Read and Interpret a Birth Chart

score for the water element to determine the score for the inward orientation and enter that number at the bottom of the grid.

Once you have completed the grid, note the element with the highest score and the modality with the highest score. These will determine the signature sign of the chart. In other words, if the element of water gets the highest score, and the modality of mutable gets the highest score, the sign of Pisces will be the signature sign.

There may be times when this process does not result in one single definitive signature sign. The scores for two or more elements or modalities may be equal, for instance. I suggest that you experiment with this in different ways. You can simply accept that the native has shared signature signs, or you can let the rising sign make the determination.

And the signature sign is only the first thing you can learn from an Element-Modality grid. Learn to note and think critically about any and all imbalances you see in the grid. Are there no fire signs represented? Is there an overabundance of air? These are terribly important factors when considering an individual's chart.

Let's test this technique by analyzing the chart of Angela Davis, born January 26, 1944, at 12:30 PM CWT in Birmingham, Alabama (see Figure 11 on page 166). This chart presents no surprises regarding the signature sign, since both the Sun and the Moon are in Aquarius. I chose it specifically to demonstrate other important information it can provide.

Angela Davis is an American political activist, scholar, and author best known for her involvement in the civil rights and Black Liberation movements of the 1960s and 1970s. Her work in advocating for prisoners' rights, racial equality, and social justice has had a lasting impact on these issues.

First, look at the balance of elements in the grid, as well as the resulting imbalance between the two orientations. This woman is almost all fire and air. Notice that Mercury is the only planet in the earth element and cardinal modality, as well as the only inward planet in this chart. Look carefully at Mercury's house placement, essential dignity, aspects, and dispositors (see Guidepost 17). Because this chart is so heavily focused on the intellectual element of air, Mercury is very important to Davis's life. You may even wonder whether Mercury in Capricorn is up to its job of starting (cardinal) and stabilizing (earth) the efforts that are important to her.

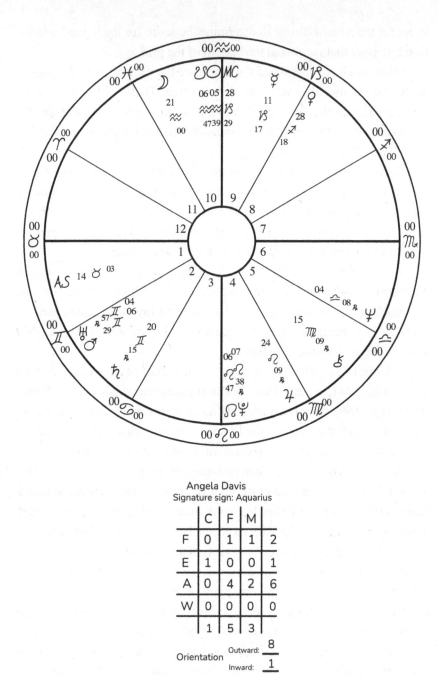

Angela Davis
Signature sign: Aquarius

	C	F	M	
F	0	1	1	2
E	1	0	0	1
A	0	4	2	6
W	0	0	0	0
	1	5	3	

Orientation   Outward: 8 / Inward: 1

Figure 11. Chart and Element-Modality grid for Angela Davis, born January 26, 1944, at 12:30 PM CWT in Birmingham, Alabama.

There is a lot to consider in this grid that you could easily miss without this simple tool. Her orientation is almost entirely outward. There is no doubt that she is a go-getter, someone pushing forward with great drive and determination. No shrinking violet here.

When you see an element or modality with a score of 0 or 1, that can tell you something as well. With no water in Davis's chart, you can anticipate that she will not be swayed by emotion, sensitivity, or nostalgia. In fact, she may struggle to understand others who are. With a score of only 1 in the cardinal modality and a score of 5 in the fixed modality, she is likely to attach herself to efforts that have been begun by others. She will take on the role of keeping those efforts going with a consistent fixed drive.

Create an Element-Modality grid for every chart you encounter. The benefits far outweigh the very minimal effort it takes.

GUIDEPOST 11

Retrograde Motion

When planets are retrograde, it simply means that they appear to be moving in a direction contrary to their normal path. In short, they appear to be going backward. In astrological terms, you can think of retrograde planets as working contrary to normal expectations. Because they are "moving against the grain," so to speak, the energies of these planets will be experienced or expressed in a unique or inward manner.

With the exception of Mercury and Venus, planets that are retrograde are found on the opposite side of the horoscope from the Sun's position. Since Mercury and Venus are closer to the Sun than the position from which we observe them, they can display retrograde movement even when they appear close to the Sun in the horoscope. Retrograde motion is shown in the chart by the letters "rx" beside the planet, indicating its current retrograde movement. The retrograde movement will dynamically change the way these planets function, making adaptations to the energies quite different from what they would be if the planet were in direct, or forward, motion.

When the personal planets are retrograde in a natal chart, an important factor to consider is secondary progressions. In astrology, secondary progressions are a predictive technique where each day after a person's birth represents one year of life. We use this method to track the inner unfolding of the chart and the native's life over time. If you use secondary progressions in your astrology work, pay particular attention to planets that are retrograde in the natal chart, as they reveal significant insights when they turn direct by progression. Keep your ephemeris close at hand to observe the path the planet has traveled in the days and weeks before and after the individual's birth.

We looked at the impact of Saturn's retrograde motion in Guidepost 4. Now let's take a look at how it affects the influence of the three most personal planets—Mercury, Venus, and Mars.

Mercury Retrograde

Because Mercury is retrograde for an average of nine weeks each year, this is the personal planet that you will encounter most often in retrograde motion in the natal charts you consider. When Mercury is retrograde in the birth chart, it suggests a different focus of the mind—the thoughts turn inward. One colleague of mine refers to this as a "ruminating mind," because those with Mercury retrograde tend to ruminate a great deal before attempting outward communication. They may have difficulty making themselves understood or understanding their own mental patterns. They may have a difficult time articulating what they mean or experience communication itself as difficult or awkward.

As the messenger of the cosmos, Mercury is expected to move from place to place quickly, delivering messages without delay. But when the messenger slows down and goes the other way, there are things you need to consider. Was something left behind that needs to be retrieved? Did a message go undelivered? Is there something you need to clarify in your mind or communication? In retrograde motion, what you normally expect of a planet is generally not what you find.

Mercury retrograde also suggests that individuals think and speak about issues that others don't deem important or necessary. Perhaps they think about astrology, while those around them consider it bunk. There are many ways that Mercury retrograde can manifest. Think about individuals whose voices just don't seem to fit them, or those who somehow surprise you the first time you hear them speak.

Consider those who grew up not trusting their own minds or their ability to express themselves. When Mercury is retrograde, the messenger may be unsure about the proper message to deliver. For these individuals, you can anticipate an insecurity regarding the contents of their minds or the ability to express what they find there. They may go over and over the implications of the communication to be delivered, unsure of what to say or how to say it. They may stand in front of the mirror trying different approaches, different word choices. Perhaps they just want to "get it right," and that uncertainty itself may be exactly what gets in the way. These are just a few possibilities, and you may encounter others. Rather than making assumptions, remember to ask questions.

How to Read and Interpret a Birth Chart

Many people with Mercury retrograde eventually find themselves in a position of using their voices in an important or significant manner. With their attention focused on this struggle, they often work hard and make a great effort to develop the mind and its ability to communicate. The aspects between Mercury and other planets will help you flesh out the story of their contribution to communication and the movement of information. Whenever working with a chart, first find the date of the person's birth in your ephemeris. Then follow the path of the various planets in the weeks before and after the individual's birth. This can help you discover all sorts of things.

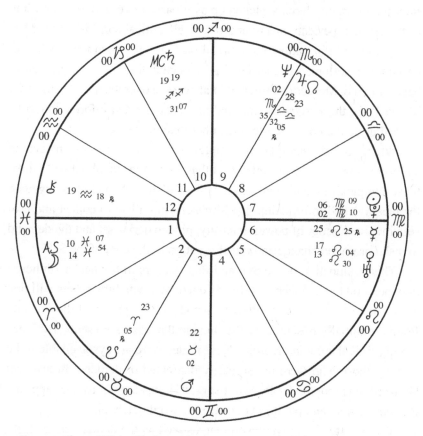

Figure 12. Chart of Michael Jackson, born August 29, 1958, at 7:33 PM in Gary, Indiana.

As an example, let's consider the chart of Michael Jackson, born August 29, 1958, at 7:33 PM in Gary, Indiana (see Figure 12). Mercury followed an interesting path as Michael's parents awaited his birth, and this in itself left a stamp on his life. Several weeks before his birth, while Mercury was still in direct motion, the planet passed the degree points of Michael's Sun-Pluto conjunction in Virgo. During its retrograde period, Mercury again passed these points as it went back into Leo, where it came to rest at his birth. In the weeks following Michael's birth, Mercury, once again in forward motion, joined with his Sun-Pluto conjunction a final time. You can explore how this will impact his life through the lens of secondary progressions.

Mercury's job is to gather, understand, and pass on information. Consider the message Mercury picked up as it passed over the Sun and Pluto in the refined, perfectionistic, and often self-critical sign of Virgo. Mercury gathered information, then turned back and revisited the area a second time, absorbing a deeper level of understanding than had previously been gathered. Mercury's third and final passage over that point came after Michael's birth, thereby leaving the final message and information to be learned or delivered in the lifetime rather than in the womb.

When you see this type of complex activity in the weeks preceding and following a birth, you can expect that the themes involved will mirror those complexities in the individual's life. With the Sun and Pluto together, the message and information that Michael's mind had to collect and process involved issues of power, intensity, hidden darkness, and the demand to make profound change and transformation to the core of the Self.

This conjunction of the Sun and Pluto occurs in Michael's 7th house in opposition to his Ascendant. In any encounter with him, others will first see the dreamy soft-spoken Pisces Ascendant. The power of the Sun and Pluto are initially obscured by the illusion that Pisces presents. But once the fog lifts, there is no hiding. These issues were always available to be seen by those who were not so easily distracted or deluded. In my own keyword notebook under Pisces, it says: "Things are not as they appear." Remember that, and put it in your own keyword notebook.

The bright shining empowerment, as well as the darker side of Jackson's story, was destined to be seen. Mercury had that planned all along. We all wish that he had played his cards differently. Remember when reading any chart not to make assumptions. Always approach any difficulties with kindness, tolerance, and nonjudgment. You may be surprised by what people tell you when you have their chart in hand. Don't underestimate the honor and privilege it is to witness the lives of others in this way.

Venus Retrograde

It always surprises me when I see Venus retrograde in a chart, because it simply is not that common. Venus spends between forty and forty-three days every eighteen to twenty months in retrograde motion, so this appears in approximately 7 percent of charts. Compare this to Mercury retrograde, which appears in approximately 18 percent of natal charts, and Mars retrograde, which appears in approximately 9 percent.

Venus is the planet we look to for information on what individuals most value in their lives. Venus focuses on love, money, resources, and things of beauty. The sign, the house placement, and the aspects to this planet provide us with information and understanding about how they experience and express love, what they create, and where they find beauty, as well as their relationship to earning, spending, and saving money. Venus represents personal and relational values. In modern Western culture, most of these values are tied up in love, money, resources, possessions, and other issues related to aesthetic beauty.

Noel Tyl referred to Venus retrograde as one of the hardest placements to have in a natal chart. I'm not sure I fully agree with him, but I certainly understand his perspective, and I mention it here to reinforce the importance of Venus's statement when in retrograde motion. You can anticipate that those with Venus retrograde will experience and understand love and beauty in ways that are not socially or culturally expected. They will likely assign a different value to beauty, to love, to money, and/or to intimacy than most of their peers.

When the relational values of an individual are at odds with the culture in which they live, it can be a challenge for them to discover, understand, and express love and beauty, and the pleasures that suit their disposition. The world around them tells them they should find beauty in sunsets. They should find love and express it in a walk down the aisle to wed their betrothed. But they may actually find beauty in the shattered hulk of a steamship and find love in a partnership that others simply can't understand.

They march to the beat of a different drum, because their internal drummer plays a very different tune. Their sense of beauty and love may seem unorthodox and may not conform to the expectations placed upon them.

There are many ways that Venus retrograde can manifest. Consider the little girl growing up in 1950s America who has no interest in marriage or being polite in the face of misogyny. Or the little boy who is unwilling to engage in "locker-room talk" and sees girls as his equal. Consider the woman who isn't stopped in her tracks by any glass ceiling and the man who supports her unconventional choices. Consider the artist who sees beauty in burned-out buildings rather than lovely landscapes, or the millionaire's child who rejects the family fortune to live on a remote island close to the earth with few creature comforts.

I think today's world supports those with Venus retrograde better than it did thirty to fifty years ago when Tyl was developing his craft. Unorthodox relationship styles find acceptance in today's world more easily than they did in past generations. We enjoy more flexibility in how we envision beauty in all its forms. We can express unusual and even radical styles of love more freely than we could in the not-so-distant past. There are so many possibilities for how this placement will manifest. As with Mercury retrograde, take the time to check your ephemeris regarding the path Venus took before and after the birth. This will give you more information regarding the complexity of the individual's path.

When you encounter someone with Venus retrograde, don't miss the opportunity to ask questions. This can be a great learning opportunity for you. It is a delight to see how creative these individuals can be in how they express their unique values of love and beauty. The chart of Brigitte Macron, born April 13, 1953, at 3:00 PM in Amines, France, is a great example (see Figure 13). Look at this chart! How exciting it would be to find this woman in my consulting room! I am certain that we would have a fascinating conversation.

Macron is a powerful woman who doesn't initially appear to be so. With that unassuming Virgo rising and the ruler of the chart in the 7th house in dreamy Pisces, you will not initially see her strength and determination. Notice how the ruler of the chart makes only a sextile to the conjunction of Jupiter and the Midheaven, and you will understand how she can easily appear to step into the shadow of her husband in her public life. But her Taurus Midheaven is ruled by retrograde Venus, which is placed auspiciously conjunct, right between the Sun and the Moon in Aries, the sign of initiation and courage. She was born shortly before the New Moon, with Venus having backed over the Sun and about to pass backward over the Moon as well.

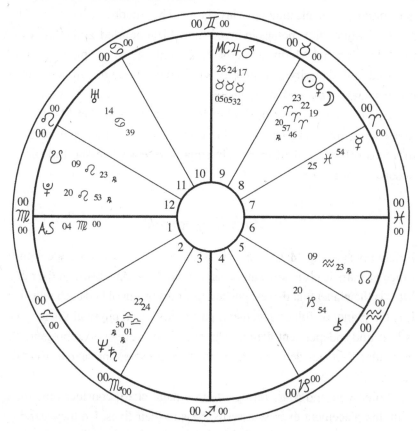

Figure 13. Chart of Brigitte Macron, born April 13, 1953, at 3:00 PM in Amines, France.

I would have many questions for Macron about her chart, not the least of which would concern her retrograde Venus. First, I would ask how she navigates other people's judgments while pursuing her own desires with determination and courage.

With this Aries gathering in her 8th house, what her heart desires will certainly raise eyebrows within her circle and in the culture at large.

Macron's Venus rules her 9th and 2nd houses, suggesting that, as she develops and acts on the courage of her values, she supports, not only her ability to navigate the opinions of others (8th house), but her understanding of the greater world (9th house) and her personal self-worth (2nd house). It is within the choices that she makes—the ones that go against the grain of others' opinions and beliefs—that she learns the strength of her courage and, ultimately, who she is. The unconventionality of her personal values and choices in love is upheld, supported, and inflamed by the Aries Sun and Moon, while Neptune and Saturn in opposition push her need to find clarity and stability within the context of soft boundaries, dreams, and, in the end, clear vision.

Uranus in a loose square to Venus further suggests that Macron will love courageously in a unique and unusual manner. Pluto in a trine aspect to Venus offers a gift of incredible empowerment when she follows her unconventional path.

Mars Retrograde

Before considering Mars in a retrograde state, let's consider the significance of Mars itself in any natal chart. What does Mars bring to the table? Mars is the planet that drives, pushes, or drags us out of bed each morning. It is the planet of full engagement, particularly in a physical sense. Mars is heat and independent action. The sign Mars resides in represents the particular flavor of determination, anger, aggression, or sexual drive the native will embody.

When you find Mars retrograde in a natal chart, consider how those with this placement express assertiveness in their lives. Do they stand up for themselves, express anger, and take risks? Or are they are fearful about taking the wrong action, and so struggle to take any action at all? Perhaps they act too quickly, without forethought.

There are many ways in which Mars retrograde can manifest. Consider the little girl who wants to climb trees and play baseball. Consider the little boy who wants to avoid these activities at all costs. Consider those whose sexual expression goes counter to what is expected by their families or the culture at large. Consider the child who is disgusted by the violence that is considered normal in the family. Or the little boy who doesn't want to hunt with his dad and brother, or the little girl who does. These manifestations are similar to those of Venus retrograde, but they involve more physicality and issues that are deemed assertive and aggressive within the family and culture involved.

One of my clients who had this placement explained that she felt as if she had more inner strength and energy than anyone she knew, but that it was somehow held tightly on a leash. She felt held back in situations related to drive, ambition, autonomy, and physicality. She thought that it was her timing that was off. But as she got older, she learned the signs of when her timing was right and she was able to move forward without being pulled back. She discovered that it was important for her to avoid competition and find her own pace.

The chart of famous Russian ballet dancer Mikhail Baryshnikov, born on January 27, 1948, in Riga, Latvia, Soviet Union, demonstrates this well. Baryshnikov has Mars retrograde in Virgo. He clearly followed his own pace and timing in his dancing, in which the precision, discipline, and perfection of Virgo are obvious. Working through an art form that is typically considered to be feminine, he expressed himself in a powerful and formative manner. His chart is particularly interesting, however, because we don't know his time of birth, so we don't have any house-based information. Others with Mars retrograde include Frida Kahlo, Martin Luther King, Jr., Cass Elliot, Jim Morrison, Mae West, Humphrey Bogart, Morgan Freeman, and Jack Nicholson.

At the risk of being redundant, I remind you: Don't make assumptions. Ask questions and learn from each and every chart and individual you consider.

GUIDEPOST 12

Aspects and Unaspected Planets

In part 1, we looked briefly at aspects and orbs and the role they play in the natal chart. Here, we'll look into these issues more deeply.

Although you do not need to use more than the five major aspects discussed in part 1—conjunction, sextile, square, trine, and opposition—the addition of minor aspects and extending orbs can sometimes help to elucidate difficult issues in a chart, provided that you do not let them distract you from the chart's main message. Here, we'll consider aspects as internal conversations. Then we'll look at allowable orbs and out-of-sign, or dissociate, aspects.

Aspects as Internal Conversations

Use your own chart to consider each planet as a distinct character, or as part of your personal internal family. Think about the chart as a large round dining room table with various characters (planets) sitting around it. Consider that the aspects represent the conversations that take place between these characters. Some will have an easier or more difficult time communicating with others because of the angle and distance between them. This is how aspects operate.

Signs of the same element (fire, earth, water, air) harmonize with each other. If they are within your allowable orb, they are in a trine aspect. Signs of the same modality (cardinal, fixed, mutable) are either square or in opposition to each other. There is stress and distrust as well as clarity between signs opposing each other. If they are within your acceptable orb, they are in opposition. If they are in a square aspect and within your allowable orb, they are at cross-purposes with each other, and action will be required to work out the differences. Signs that are in a sextile aspect to each other will be in a different element and different modality, but in the same orientation. Their elements are complementary, suggesting harmony for these aspects.

Once again, think about the planets around the chart as characters around a large round table. Put yourself in the position of each planet and scan the table, while considering the angle and distance between yourself and the other nine characters. Think about the planets with which you would be most likely to converse.

The two or more characters or planets involved in a conjunction (0° separation) have no choice but to be party to the same conversations. Everything one says, the other hears, considers, and responds to. How this works with any particular conjunction depends on the planets involved. Clearly, a conjunction between Jupiter and Venus will produce a connection and a conversation that will be a far cry from one resulting from a conjunction between Mars and Pluto. All conjunctions blend and combine the energies of the planets involved. So keep in mind that planets in conjunction look at the world from the same perspective.

The planets or characters that are seated in opposition—180° across the table from each other—share the clearest sightline, and yet are a bit too far away from each other to carry on a conversation. Because an easy conversation isn't possible, stress may seep in as each becomes suspicious of the other's motives. It is important that indiviuals keep their oppositions clearly in view, and understand that each character within the opposition is a part of them. It is all too easy for them to project one side or the other onto others in their lives, but both sides are actually part of their internal landscape.

Another simple way to understand an opposition is by thinking of it as a teeter-totter or a seesaw. The opposition represents a dynamic interaction between two characters with contrasting qualities and agendas. As one planet rises, the other descends, creating a constant back-and-forth, give-and-take motion. As each side pulls in the other direction, it requires continual effort to find a balance point between these forces—giving equal attention to each side, while seeking equilibrium and understanding between the conflicting planetary energies. Over time, this effort can lead to great clarity.

It is crucial to recognize the tendency of individuals with strong oppositions involving personal planets to project one side of the equation onto another. Consider those with a potent opposition of planets in Taurus and Scorpio. They may perceive themselves as lovely, calm, long-suffering, and loyal. When they fail to embrace the broader perspective that acknowledges both sides of the opposition as part of their inner nature, they may attribute intensity, a need for privacy, and a possessive nature solely to their partners. This not only creates an adversarial dynamic between them and others; it can also create a tension within their own inner being. Two planets in opposition will reside in signs that are in the same modality, but in different elements.

From any point at the table, there are two positions that are 120° apart (trine). Any planet or character in these positions may still be too far away to engage in conversation, but you may find that, in fact, nothing needs to be said. Everything in their manner and expression makes it easy for you to trust them. They wink at you; you wink back. And you each recognize the easy resonance. You relax, knowing you are on the same team and are there to support each other. Any character/planet that is in a trine aspect to another can be a great ally and cheerleader, always available to lend a hand and help you move forward. A trine aspect is an active gift flowing between the two.

The reason these two planets resonate so effortlessly is rooted in the fact that they are in the same element. Regardless of the starting point, moving 120° in either direction leads to the other two signs within the same element. This elemental similarity serves as a unifying force, fostering an inherent understanding and compatibility between the two characters or planets involved.

Likewise, there are two positions 90° on either side of each character at the table (square). This is an awkward and uncomfortable angle from which to carry on a conversation. You may prefer to avoid engaging with these characters altogether, but your eye keeps drawing your attention in their direction. You understand instinctively that there is something between you that must be worked on and resolved. Each time you look toward these characters, they are looking back at you. There seems to be an unspoken understanding of an unresolved tension between you that must be addressed. A square aspect demands that the two planetary characters involved engage with each other in a good-faith effort to resolve their considerable differences.

Square aspects occur within the same modality, but in different elements. While the two characters in question share the same overall approach or style in how they operate (modality), they express themselves in distinct ways and possess very different elemental qualities. This contrast brings challenge and complexity to the interaction between the two energies, requiring conscious effort and negotiation to find common ground and work out their differences.

When two planets are in a square aspect, they are at cross purposes. One wants to go in one direction, one in another. The results of the efforts made to resolve the difficulties of a square are of the utmost importance. This is where accomplishments occur and difficulties are resolved. This is where we develop strength of character and make a difference in the lives of others.

Those planets in a sextile aspect are 60° apart in each direction. In order to engage in a conversation with them, you will have to make a bit of an effort—not much, but just enough that you could choose to ignore these exchanges. Although these conversations can be easy to avoid, they can be of great value. The conversations between two planets that are in a sextile aspect open doors and provide opportunities.

Now imagine a planet that forms a sextile aspect with one planet and a square aspect with another. If both of these planets are on the same side (either east or west) of the first planet, consider what happens. As you face the planet in the sextile aspect, the planet forming the square aspect is within your field of view. While the square presents challenges and tension, your ongoing interaction with the sextile planet will help mitigate this discomfort simply because you become more accustomed to the planet in question. The supportive nature of the sextile acts as a bridge, providing opportunities for growth and resolution in dealing with the challenges posed by the square. In essence, the sextile aspect serves as a helpful intermediary, allowing you to address and navigate the complexities of the square in an easier more constructive manner.

Allowable Orbs

As we saw in part 1, the term "orb" refers to the range within which an aspect's influence can be expected to function. If aspects functioned only when the planets were at the precise degree of a particular aspect, we would have very few indeed. So we allow a certain amount of "wiggle room," which is called the orb. The less wiggle room, the tighter the orb, and the stronger the influence of the aspect.

As an example, consider a natal chart with Venus at 8° and Leo and Saturn at 14° Scorpio. Because you know that Leo and Scorpio are fixed signs that are separated by 90°, you can expect a square aspect between these two if the orb is close enough. The difference between 6° and 14° is 7° degrees from exactitude, which may or may not be within your allowable orb. This "orb of influence" tells you the range—the distance before and after the exact aspect—in which you can expect the aspect itself to function.

Astrologers all have their own opinion about what is an allowable orb. There is no magic number, and different astrologers use different orbs. Over time, you will settle on what works best for you. I tend to use a slightly wider orb for the Sun and the Moon than for the planets. For conjunctions, oppositions, squares, and trines, I use an orb of 8° for aspects that are formed to the Sun and Moon, and 7° for aspects formed between the planets. For the sextile, I use 7° for those that are formed to the Sun and Moon, and 6° for those formed between the planets.

Dissociate (Out-of-Sign) Aspects

A question arises when planets are in aspect by orb, but not by element, modality, or orientation. As an example, consider a chart in which Mars is at 2° Gemini and Uranus is at 28° Taurus. By orb, these planets are conjunct. However, since they are not in the same sign, the impact of this aspect will be reduced. In a chart in which Pluto is at 3° Virgo and Venus is at 27° Aquarius, these planets are in opposition. But they are not in the same modality, so the impact of this aspect will not be as significant as you may expect. It is important to consider this when you see planets at very early or late degrees of a sign. Be sure to remain fully aware of these complexities when you are dealing with out-of-sign aspects.

Should you ignore these aspects? Or are they important in their own right? This is one of those times when you get to choose. Generally, I tend to tuck them aside while remaining aware of them. There are always more pressing things to discuss in a chart than an aspect that is out-of-sign. But if, within the context of your conversation with the individual, you find that the out-of-sign aspect is relevant, then use it. Just be sure not to be caught off-guard.

Unaspected Planets

Now that you understand the types of conversations represented by aspects between planets, let's turn our attention to the occasional planet that is out-of-touch and disconnected from the others. Some use the term "peregrine" or "feral" to describe these planets. But those terms have other astrological meanings, so let's simply call them what they are—unaspected planets.

There are a few things to consider when determining if a planet falls into this category. First, the term refers only to the five major aspects between planets. Do not consider minor aspects or aspects to angles, asteroids, nodes, or other points in the chart. Second, because a planet without an immediate conversational partner will reach out farther than normal to establish a connection, it is advisable to widen the orbs used in this assessment. You have to think beyond the aspect grid. Although I encourage you to widen the allowable orbs you use, do not extend them into out-of-sign aspects. Always ask about the issues of the house containing the unaspected planet, as well as the house(s) ruled by it. This will clarify how it functions in a particular chart, and how well people have integrated it in their lives.

Back to the Table

Once again, imagine the planets as characters sitting around a large round table. Notice how they are gathered in various configurations, having different types of conversations (aspects) among themselves. Several may be huddled together talking intimately; a few may be arguing about something terribly important; others may be eyeing each other across the table with distrust; some may seem to be excited and making plans for the future. Knowing that the planets in their orbits move counterclockwise around the chart, you can see which ones are reaching out toward each other and which are moving away. Always visualize the planets moving counterclockwise around the perimeter of the chart. You can deepen your understanding of them by considering the speed and direction of their movement.

If you notice that one planet is all alone and that, even by stretching the orb a few degrees, there are no conversation partners by any major aspect, this is an unaspected planet. Due to its placement at the table, it is alienated and not included in or engaged in any conversations. How would this make you feel and what would you do about it if you were the planet in question? The answer depends, to some extent, on which planet is in this solitary placement, the sign and house position it holds, and the house(s) it rules.

Integrating the energy of unaspected planets is of great importance. Because they are not taken into consideration by their cohorts, they may feel invisible or highly misunderstood. Those with unaspected planets in their chart may feel that they are "marching to a different drummer" in the area of life indicated by the placement or rulership of these planets. Generally speaking, particularly early in life, unaspected planets will seek attention by becoming loud and possibly overbearing because they are alone, disconnected, and isolated. In the resulting vulnerability, their expression may become overwhelming and discordant to the rest of the personality. Thus they commonly take on the role of mavericks, becoming dominant players in the chart. This dominance may be expressed in a wide variety of ways—as anger, arrogance, sadness, despondency, or overexcitement. Feeling misunderstood, they have little to lose and may become preoccupied with their own issues, expressing them in an untamed, raw, and/or unfiltered way.

As life progresses, however, transits to unaspected planets will encourage and allow integration of the energies involved. As a result, all that they represent can become a source of great strength over time. These areas of the life are ripe for the development of a unique and highly individual path.

Without social or familial validation, those with unaspected planets must cultivate a deep sense of self-acceptance and self-reliance. When allowed to mature, these planets grant them the freedom to find their own path forward beyond expectations or norms.

Let's take a closer look at how this might play out in each of the planets.

Unaspected Sun

An unaspected Sun suggests a distinct and independent expression of the core identity. Those with this placement may struggle with feelings of disconnection and being misunderstood. Through personal growth and self-reflection, they must learn to embrace their unique individuality and develop a strong sense of self apart from societal or family expectations.

These individuals must make the effort to cultivate self-acceptance and belief in their own worth and capabilities. They are driven and dedicated in pursuing their passions and goals, because their unwavering determination propels them forward. They will need to develop introspection as they come to a healthy state of self-acceptance. As they embrace their true self and radiate their authenticity, they become a source of inspiration for others.

Vincent van Gogh, born March 30, 1853, at 11:00 AM in Zundert, Netherlands, is a good example. His Aries Sun is unaspected in the 10th house ruling the 2nd. In trying to assert himself directly to boost his ego, he encountered difficulty both in supporting himself financially and in developing his self-worth, leading to struggle and discord. During his life, he was considered a failure and even a madman.

There is little question that, at the very core, van Gogh was misunderstood by and disconnected from the artistic community of which he longed to be a part. The expression of his Aries Sun, his life force, manifested in ways that others did not understand. With his Sun ruling his 2nd house, his inability to connect left him financially dependent and living in poverty throughout his life. His self-esteem must have suffered mightily.

But van Gogh's unaspected Sun also granted him the freedom to explore his unique interests, passions, and creative instincts without being influenced by societal expectations or norms. He had little choice but to embark on his own profound introspective journey, to discover and embrace an authentic path in his work and his life. We are grateful for the gifts his unaspected Sun provided. Without it, he never would have created the masterpieces that he left behind.

Unaspected Moon

An unaspected Moon in a natal chart reveals a unique emotional land-scape. These individuals experience their emotions in a distinct and solitary way, as their feelings are not easily swayed by external influences or connections with others. With a pronounced sense of emotional independence, they may find solace in a deeply solitary emotional world, unburdened by the expectations or judgments of those around them. This introspective quality leads them to engage in deep self-exploration, and allows them to gain a profound understanding of their inner emotional workings. Their emotional responses tend to be deeply personal, and they may have a unique approach to handling and processing their feelings. You can also consider what this unaspected Moon suggests about their relationship with the mother and their own ideas about nurturing others.

Chelsea Clinton, born February 27, 1980, at 11:24 PM in Little Rock, Arkansas, demonstrates this well. Her unaspected 10th-house Leo Moon is quite interesting. We know who Chelsea is because of her politically famous parents. Looking at her chart, we see Saturn retrograde ruling her 3rd house and opposing Mercury, also retrograde. She likely has to work very hard to shape her thinking in a way her father will approve. But her mother is another story. With her unaspected Leo Moon in the 10th house ruling the 9th, it is her mother with whom she aligns herself and her mother's worldview that is powerfully amplified in her life.

As a young woman, Chelsea Clinton was clearly in the public eye and yet paradoxically hidden away. There was a great deal of respect and privacy given to her during the years that her father was in the White House. Beyond the time spent under parental control, her focus has been on 9th-house issues of higher education, personal worldview, philosophy, and global concerns. In 2003, she completed a graduate degree in international relations from Oxford University, with her thesis focused on global initiatives to fight AIDS. In 2014, she completed doctoral work that focused on global governance. In the years since, she has published several children's books that introduce middle school children to a range of social and global 9th-house issues, and co-founded an independent production company with her mother that is dedicated to creating films that empower women and activate audiences through understanding of the world we live in.

Clinton's chart is a powerful one. Her relationship with her mother and the work they do together will always stand outside of social expectations. Regardless of what it may look like to the outside world, I expect that she has done deeply personal emotional work. She may indeed be working with her mother (Moon), but make no mistake—it is her own unique individual work that she is doing.

It is also important to note that Chiron is in a close square aspect to Chelsea's Moon. Because Chiron is an asteroid, this does not disrupt the unaspected status of her Moon, but it certainly suggests her need to face deep wounds connected with her mother or her relationship with her. Her accomplishments, particularly the ones connected with or in response to her mother, will bear watching over the coming years.

Unaspected Mercury

An unaspected Mercury in a natal chart signifies a distinctive pattern of thought and communication. Individuals with this placement tend to be highly independent thinkers, forming ideas and opinions that are not easily influenced by others. They possess a strong desire for knowledge and engage in self-directed learning, constantly seeking intellectual stimulation. Reflective by nature, they dedicate significant time to analyzing information and pursuing deep understanding. This introspective focus contributes to their intellectual depth and self-awareness. Moreover, they have a knack for approaching issues and problems from various perspectives, leading to a unique approach to problem-solving.

As we might expect, Mohandas (Mahatma) Gandhi's chart provides a fascinating study of this. Born October 2, 1869, at 7:08 AM in Porbandar, India, Gandhi is best known for advocating for the civil rights of Indian citizens and as the leader of India's nonviolent movement for independence from British rule in 1947. His method of nonviolent protest was called *satyagaha*, a Sanskrit word that means "insistence on truth." In all of this, we see his Libra Sun rising, ruled by Venus in Scorpio conjunct Mars opposing Pluto and Jupiter—and so much more. But let's slow down and look more closely at his unaspected Mercury, which is in Scorpio in the 2nd house, ruling the 9th and 12th.

How does this placement play out? It is relatively easy to understand Gandhi's work when we consider that his chart brings together issues of the 2nd, 9th, and 12th houses with the dark intensity of Scorpio. He lived a life of purposeful poverty, being a true minimalist long before that term was coined. He believed that true poverty was akin to violence, and that any wealth beyond what was necessary should be given away to those in greater need. Clearly, his thinking carried the deep intensity of Scorpio, bringing topics of money and resources (2nd house) to a global view (9th house) and highlighting how these issues impact the suffering of the collective (12th house).

Moreover, Gandhi's Mercury is conjunct his Ascendant by degree (an out-of-sign aspect). Because the Ascendant is not a planet, this aspect does not disrupt the unaspected status of his Mercury, but it does show how directly his voice is used in the full expression of his personality.

Unaspected Venus

An unaspected Venus in a natal chart signifies a distinctive approach to love, relationships, pleasure, and aesthetics. Individuals with this placement possess a strong sense of independence when it comes to matters of the heart and matters of pleasure and beauty. They tend to forge their own path in these issues and are not easily swayed by societal expectations or external influences. This independence allows them to define their own standards, often appreciating unique and unconventional forms of love, art, beauty, pleasure, and aesthetics.

Hugh Hefner, born April 9, 1926, at 4:20 PM in Chicago, Illinois, was an American publisher who founded *Playboy* magazine and the Playboy empire. These enterprises were wildly successful throughout the 1950s and 1960s, and beyond. In the years that followed the birth of the magazine, Hefner (Mercury rx rules the Midheaven) built his brand from a comparatively modest beginning to include a worldwide network of casinos, hotels, and clubs.

Hefner's unaspected Venus is in the 7th house ruling the 2nd and 9th. The issues of the 2nd and 9th houses join together with the dreamy imagination and questionable hold on reality of Pisces. This is quite clear in Hefner's dreamy image of women, love, and relationship, which was decidedly unhinged from reality. Venus ruling his 2nd and 9th houses suggests that how he uses his understanding of value and beauty impacts his finances, his own sense of self-worth (2nd), and his worldview (9th house). Given that he created an entire worldview from his overblown unrealistic perspective on women and made a fortune from that frame of reference, this is crystal clear.

Hefner surrounded himself with Venus in the form of luxury, opulence, and beautiful women. He advocated for freedom in areas of sexuality and self-expression. Along the way, he became politically active as he battled for freedom of the press, freedom of speech, and sexual liberation. His patriarchal, male-centric position (Aries Sun and Mercury ruling his personality, career, and unconscious mind) is clear and ever-present in his life. His unaspected Venus contributes to a disconnect from and lack of understanding of actual women and the true value of sexuality and human connection. The beat of his "different drummer" in this area became his strength and his gift, impacting the culture in both positive and negative ways. It is also interesting to note that, when the first issue of *Playboy* was published, Jupiter was conjunct his Midheaven and Uranus was conjunct his north node.

Unaspected Mars

An unaspected Mars in a natal chart suggests a distinct and individualistic approach to assertion, action, anger, and drive. Individuals with this placement tend to exhibit a strong sense of independence and self-motivation. Their energy, ambition, and assertiveness are not easily influenced or directed by external factors or societal expectations. They may also possess a unique way of pursuing their goals and desires. They can be highly self-directed and may not conform to traditional methods of achieving success. Their assertiveness is marked by a willingness to blaze their own trails and take unconventional approaches to problem-solving and accomplishing their objectives.

The chart of Emily W. Davison, born October 11, 1872, at 12:30 AM in London, England, demonstrates this clearly. Her unaspected Mars makes her unimaginably difficult life easier to understand. Davison was an English suffragette who fought for the vote of women in the early 20th century. As a member of the Women's Social and Political Union (WSPU) and an unrestrained radical militant warrior for the cause, she was arrested nine times, went on seven hunger strikes, was brutally force-fed on forty-nine occasions, and was once fire-hosed for fifteen minutes. Her death beneath the hooves of King George V's horse during the 1913 Epsom Derby catapulted her to the status of suffragette martyr. Whether that was her intention is unclear to this day.

Davison's unaspected Mars is in Virgo, in her 2nd house ruling her 4th and 9th. How does Mars in Virgo play out? Virgo knows what is right and proper, but Virgo also wants to be of service in a practical way. Davison's chart shows that her sense of self and her worldview prevent her from relinquishing righteous indignation and rage regarding her treatment at the hands of the patriarchy. Pushed into overdrive, Mars moves her to take a wildly bold action in the service of the cause of the suffragettes. Her profound rage at the injustice she sees and experiences demands that her deepest core values (4th, Scorpio) be fully expressed in the political arena (9th, Aries). Her rage was indeed extreme; her view of necessary action was misunderstood; and she was most certainly marching to a different drummer than most. Great causes often need, and ultimately attract, martyrs. And Davison's unhinged and unaspected Mars put her clearly into this role.

Unaspected Jupiter

An unaspected Jupiter in a natal chart reveals a strong sense of individualism in matters of expansion, growth, beliefs, luck, and optimism. These individuals tend to chart their own course for personal development and often embrace unique opportunities for growth. They have a distinct, self-directed approach to seeking knowledge, wisdom, spiritual understanding, and abundance. They are not readily influenced by external expectations or conventions. This further suggests a powerful independence and willingness to go their own way, shaping their destiny in a manner that reflects their unique beliefs.

Janis Joplin, born January 19, 1943, at 9:45 AM in Port Arthur, Texas, is a good example of this. Joplin brought an electric intensity to the culture of the late 1960s. Hers is a powerful chart with many factors that reflect her life, how the world understood and grappled with her personality, and how she lived and died.

Jupiter is unaspected in Joplin's chart; it is also retrograde. But look again. Mars is also unaspected and is disposed by Jupiter. In astrology, a "dispositor" is a planet that rules the sign that another planet occupies. We will discuss them in more detail in Guidepost 17. For our purposes here, suffice it to say that this disposition points to the primacy of Jupiter's unaspected state. The unaspected Mars may be important; but Jupiter holds the key.

Joplin's unaspected Jupiter in Cancer is in her 6th house, ruling the 2nd and 11th. How would Jupiter in Cancer play out? Consider how the vulnerability of unhinged extremes in the day-to-day routines of the 6th house are reflected in her overindulgence in drugs, alcohol, and sex, and her lack of stable self-care. By extension, when we bring these issues to the houses that Jupiter rules, we see how her overindulgence impacts her resources and self-worth (2nd house), along with her ability to feel loved by her community of fans and musicians (11th house).

The depth of Joplin's vulnerability is crystal clear in her life. She seems simply unable to tamp down her push toward excess and demonstrates a clear disregard for the risks she takes. She also displays an inability to know (or take action on) when enough is enough. Her day-to-day vulnerability and indulgent extremes (Cancer, 6th house) result in and from her need for love (11th house) and expressly challenge her self-esteem and ability to support herself financially (2nd house). She created her entire career out of extremes that profoundly impacted her relationship to money, her personal self-worth, and her ability to experience the love of her fan base (11th house).

But let's not neglect the other side of this run-away Jupiter. Joplin's buoyancy, her enthusiasm, and her exuberance were palpable. She was accepting of people from all walks of life in an era when that was not common from a white girl who grew up in a small city in Texas. I miss her raw unfiltered vulnerability and her palpable energy. Just imagine how much more her voice could have brought us if only her overindulgence had not taken her from us at such an early age.

Touching briefly on Joplin's unaspected Mars, we see that her Sagittarius Mars is disposed (ruled) by Jupiter, putting Mars "in service" to Jupiter. Note the house where Mars resides and the houses that it rules. Her raw, unfiltered, opinionated energy is expressed first in the community that supports her (11th house). The house rulership of this dominant Mars is expressed through the projection of her voice (3rd house) and her social reputation (10th house).

Unaspected Saturn

An unaspected Saturn in a natal chart signifies an individualistic approach to discipline, responsibility, hard work, and structure. Individuals with this statement in their natal chart take self-reliance and self-discipline to heart, adhering to their own set of rules and principles. They may approach challenges and obligations with a unique sense of responsibility and self-imposed structure, making them highly self-sufficient in navigating life's demands. With this planet of authority unaspected, you can expect individuals to demonstrate a fierce independence and a willingness to forge their own paths regarding how they manage work and responsibilities. They will probably work hard to shape their destinies in a unique manner that reflects this.

Jim McElreath, born February 18, 1928, at 8:00 AM in Arlington, Texas, is a good example. Unfortunately, we don't know much about his early life, so it is difficult to say anything about how his father played into the Saturn archetype. But it is worth noting that this archetype represents, not only the native's father, but also the capacity to father children.

McElreath began racing cars at seventeen and went on to have a wildly successful career. In 1977, he and his son attempted, without success, to become the first father/son team to qualify for the Indy 500. They never had another opportunity, because his son died in a crash later that year. In 2000, his daughter died in another car accident along with her husband, who was also race car driver. Shortly after this, his wife suffered a stroke that confined her to a wheelchair.

It's a good thing that an unaspected Saturn is expressed through stoicism, effort, and hard work, because these issues clearly played a larger-than-life and very public role in McElreath's story. The tragedies in this life have been very public, yet they never diminished his commitment to his career. He continued to drive and win titles. In 2002, he was inducted into the National Sprint Car Hall of Fame.

Saturn is conjunct the Midheaven in McElreath's chart, putting his focus, his efforts, and his parenting clearly in public view. Saturn rules his 11th house, the community that supports and loves him for his dominance on the racetrack. I have included this chart for a couple of reasons, despite the fact that, if we stretch the orbs in it, Saturn loses its unaspected status. For one thing, it was difficult to find a chart with an unaspected Saturn. And for another, take a look at Jupiter!

Jupiter disposes Saturn in this chart, causing me to look at it immediately in relation to Saturn. Jupiter and Uranus are conjunct in the 2nd house and neither form any major aspects beyond their joint conjunction. They sit together, speaking only with each other, without input from anyone else at the table. This is called an "unaspected island" (see below) and it puts a clear spotlight on McElreath's uniquely inflated feelings of self-worth, as well as his money-making capacity. This is a great reminder that we need to keep an eye out, not only for individual unaspected planets, but for unaspected islands as well. We'll talk about these a bit more at the end of this guidepost.

Unaspected Uranus

An unaspected Uranus in a natal chart suggests an unusual and individualistic approach to innovation, change, and originality. People with this placement tend to be free thinkers who embrace their own unique perspectives on life. They're often trailblazers, unafraid to break from tradition and explore unconventional ideas and experiences. This independence

How to Read and Interpret a Birth Chart

from societal norms can lead to unexpected and innovative solutions to challenges, as they approach problems from a fresh and unorthodox angle. Their natural rebellious spirit fuels their desire for personal freedom, making them fiercely independent and open to embracing change in all aspects of life.

Meghan Markle is a clear example of this. Born August 4, 1981, at 4:46 AM in Canoga Park, California, Markle is the daughter of a television lighting director and a clinical therapist and yoga instructor. At age eleven, she took her first feminist action by participating in a writing campaign that targeted a television advertisement that suggested that women were "bogged down by greasy cookware." She sent the letter to then–First Lady Hillary Clinton. The advertisement was subsequently changed.

Following a career as an actress and a short-lived first marriage, Markle came into sudden and unusual prominence when, in May 2018, she married Prince Harry, grandson of Queen Elizabeth II, thus becoming Duchess of Sussex. But her mixed-race identity and her wildly independent spirit soon brought her into conflict with the British royal family. As a result, in the spring of 2020, she and Harry renounced their royal duties and left England.

Markle's unaspected Uranus appears in her 5th house, co-ruler of her 8th house and her south node. Consider how the energy of a raw, unfiltered, or misunderstood Uranus might dominate in these circumstances. Her creativity and manner of expressing love (5th house) are highlighted as she navigates intense differences of values with others (8th house). We can expect that this will be a theme throughout her life. As co-ruler of her south node, a karmic element is likely to run like a river beneath this theme. Her deep creativity sets her on an alternate path as she marches to a very different drummer by setting boundaries (8th house) to support her most authentic and unique life.

For supporting information, look to Saturn as the other ruler of the 8th house and to Mars as the planet that disposes Uranus in the chart. When we see that Mars and Saturn are in a square aspect to each other, we begin to unravel the story behind what we see in the tabloids.

Unaspected Neptune

You can expect individuals with an unaspected Neptune to possess a highly developed and unique imagination, strong intuition, or deeply felt and expressed compassion. They are drawn to the intangible side of life—dreams, imagination, and spirituality. They may excel as artists, filmmakers, or poets. On the other hand, they may face challenges of confusion and delusions, or may struggle with addiction and substance abuse. It will likely be a great struggle for them to navigate both the positive and negative dimensions of this unhinged Neptune influence. Lewis Carroll, born January 27, 1832, at 3:45 AM in Daresbury, England, provides a good example.

Lewis Carroll is the pen name of Charles Lutwidge Dodgson, an English writer of children's fiction—specifically in the genre called "literary nonsense." He is best known as the author of *Alice's Adventures in Wonderland* and its sequel *Through the Looking Glass*. As you delve into the details of Carroll's biography, you can see how his untamed preoccupation with issues related to Neptune dominated and reflected many aspects of his life, which was filled with controversies and mysteries.

Because Neptune is the planet directly east of the Sun in Carroll's chart, it is the last planet that rose over the horizon before the Sun on the day of his birth. As Tyl observes in *Synthesis and Counseling*, this gives Neptune an additional brushstroke of importance in his career and life. There is much about this author and his life that we will never know. And that seems quite appropriate with Neptune being disconnected, misunderstood, and dominant. He certainly marched to a different drummer in his life and in his career.

Carroll included a delightful acrostic poem at the end of *Through the Looking Glass* in which the first letter of each line spells out the name of Alice Pleasance Liddell. If you are interested in going down a Neptunian rabbit hole, you can explore the role that this Alice played in his life.

Unaspected Pluto

Those with Pluto unaspected in their natal chart tend to have an individualistic and intense approach to power, change, and deep psychological processes. They can be expected to have a strong, independent drive toward their own personal growth and ability to change. They navigate the depths of their own psyche with a fierce determination and are often unyielding when it comes to pursuing and healing their inner demons. Independence from external influence allows them to uncover profound insights into their own motivations and desires, often leading to a unique and deeply personal journey of self-discovery and empowerment. Let's look at two charts to see how this plays out—those of Sigmund Freud, born May 6, 1856, at 6:30 PM in Freiberg/Mähren, Czech Republic, and Kenny Rogers, born August 21, 1938, at 11:29 AM in Houston, Texas.

Austrian neurologist Sigmund Freud is known for developing psychoanalysis as a means of treating psychopathology. Kenny Rogers is an American singer, songwriter, actor, and record producer. I suspect that most of you have never wondered what these two might have in common. In my search for an unaspected Pluto, however, I discovered that they both have, not only an unaspected Pluto, but also a Scorpio rising that places Pluto as the co-ruler of the personality and the entire chart. Moreover, their Uranus is at nearly the same degree of Taurus in the 7th house—indicating that they were born a Uranus cycle apart, approximately eighty-four years.

While it may seem rather humorous and almost unthinkable to consider what similarities might exist between Freud and Rogers, when you take a closer look at their lives, you will find that they share a similar deep passion and intensity. Freud's Pluto in Taurus is in his 7th house; Rogers's is in Leo in his 10th. That immediately speaks to what is most intensely important to these individuals. Freud is deeply concerned, passionate, and marching to a different drummer regarding human relationships (7th) and their connection to the physical body and senses (Taurus). Rogers is deeply concerned, passionate, and marching to a different drummer regarding his personal self-expression (Leo) in his career (10th).

This comparison illustrates the importance of co-rulers and dispositors. When you find that one ruler of the chart is unaspected, be sure to examine the other ruler. This opens another perspective and a new dimension you can explore for deeper understanding. We'll address how the impact of an unaspected planet can be extended by dispositors in Guidepost 17.

With Scorpio rising in both of these charts, Pluto and Mars are co-rulers of each. The unaspected Pluto shows the depth of the passionate need to march to a different drummer, to function in a dominant fashion even when misunderstood, and to be preoccupied with issues of power and empowerment. With Mars as the primary ruler of each man's Ascendant, its placement offers a more complete story of their personalities.

In Freud's chart, Mars is retrograde in Libra in the 12th house—the planet of physicality, drive, and sexuality (Libra) hidden away in the unconscious (12th house). Mars retrograde suggests that it will not function as expected. Both rulers of the Ascendant, Pluto and Mars, are disposed by Venus, which is then disposed by Mars, bringing us to what astrologers call a "mutual reception" between Mars and Venus (see Guidepost 17). This is a situation in which two planets appear in each other's signs. In this instance, Venus, representing the feminine principle, is living in Mars's home, and Mars, representing the masculine principle, is living in Venus's home. Issues of relationship, sexuality, and the unconscious are prominent in all that we know about this man.

In Kenny Rogers's chart, we find very little complexity. Both Mars and Pluto are in Leo in the 10th house, with the Midheaven positioned between the two. Mars, Pluto, and the Midheaven are all disposed by his Leo Sun, also in the 10th. And the buck stops there. Rogers enjoyed great fame and popularity, rising from humble beginnings to become one of the top-selling music artists of all time. I think you could truly say that his fame and the path of his life were "written in the stars."

Unaspected Islands

Unaspected islands occur when two conjunct planets don't form any major aspects beyond their joint conjunction. Returning to our table metaphor, they sit together, speaking only with each other, without any input from anyone else at the table. A startling example of this placment appears in the chart of Tom Waits, born December 7, 1949, at 7:25 AM in Pomona, California. Waits has a truly unique chart that contains, not one, but two unaspected islands—one between the Moon and Neptune and one between Venus and Jupiter. Granted, if we stretch the orb allowance, the Moon and Neptune come into a square aspect. So here, we will (mostly) focus on the placement of Venus and Jupiter in Aquarius's 3rd house.

For this example, let's put a new twist on the table metaphor. Think about the Ascendant as a character with whom the wait staff converses as they come and go. Think of the Midheaven as the gossip that the kitchen staff hears. Notice that the Ascendant is ruled by Jupiter, while the Midheaven is ruled by Venus. These are the two planets that form an unaspected island, residing in the cool detachment of Aquarius in the 3rd house. They are huddled together, isolating themselves from the rest. They will however, express their unusual voice (Aquarius, 3rd house) in the areas of personality (Ascendant) and career (Midheaven).

Waits married in 1980 and has remained married ever since, which is very uncommon in the music industry. He and his wife have been diligent in keeping their personal and public lives decidedly separate. The persona he has presented of the low-life, alcoholic, bad boy is quite at odds with the reality of the family man living a conservative and privileged life. Because of his insistence on remaining detached from public view, we know very little about his personal life. It is clear, however, that his work and his music have had a profound impact on the cultural music scene.

GUIDEPOST 13

The Aries Point

The Aries Point—which should really be called the Cardinal Point because it is found at 0° of each cardinal sign (Aries, Cancer, Libra, and Capricorn)—is a point of public significance. Put it on your list of things to notice right up front in any natal chart. This powerful point holds the greatest concentration of cardinal energies. It is a portal to a tremendous power associated with action, ambition, assertiveness, and independence. It represents the spark of new beginnings and the intense drive needed to propel us forward.

When a planet, the Ascendant, or the Midheaven align with the Aries Point in a birth chart, it indicates a potential for strong leadership qualities, fearlessness, and a pioneering spirit. Individuals with these placements are inclined to take risks, embrace challenges, and consequently leave their mark on the world. They possess a natural urge to take initiative and are not afraid to venture into uncharted territory.

When the Aries Point is emphasized in a birth chart, it suggests a path of influence and success—not due to magic, but to a fully engaged pioneering spirit. Those with this point highlighted are likely to have the *chutzpah* necessary to lead change and make a notable impact as they pursue their goals and desires with confidence. This special point acts as a gateway to potential manifestation, enabling them to find themselves on a journey of growth, accomplishment, and recognition for the bold actions they take with the energy of whatever planet is found in this position.

Those with a planet or an angle at the Aries Point are pushed into direct action and this will likely be expressed publicly. The house in which this planet resides will represent the area of the life through which the energy of the planet is expressed. The houses ruled by the planet will be impacted by the actions taken.

The Aries Point is sometimes considered a point of fame. While this fame is not predestined, individuals with this placement will express the energy of a planet positioned there strongly and publicly. Anything for which they are well known will be connected to the planet or point held there. Always consider the sign, house, rulership, and aspects of any planet residing at this point to gain a richer understanding of the chart. The manifestation of the Aries Point will run the gamut from the most positive to the most difficult or challenged expression.

The natal charts of famous people can be a powerful resource for learning to understand how charts work in real life. The birth data of influential people is often available and their lives are quite public. In reality, however, the majority of charts you will work with directly will be those of ordinary individuals. But even normal individuals like ourselves will be known in our communities by the planets on the Aries Point. The leader of the school board or the owner of the local newspaper, for instance, may have Mercury conjunct the Aries Point, causing them to be known in their communities for their communication skills.

When considering the Aries Point, include only planets or points that are between 0° and 3° of the cardinal signs (Aries, Cancer, Libra, and Capricorn). Some astrologers include the last few degrees of the mutable signs as well. I do not encourage this, but, as with orbs, do your own research and make your own decision.

Let's look at how the expression of each planet manifests when it is at the Aries Point, which we'll refer to below as simply the AP.

Sun—Ego on Display

Those with the Sun at the Aries Point will be publicly known for the expression of their egos. They will show strong initiatory energy, leadership qualities, and a trailblazing spirit. They will probably have endless amounts of energy, a strongly competitive nature, and a powerful need for self-expression. Always consider the sign and house the Sun is in, as well as the house that it rules.

Meryl Streep and Elizabeth Warren were born on the same day at a distance of 1,400 miles. When you look at them side by side, however, you can immediately see the similarities between them. Without an accurate birth time for Elizabeth Warren, I am using a sunrise chart here. Some astrologers use a chart with the Sun conjunct the Midheaven, but I find that the Sun conjunct the Ascendant works best. The sunrise chart with Cancer rising works very well for Warren.

Streep, born June 22, 1949, at 8:05 AM in Summit, New Jersey, has the Sun at the Cancer AP in the 12th house, ruling the 1st. She is a powerful, brilliant, versatile American actor with an innate ability to inhabit whatever role she is given. With the Sun tightly conjunct Uranus (also at the AP) in the 12th house, consider what is on display. Her ability to take on a wide variety of roles seamlessly is extremely powerful. Perhaps it is her ability to partake in or access a universal mind that enables her to express herself by leaving herself behind. That is very "12th house" indeed. With this powerful Sun being expressed through the Leo Ascendant, her role as an actor is certainly a natural fit.

Streep is considered to be one of the greatest actors of her generation. She has received a record twenty-one Academy Award nominations and thirty-two Golden Globe nominations. Notice that her Sun at the Cancer AP rules, not only her Ascendant, but also Pluto, which is in a powerful trine aspect to the Midheaven, further suggesting the power of her career.

In Elizabeth Warren's case (born June 22, 1949, without an accurate birthtime, in Oklahoma City, Oklahoma), the Sun again is tightly conjunct Uranus (also at the AP), clearly suggesting that what is on display is her powerful ability to engage her inner protective "mother bear" nature (Cancer). Working with a sunrise chart, the Sun would rule her 2nd house, the house of money, resources, and self-worth. As a Democratic senator representing Massachusetts, she has consistently prioritized issues of affordable healthcare, income equality, student-loan debt relief, and tax reform to benefit working families.

Moon—Emotions on Display

The Moon conjunct the Aries Point in a natal chart accentuates the public display of emotions. These individuals will initiate an emotional response from others while seeking security through outward action and independence. They will have a fearless pioneering spirit and a passionate and competitive nature, and be best known for the expression of their emotions. Consider the sign the Moon is in, the house of its tenancy, and the house that holds Cancer (being ruled by the Moon).

We see this in the chart of Alexandria Ocasio-Cortez, born October 13, 1989, at 11:50 AM in Bronx, New York. Her Moon is at the Aries Point in the 5th house, ruling the 8th. Thus her public display of emotions may not manifest the way you expect it to. She certainly does not bring to mind the emotions of nurturing or mothering care. But remember that the Aries Point includes all of the cardinal signs. And the emotions of Aries will be vastly different from those of Cancer, Libra, or Capricorn.

This American politician and activist is popularly known by her initials, AOC. Keep in mind that anyone with an Aries Moon carries a deep inner need to be important as well as "first" in some manner or area of life. AOC is one of the first members of the Democratic Socialists of America, as well as the first woman of Puerto Rican descent to be elected to the US Congress. She made history when, less than a month after her twenty-ninth birthday, she defeated a ten-term Congressman to become the youngest woman ever elected to Congress. She has proven herself to be a passionate and intelligent woman of unusual fortitude.

AOC's Aries Moon is square Uranus, which is also at the AP and co-ruling her north node. Her Sun is conjunct Mars, ruler of her Moon. This puts her immense emotional creativity and drive on clear display as she learns to navigate the values and beliefs of others (8th house). The Moon and Uranus form a challenging T-square with her Midheaven and Mercury, also at the AP in Libra. This clearly shows the difficulties she encounters due to the expression of her dominant emotions as she learns to set boundaries and navigate the beliefs of others. This is the work of her lifetime.

Mercury—Intellect on Display

You can anticipate that individuals with Mercury at the Aries Point will be publicly known for their intellect, their ideas, and their communication skills. They will be assertive in expressing their thoughts and ideas, and will exhibit strong leadership qualities and great determination in their use of words and thoughts. They tend toward a quick, direct, and possibly aggressive communication style as they courageously embrace whatever challenges they encounter. They are anxious to initiate change and take risks with their restless, independent minds and the decisive direct expression of their voices. Consider the sign Mercury is in, the house of its tenancy, the aspects it makes, and the houses that hold Gemini and Virgo.

Rona Barrett, born October 8, 1936, at 4:15 AM in New York, New York, is a good example of this type of individual. This American gossip columnist has Mercury at the Libra AP in the 2nd house, ruling the 1st and 10th. In 1966, she began broadcasting Hollywood gossip on stations around the country, making a number of famous enemies along the way. She developed television specials about film, music, sports, and political celebrities, and produced several magazines that reported on the entertainment industry.

Barrett's Mercury is retrograde at the AP, and in her 2nd house. Mercury rules her Ascendant and her Midheaven, making only one aspect—a sextile to Pluto. Due to Mercury's apparent retrograde motion, her mind functions in a way that is contrary to what others expect (see Guidepost 11). And yet, it is the function of her mind and voice that rule her personality and her career, and make her the unique individual that she is.

Venus—Personal Values on Display

Those with Venus at the Aries Point will be publicly known for a bold and assertive approach to, and public expression of, all things Venus. They may be known for their personal beauty, their artistic expression, their lavish lifestyle, or their philanthropy. They may lead an opulent and glamorous life, prominently displaying their wealth and exhibiting strong leadership qualities aligned with their values. The values they express will likely revolve around the themes of women, beauty, money, or love. Their independent beliefs on these issues can have a great impact on others. A more negative expression may manifest in the form of gluttony and hubris, or the denial and turning away from all things Venus-related. Consider the sign Venus is in, the house of its tenancy, the aspects it makes, and the house that holds Taurus and Libra.

The chart of Betty Friedan, born February 4, 1921, at 4:00 AM in Peoria, Illinois, illustrates this. This feminist, writer, and activist has Venus in Aries at the AP in the 5th house, ruling the 6th and 12th. She spent her life engaged in the battle for women's equality, changing the course of history with her demanding and assertive pursuit of feminist principles. Her chart demonstrates the battle that exerted such influence over her life. Venus at the AP is conjunct Chiron, and is the focal planet in a T-square with Pluto and the Moon. Even a brief consideration of this configuration indicates anger, determination, and demand for action in any consideration of her needs, values, and beliefs regarding women, beauty, or resources.

Mars—Courage on Display

Mars is the planet that represents how we go about asserting ourselves. You can expect those with Mars at the AP to be publicly known for the way in which they express their assertive drive. They will possess a powerful determination to initiate new projects and take on difficult challenges with passionate boldness and fortitude. Their assertiveness and willingness to lead often propel them into positions of authority and prominence, where they make a mark on the world and leave a lasting impression. They thrive in situations that demand courage, risk-taking, competitiveness, and a pioneering spirit. On the other hand, this configuration may be expressed negatively as anger or even violence. As always, consider the sign Mars is in, the house of its tenancy, the aspects it makes, and the house that holds Aries and Scorpio.

Gloria Allred, born July 3, 1941, at 10:56 PM in Philadelphia, Pennsylvania, is a perfect example. Allred is a powerful attorney who is known for taking controversial high-profile cases, particularly those involving women's rights. Her Mars is in Aries at the AP in the 3rd house, ruling the 3rd and 10th. Imagine the combativeness of her voice (3rd house) as she passionately defends her clients! This quote alone puts her Aries Mars on full display: "I start every day with the knowledge that helping people and fighting for justice is my duty, and that nothing worthwhile comes without sacrifice, self-discipline, and courage." The title of her 2007 book—*Fight Back and Win*—says it all.

Allred's Mars is indeed in a powerful position to make a difference in the world. The trine to her Venus-Pluto conjunction points to how her strength and determination are a fully empowered gift to women and justice. You can learn a lot from considering her chart as you read her book.

Jupiter—Opinions on Display

An individual with Jupiter at the AP will be publicly known for something excessive and over-the-top. They will express their beliefs, opinions, optimism, success, or humor in a direct and determined way and will possess an expansive and publicly evident exuberance. Their optimistic outlook and enthusiasm suggest the ability to be natural leaders, and their thirst for adventure may drive them to great experiences of exploration. On the other hand, they may be known for exaggerated beliefs or opinions, overindulgence, and a lack of self-control or restraint when it comes to satisfying their desires or appetites. Consider the sign Jupiter is in, the house of its tenancy, the aspects it makes, and the house that holds Sagittarius and Pisces.

Consider Jim Bakker's chart. This former American televangelist, born January 2, 1940, at 11:00 AM in Muskegon Heights, Michigan, has Jupiter at the AP in the 2nd house, ruling the 1st and 10th and the Midheaven. He gained fame through *The PTL Club* (Praise the Lord club), a popular television program that attracted millions of viewers and brought significant wealth to him and his flamboyant wife. He was brought down by scandal in 1989 when he was convicted on multiple counts of fraud and sexual misconduct. This led to intense scrutiny of his extravagant lifestyle and lavish spending, leaving a tarnished reputation in its wake.

Bakker's Jupiter in the 2nd house rules his Ascendant and Midheaven, and forms a powerful trine aspect to Pluto. This certainly puts issues of money, belief, and power front and center in his personality and his career.

Saturn—Discipline on Display

With Saturn at the Aries Point, you can expect that individuals' public contribution will be of a serious and disciplined nature. They will be publicly known for strong ambitions, a highly disciplined nature, and a serious demeanor. They will face their public responsibilities with self-restraint and determination, and have a powerful work ethic. This results in the development of personal power within their community or professional sphere, where they will be recognized for their authority and achievements. Consider the sign Saturn is in, the house of its tenancy, the aspects it makes, and the houses that hold Capricorn and Aquarius.

The chart of author and philologist J. R. R. Tolkien demonstrates this. Born January 3, 1892, at 10:00 PM in Bloemfontein, South Africa, Tolkien had Saturn at the Libra Aries Point in the 2nd house, ruling the 5th and 6th. He is best known for his popular fantasy works *The Hobbit* and *The Lord of the Rings* trilogy. A professor of Anglo-Saxon at Oxford University, he made unparalleled contributions to the world of fantasy literature through his mastery of languages and his powerful understanding of mythology, which led him to create the intricately crafted realms of Middle Earth. His effort, dedication, and self-discipline resulted in his being considered one of the most influential and beloved fantasy writers of all time.

In Tolkien's chart, Saturn squares and disposes Mercury in the 5th house, which is retrograde and rules both the Ascendant and Midheaven. This demands that he make an effort to express his serious mind through his personality and his career or social reputation. Saturn is also in a powerful trine aspect to Pluto and Neptune at the top of the chart. The gift of empowerment and imagination brought into public view is clear in this chart, as well as in Tolkien's life.

Uranus—Individuality on Display

Those with Uranus at the Aries Point will enjoy public reputations marked by innovation and a maverick style. They will be known for their unique and progressive vision that challenges cultural norms. They have a strong trailblazing spirit, the ability to think outside the box, and the determination to place their vision in the public eye. Their achievements come through their willingness to embrace the unorthodox, to take risks, and to push assertively for change and social advancement. Consider the sign Uranus is in, the house of its tenancy, the aspects it makes, and the house that holds Aquarius, of which it is the co-ruler with Saturn.

Mary Baker Eddy, born July 16, 1821, at 5:38 PM (rectified birth time) in Bow, New Hampshire, is a good example to consider here. Eddy, whose Uranus is at the Capricorn AP conjunct Neptune, which is also at the AP, was the last of six children born on a tiny New England farm in 1821. From these humble beginnings, and before women were even allowed to vote, Eddy became one of the most influential women in religious history. She founded the First Church of Christ, Scientist, which currently has over 1,700 congregations worldwide. As an author and teacher promoting physical healing through spiritual teachings, she launched the still-influential international newspaper, *The Christian Science Monitor*.

Both Uranus and Neptune are at the AP in this rectified chart. This is indeed a unique statement that suggests a highly public expression of revolutionary spiritual beliefs. If you resist the urge to include out-of-sign aspects, you see only a sextile to her north node, which suggests an amazing opportunity for her to move forward on her given path. Eddy's nodal axis pushes her from common practical concerns (Virgo, south node) to deeply mystical concerns (Pisces, north node). This indicates an intensely unusual self-expression involving revolutionary spiritual beliefs.

Neptune—Dreams and Imagination on Display

Those with Neptune at the Aries Point are known for their ability to express imagination, spirituality, or compassion. The strength of their expressed vision brings awe and inspiration to others, dissolving boundaries and bringing people together in a shared sense of unity. Their considerable creative talent or spiritual insights resonate with others. They will be known publicly or in their families and communities for their ability to touch the hearts and souls of others. Consider the sign Neptune is in, the house of its tenancy, the aspects it makes, and the house that holds Pisces, of which it is the co-ruler with Jupiter.

The chart of beloved animator, film producer, and theme-park designer Walt Disney demonstrates this well. Born December 5, 1901, at 12:35 AM in Chicago, Illinois, Disney has Neptune at the Cancer AP in the 11th house, co-ruling the 7th. The characters, films, and songs he created during his long career have populated the dreams of children for generations. Cartoon figures like Mickey Mouse and full-length animated features like *Snow White and the Seven Dwarfs* will live forever as a part of our popular culture. It is easy to imagine him as a boy daydreaming and doodling during class, and entertaining his classmates with tales and illustrations.

In Disney's chart, Neptune at the Cancer AP is widely opposed by Mars in the 5th house of creativity. We see an overwhelming desire to be known for his powerful creative imagination. The dream and vision that he brings to others were certainly well received.

Pluto—Power or Transformation on Display

Those with Pluto at the Aries Point will be known for the embodiment of power and the ability to transform their lives or the lives of others. They will be catalysts of change, and their contribution to the world will center on dismantling established structures. They fearlessly express what is normally hidden and command respect from others in the process. The power of their presence influences psychological exploration or social justice. Their lives leave a lasting impact as they dismantle the old to make way for the new. Consider the house Pluto is in, the aspects it makes, and the house that holds Scorpio, of which it is the co-ruler with Mars.

For an example of this, let's look at the chart of Billy Tipton, born December 29, 1914, at 2:00 AM in Oklahoma City, Oklahoma. Tipton, whose Pluto is at the Cancer AP in the 10th house, co-ruling the 2nd, lived a seemingly conventional life as a trumpet player, jazz musician, husband, and father. After his death in 1989 at seventy-four, it was discovered that he had lived his life in a female body. His life-long secret, which was on constant public display, was entirely unknown to his many fans. Posthumously, he became a poster child for raising awareness about the difference between biological sex and culturally constructed gender.

Tipton's Pluto is at the Cancer AP in the 10th house, in opposition to Mercury, Mars, and the Sun in 4th-house Capricorn. Pluto, the transformed self, is expressed in his career and public life. What is hidden in life is revealed in death. Unrelated to this placement, but strikingly significant, is the fact that Venus is ruler of the Ascendant, forming a perfect trine to Neptune at the Midheaven.

The Two Faces of Pluto

Pluto is our friend. It is important—but not always easy—to remember that, because Pluto is not the friend you bring home to impress your parents, or the friend you bring along on a first date. Nor is Pluto the friend you introduce to other friends over brunch. Rather, Pluto is the friend you curl up with in bed when you are alone in the middle of a global pandemic. Pluto is the friend you know will be with you at the end—the very end. You can trust Pluto to push you over the edge when you know you must allow yourself to topple into the abyss.

To grasp the function of Pluto in the natal chart, you must understand that this planet has two very distinct faces—the face of destruction and the face of empowerment. Pluto is the tsunami that washes away whatever it encounters, the earthquake that swallows villages whole. Pluto can destroy a life that has been built brick by brick, resulting in breakdown, annihilation, and decay. But Pluto also has another face—the face of empowerment. Pluto may come in the guise of someone who brings the bricks you need to rebuild, sustain, and empower the entire system that ultimately supports your life. This planet can offer gifts that propel you to the top of your game. You may find yourself on stage, powerful and alive, with the whole world watching. That is a Pluto gift indeed.

As a major component of becoming truly empowered in any aspect of our lives, Pluto must and will destroy what stands in the way of the change that will bring us there. This planet forces us to dig deeply beneath the surface to the dark roots at the core of the matter at hand. Once we are forced into a position where we must look unflinchingly at the core issue—probably with our backs against a wall or our hands tied behind our backs—the true task of transformation begins. Keep in mind that Pluto always has the upper hand and will, without question, get the job done.

The biggest challenge for those of us in Pluto's grasp is to accept what is coming and resist fighting against the powerful change at hand.

Dark Night of the Soul

We all have dark times in our lives—times we don't often talk about with others. They have been called "the dark night of the soul." Times when all you can do is keep breathing as the child rips forth from your body, or hang on as your skin is shed whether you like it or not. These difficult times come as Pluto approaches a transit to a personal planet or when a configuration in the natal chart that involves Pluto is impacted by other transiting planets. These times change us profoundly and permanently. Once we've gone through them, our lives will never be the same. That's why it is important that we regard Pluto as a friend and find ways to work with this planet's position in our natal chart.

When working with a natal chart, it is important to consider how the experience of the dark night of the soul is baked into the very structure of certain lives. To do this, you have to consider what Pluto's natal position offers, as well as the aspects it forms to the personal planets and angles.

Because Pluto is a generational planet that spends many years passing through each sign, the sign it holds in a natal chart is not of great individual importance. In fact, everyone in a particular generation will have the same sign placement. Pluto's importance lies in its house placement and the aspects that it makes to the personal planets and angles. Even though Pluto's impact feels very personal when in aspect to a personal planet, the impact comes from an impersonal cultural or societal issue or influence. As an example, consider someone with Pluto conjunct the Moon. That person may experience personal and devastating difficulties in the relationship with the mother, but you can be pretty sure that those difficulties stem from a societal pressure on the mother. Whatever comes from Pluto, Neptune, or Uranus derives from the bedrock of the society or culture into which individuals are born or encounter along the way.

When you look at Pluto in a natal chart, consider how much devastation the person must endure in order to reach the full potential of empowerment in life. When you see challenging aspects from Pluto to personal planets (squares, oppositions, conjunctions), you know that something (or many things) in that life must be dismantled and destroyed in order to be reconstructed so that person can come to full potential. When you see flowing aspects to personal planets (sextile, trines), these will show you where empowerment comes more easily, perhaps offered as a gift or an opportunity ripe for the taking.

Pluto is a tiny planet that was discovered not even a hundred years ago, in 1930. It is positioned the farthest in distance from Earth. Pay close attention to how Pluto interacts with other planets. Although primarily ruled by Mars, Scorpio is co-ruled by Pluto, which adds more intensity and a darker edge to the house it occupies. The house that holds Pluto will feel powerful Plutonian forces, but the most significant impact will be on houses ruled by planets that are in difficult aspects (square or opposition) to Pluto.

Destruction and Empowerment

Let's return to two charts we have considered before that demonstrate the ability of Pluto to both destroy and empower—those of Louis Armstrong (see Figure 8) and Michael Jackson (see Figure 12).

Pluto resides in Armstrong's 3rd house of communication, suggesting a powerful and transformative voice. Pluto sextiles his Leo Sun in the 5th house of creativity, his Aries Moon in the 1st house of self, and the Ascendant as well. But sextile aspects offer opportunity, not the automatic gift of a trine aspect. They require the effort of paying attention and taking action, although they don't require that the native pass through the grueling transformation that a square aspect would. Thus Armstrong had to take a conscious stand and make a concerted effort in order to receive the opportunities that Pluto offers. He had to show up and use his powerful voice. The gifts offered come from his voice as well as his environment (3rd house). These potential gifts (sextile) are offered to the personality (1st house) and include the ability to pour love into his creativity (5th house).

In Guidepost 7, we discussed the importance of Mars as the ruler of Armstrong's Ascendant. Now note the relationship between his Mars and Pluto. A trine aspect from Pluto to Mars offers him the undeniable gift of a very powerful personality (Mars ruling the 1st). This gift comes through his understanding of the cultural times in which he lives, which dictate how he must engage with others diplomatically (Mars in Libra, 7th house) through the gift of his voice (3rd house). Uranus in opposition to Pluto highlights the generational importance of the times in which he was born, as well as his own impact upon his generation and culture. His personal story is intimately tied into the larger cultural story of his generation.

Armstrong had a powerful voice (both literally and metaphorically) in a unique cultural time (Pluto opposite Uranus), and he used that voice to overcome great personal odds as well as to have a huge impact on the larger culture. Note also that Mars and Pluto are co-rulers of the 8th house where Armstrong's north node is positioned, another powerful statement regarding his ability to break through the cultural barriers of other people's beliefs.

It is also interesting that Uranus is part of a very significant grand trine configuration and is at the exact midpoint of the Sun and Moon. We will talk about grand trines in Guidepost 15. At this point, suffice it to say that Pluto adds its considerable power to the entire structure of Armstrong's fire grand trine. This is a chart that displays enormous power potential. It would take this kind of strong empowerment for a Black man born in the American South in 1901 to attain the cultural and professional heights that he reached. Imagine who he could have been and what he could have accomplished in a world without racism.

Pluto in Michael Jackson's chart is conjunct his Virgo Sun in the 7th house. If we stretch the orbs, we can consider its impact reaching for an opposition to the Pisces Moon in the 1st house as well. The full power of Michael's Full Moon chart became evident when The Jackson 5 made their first national TV appearance, performing at the Miss Black America Pageant at Madison Square Garden in 1969. However, that auspicious beginning fell prey to dark forces early on.

Both Jackson's promise and his eventual fall are reflected in the Sun-Pluto conjunction. We can see them together, whether holding hands in a great show of empowerment or in a battle for power and control. Think of the Sun's power to incinerate and Pluto's power to smother. With all that we now know about Michael Jackson, we can interpret both sides as an accurate depiction of his life and experience.

Any planet that is in aspect to Jackson's Sun is also going to be, by default, influenced by Pluto. Conjunctions function as a unit that cannot be separated. Therefore, I feel comfortable stretching the orb to accommodate Pluto's opposition to Jackson's Moon.

There is so much to explore here, but let's keep to the basics. Pluto conjunct the Sun indicates, among other things, the power dynamics between Michael and his father. With the Sun ruling the 6th house, this power dynamic will directly impact every element of Michael's day-to-day routines and his lifestyle. His routines of self-care, as well as the practices he engaged in to develop his craft, were impacted in childhood by his being under the thumb of a powerful and controlling father. Moreover, his Pisces Moon in opposition to the Sun suggests a passive mother at the mercy of the demands of the powerful father.

With generational Pluto in such close aspect to the Sun, Jackson's life was likely to have an impact on the larger culture, even as that culture had an outsized impact on his personal life.

GUIDEPOST 15

Grand Trines

As we learned in part 1, trines are formed when two planets are positioned 120° apart. Ideally these planets will be in signs that are of the same element, allowing for an easy resonance and natural understanding between them. There is no need for extensive discussion or discord, as they have the simple ability to move forward toward the same goals. They are able to relax because each understands that the other has its back. They are on the same team, so to speak, and will readily support one another.

Grand trines are formed when three planets, each separated by 120° (plus or minus the allowable orb), create a full three-sided triangle. Additional planets may be involved by conjunction with one or more points within this triangle. When I find a grand trine in the chart of a new client, I feel as if I have struck gold. I am confident that the client and I will have a rich and meaningful conversation, because the gifts and challenges of this configuration are powerful, life-affirming, and life-altering. Arming the individual with the information it provides can result in powerful self-understanding and great practical benefits.

Elemental Energy

The first thing to notice in a grand trine is the element involved. Ideally, each planet in the configuration will occupy the same element. When they do, this results in what we (appropriately) call a fire grand trine, an earth grand trine, an air grand trine, or a water grand trine. Grand trines in which one planet, by nature of orb, is in a different element than the other two are named for the element that holds two of the three planets. Because a grand trine containing an out-of-element planet is weakened, ask questions of the native to determine its strength.

The fact that grand trines always fall predominantly in one of the four elements suggests a pronounced self-sufficiency within that element. The general approach and response to the life of those with this configuration will be specifically related to that element as well.

A fire grand trine points to a spirited, dynamic self-sufficiency. There is no need for others to motivate, drive, or even encourage these people to take action. They do not need others in order to develop or enjoy an enthusiastic or passionate life. They tend to approach life energetically and respond to it with excitement and optimism.

An earth grand trine indicates practical self-sufficiency, and little need for the input of others in managing the practical realities of life. With little effort, these individuals will make sure they have money in their wallets and food in the cupboards; they always pay their bills and never forget to feed the cat. They tend to approach life soberly and respond to it with practicality and determination.

An air grand trine suggests an intellectual self-sufficiency. Those with this configuration are able to entertain themselves all day long with their own curiosity and intellect. They do not need others to engage their minds or their thinking processes. They tend to approach life with interest and respond to it with curiosity and analysis.

A water grand trine promises emotional self-sufficiency. These individuals are deeply sensitive and highly emotional. They feel so much love and expansion within their own hearts and don't really need the reflection of others to do so. They tend to approach life with deep feelings and respond with profound sensitivity and heart.

Upsides and Downsides

In the early days of my studies, the only information I could find about grand trines was the common idea that a grand trine is a configuration of auspicious wonder. I learned that those lucky enough to have one in their natal chart would experience good luck and good fortune, and that everything wonderful would come their way. Although there is a certain amount of truth in this glowing expectation, it is never that simple. Indeed, we can anticipate that those with a grand trine in their natal chart will experience more flow, ease, and good fortune in many areas of their lives than the rest of us. Given that trines reflect an easy free flow of energy, even a single powerful trine in a natal chart will provide wonderful gifts to those who possess it.

However, life is always more complicated than we may wish it to be. Ease, flow, and simplicity are never the end of the story. When I find this configuration in a chart, I begin my conversation with the native by saying something along these lines: "When astrologers see a grand trine in a natal chart, they often speak of good luck and good fortune, suggesting that everything wonderful will come your way. But we know that life is complex and there is always more to a story than what we see on the surface." In order to understand the areas of life where the native will experience ease and good fortune, look to the houses that are tenanted by the planets involved, as well as the houses that are ruled by those planets.

With a minimum of three single planets or angles creating the grand trine, its gift is intensified and increased by tenancy and house rulership. A grand trine is a fully self-contained system that actually turns back into itself. Consider one flow of energy meeting another, which in turn meets a third, which finally rejoins the original flow. This generates a powerful force of forward motion. But resist any temptation you may have to leave the conversation there.

The downside of a grand trine lies in the way others percieve the native and how that perception impacts the individual's relationships. The self-sufficiency that others see does not easily allow space for connection. This creates a situation in which energy flows easily, but does not escape the confines of the Self or allow access to or input from others.

As powerful, advantageous, and lovely as a grand trine is, it can clearly work against relationships. These individuals appear entirely independent and self-sufficient, as if they do not need others. The people in their lives can easily think that they "have it all together," and are too occupied with their own experiences to bother with them. In this way, a distance is created between those with this configuuration and the others in their lives.

In fact, those with grand trines in their charts risk spending a lifetime feeling misunderstood, isolated, and potentially quite lonely. They may be living lives of great ease and self-sufficiency, and yet find themselves quite lonely, trying to understand how to invite others into their lives or include them in a meaningful manner.

Another problem with the grand trine is its ability to pull the attention of those who possess it away from everything else in their lives. They risk letting themselves become stuck in its wonder and flow. It is wonderful to have this flow to rest within and yet it is important to understand that being exclusively engaged in the easiest aspects of life can be counterproductive and distract the native from the greater purpose and necessary efforts of life.

We all have work we must do and lessons we must learn. Squares, oppositions, the more challenging conjunctions, and the nodal axis point us to that work and those lessons. Remaining exclusively focused on the easy flow of a grand trine can effectively keep us from necessary effort, the satisfaction of accomplishment, and a life well lived.

Defense Mechanisms

A defense mechanism is an automatic way of thinking or behaving that we use to protect ourselves from experiencing difficult and unpleasant emotions. A grand trine can easily become a highly effective defense mechanism for those growing up in difficult or extreme circumstances. Its ease and flow provide a place of safety where they can separate from their difficulties and focus on simply moving forward. This can be a powerful tool for children growing up in unhappy, abusive, or simply uncomfortable circumstances. It can take them to a place where they can keep difficult circumstances and difficult people at bay, saying: "I don't need you. I'm fine on my own."

For some children, a defense mechanism may be a necessary means of survival and therefore a gift. However, when we continue to use them as adults, they can isolate us and prevent us from doing the work that the rest of the chart asks of us. It is understandable that those strategies that protected us and made our lives easier as children might seem to be an effective means of protecting us as adults as well. But make no mistake—remaining focused exclusively on these behaviors can put you on a path that will not lead you where you want to go.

Imagine a young boy with a water grand trine as well as Saturn retrograde squaring Venus, and a deeply difficult relationship with his father. Early in his life, this child learned to hold his head high and say: "I don't need anyone." He learned to do an excellent job of self-soothing and caring for his emotions on his own. In adulthood, this young man has spent a lifetime keeping others at an emotional distance. The ease of the grand trine both highlighted and enabled him to sweep the Venus-Saturn difficulty under the rug. Without self-understanding and moving beyond the ease of his grand trine, he risks drifting along on a lonely path.

When individuals use the gift of a grand trine as a defense mechanism for many years, they may be tempted to ignore the areas of work and effort that are being asked of them by the rest of the chart. It is important to understand that self-sufficiency brings its own dificulties. Relationships with others bring practical benefits; they bring wisdom, comfort, and excitement into our lives. People want to be needed, and will simply pull away when they encounter someone who does not accept or reach out for connection.

When you speak with an individual with a natal grand trine, bring the conversation to the difficulties of the grand trine as simply and directly as possible. Pay careful attention to the reaction you receive as you reach this turning point in the conversation. What response do you get if you point out a particularly gnarly dynamic? Has the person been working on this issue or have they allowed the ease of the grand trine to keep them functionally unaware of the challenge at hand.

No matter how obvious the challenges in a chart, if the individual has no apparent recognition of them and you feel resistance, it is time to back off. It is not your job to push others beyond what they are ready to acknowledge or work with. The best you can do is to plant the seed. Unless you are in a therapeutic relationship with them, that is enough. It is always their choice to work with their demons in their own time—or not. You can gently show them the door, but it is never your job to blast it open. Your job is to gently point the problem out to them and allow them to absorb that knowledge in their own time.

Speak to them about the need to let their guard down and allow others to support them. Show them that, when they allow themselves to be supported by others, it deeply enriches their lives and makes them more effective as they work with their deeper challenges. This will ultimately give them more satisfaction than staying on the easy path of the grand trine.

Here are a few suggestions for managing this conversation with an individual with a natal grand trine:

- Encourage those with a fire grand trine to allow others to initiate activities and bring new interests to share. Suggest that they step aside and let someone else take the lead to move an action or project forward.

- Encourage those with an earth grand trine to release control of the family finances or the organization of an event. Advise them to ask for someone's help or support on another practical project or issue.

- Encourage those with an air grand trine to listen with full attention to the ideas of others, or to step aside and allow someone else to spearhead the intellectual side of a project without interference.

- Encourage those with a water grand trine to turn toward their vulnerability in the presence of a friend and allow themselves to be soothed or comforted. Perhaps they could notice, support, and comfort the vulnerability of another. They may learn that suffering teaches a great deal when it is a shared experience.

Let's take another look at the chart of Louis Armstrong (see Figure 8) as an example of this. Armstrong's fire grand trine is a powerful one indeed and includes his Sun in Leo, his Moon and Ascendant in Aries, and Uranus at the top of the chart in Sagittarius. This alone provides us with a significant understanding of who Armstrong was and what propelled his life.

As you examine his chart, think about the hot summer night of Armstrong's birth in New Orleans. Shortly before his birth, the Aries Moon rose over the horizon. The Sun, in its own sign, resides in and rules the house of creativity and the giving of love. Think of that powerful Leo Sun with the free flow of the trine aspect pouring its energy unimpeded to the

Moon in the 1st house of Self and Uranus in the 9th. Consider how the Moon and Uranus pour energy back to the Sun, as well as between each other. Here we see the empowerment of focused fire. Armstrong exudes the power of innovation, drive, and determination within his particular and unique time and place in history.

Note, as well, Pluto's opposition to Uranus as it forms sextile aspects to both the Sun and the Moon. The stress between Uranus and Pluto suggests the particular cultural stress of his time and clearly shows Armstrong's powerful and unique role in cultural history. Moreover, the outer planets interact with his Ascendant and his Midheaven, as well as with the Sun and the Moon and the inner planets. These interactions provide a window into his impact on the culture as well as how the larger culture impacted his individual life. It is also significant that this chart has Neptune opposing Chiron at the Aries Point.

Separated Grand Trines

I call a grand trine in which neither the Sun nor the Moon is involved a "separated grand trine." These are perhaps the most interesting and the most challenging for individuals to manage and integrate into their lives. Whether or not the Sun or the Moon is involved in the trine tells you a lot about how the native will experience this important configuration.

Without the involvement of the Sun or Moon, the flow of a grand trine—and potentially the defense mechanism that has built up around it—operates separately from the essense of the individual represented by the Sun and the emotional needs represented by the Moon. This results in what Noel Tyl called a "discernible schism" between the theme of the Sun-Moon blend and the parts of the native's life represented within the grand trine (see *Synthesis and Counseling*). These two parts of the life are likely to be alienated from each other. This creates a difficult challenge for those trying to manage and integrate two profoundly different parts of themselves and their lives.

In order to understand this configuration, I have turned to the work of Richard Schwartz, a family therapist, academic, author, and creator of the Internal Family Systems therapeutic model. His approach opens a perspective that allows us to understand this astrological configuration. In his 2021 book *No Bad Parts*, he describes a way to work with this dynamic without pathologizing it. Rather than emphasizing the separation of these themes, he suggests that the key is to *integrate* them.

Viewing an individual life through the lens of Schwartz's therapeutic model can be quite useful, because it makes apparent the fact that we all have different internal parts. We do not travel through this life as one simple whole, moving in harmony. We each have multiple parts, disparate needs, and separate internal personalities and voices that demand our attention and can often contradict each other. These parts—which may be represented in astrology by individual planets or by whole planetary configurations—do not always work well together and can cause great internal conflict. We are all born with various internal parts that exist as an internal family within us. The key to healing the wounded or separate parts is to honor, understand, welcome, and love every part.

When I encounter clients with a powerful grand trine that does not involve the Sun or the Moon, I anticipate that they will be living lives of great complexity. In the recent past, they may have been diagnosed with a multiple personality disorder—what is known today as a dissociative identity disorder. They feel the presence of two or more distinctly separate internal beings within. Luckily, we now know how to work with this phenomenon without pathologizing it. There are many ways that individuals who live with the complexity of this configuration can switch between alternate internal perspectives and even disparate identities.

It is easy to see how a separated grand trine might have been seen as a dissociative identity disorder. Think about the self-sufficiency and the potential for defensive behaviors present in all grand trines. When the easiest path available does not take into consideration the two lights of the Sun and the Moon, a separation is created. The core self and the greatest needs of the personality are asking very different things from the easy path that the grand trine offers. This moves the native in two very different directions.

When an individual is able to travel an uncomplicated and effortless path—a path where they feel comfortable and rewarded—it is easy to understand their reluctance to turn to the parts of their lives that potentially hold great difficulty and challenge. When the path of least resistance has also been used as a defense mechanism distancing them from pain, you can imagine it would be difficult indeed to follow another path. The longer they spend on the easy path, the harder it becomes to forge another. If they do not find a way to support both the flow of the grand trine and the prominence of the Sun and Moon, it can certainly become a pathology.

However, I have encountered many people over the years who have found amazingly creative ways to support both the flow of the separated grand trine and the effort suggested in the dynamics of the Sun and Moon. When you encounter this in a chart, you must actively support curiosity and creativity in its management. Ask clients how it feels to be living two lives simultaneously. They may never have thought of it in that way before, but your question will help them to do so. This supports understanding and self-acceptance: "Why, yes, that is my life!"

Separate Lives

This may play out in individuals who refuse to mix their home lives with their careers. They don't bring their spouse to office parties, and they don't talk about work when they are at home. In essence, they live two very separate lives within the one life. When they are at work, their connection to home and family fades away, as their entire being becomes focused on their work and social reputation. Their work colleagues will probably describe them very differently from the way their neighbors or family members will. In this case, the challenges of the Sun and the Moon dominate their home life, while the flow of the grand trine plays out in their work world, or the other way around. The house placements and planetary rulerships will show you where the ease resides and where the challenges arise. This same dynamic can be seen in actors who express very different personalities depending on whether they are onstage or not.

In my client files, I have several transgender individuals who continue to identify with the sex they were assigned at birth in some aspects of their lives, while living completely different lives identifying as another gender in other aspects of life. They have developed creative ways to manage this situation and are leading healthy lives within this framework. I've also encountered examples of individuals who essentially maintain two separate lives in two different cities—sometimes at a distance of hundreds of miles. In one place, they live an independent existence; in the other, they reside with a partner. You can see a shadow of this dynamic in individuals with a very focused and powerful single trine aspect that does not include the Sun or Moon as well.

The lives of those with a separated grand trine will have two very distinct pathways, two very different modes of expression and ways of life. If one side of the personality is being held in secret or if they are using defense mechanisms as a way to avoid addressing important issues that are clear in the chart, they may have important inner work to do in order to live a fully integrated life. Point these things out gently. As we work with individuals who have this statement in their natal chart, we can help them find creative ways to work with this dynamic.

Dorothy Day, born November 8, 1897, at 6:50 PM EST in Bath Beach, New York, is a wonderful example of a grand trine without involvment of the Sun or Moon (see Figure 14).

As we saw in Guidepost 7, in her youth, Day was a fully engaged Bohemian, anarchist, and social activist. Imagine the surprise of those who knew her when she became a devout Roman Catholic! Imagine the difficulty she herself experienced as she tried to integrate her political activism and her devout spiritual nature into one cohesive life.

Day was a highly intellectual and humanitarian woman with a powerful air grand trine that included her Ascendant, Neptune, Pluto, Venus, and the Midheaven. Here we see her very public intellectual self-sufficiency, her activism, and the unique vision of her values. But the opposition between the cluster of planets in Scorpio (including the Sun) in her 6th house and the Taurus Moon in her 12th tells a very different story of her life. Here we see a powerful emotional intensity and a deeply private nature.

Day's 12th-house Taurus Moon is ruled by Venus, which is a part of her air grand trine. Perhaps it was through this connection that she "heard the voice of God." My understanding of 12th-house placements suggests that they can allow the unconscious to open to hidden information, symbolic languages, and voices from other dimensions. Through her wild air grand trine, she was attracted to Bohemian and anarchist sensibilities. Taurus and Scorpio brought her to the traditions and spiritual pleasures of Catholicism. Together, they made her the best-known radically political American Catholic.

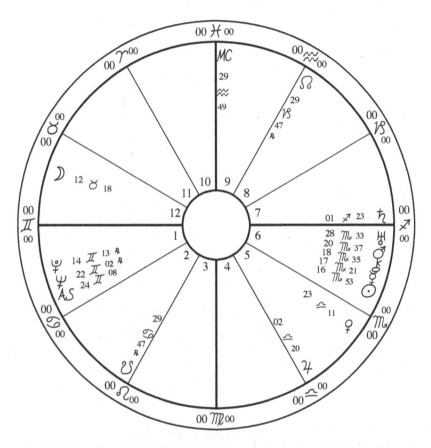

Figure 14. Chart of Dorothy Day, born November 8, 1897, at 6:50 PM EST in Bath Beach, New York. Notice the grand trine that is separate from the Sun and the Moon.

Day now carries the title of "Servant of God," as the Catholic Church considers her for canonization. That certainly says something about the power of her life, her air grand trine, and her determination and creativity in making a powerful and authentic life for herself.

GUIDEPOST 16

Stelliums

A stellium is simply a gathering of planets in a single sign or house that denotes a heightened level of focus on the sign and house in which they fall. The qualities associated with the sign and the topics associated with the house are thus rendered prominent in the native's life, to the extent that they become dominant factors in the chart as a whole.

Everyone has their own opinion as to what constitutes a stellium. Some say it is a gathering of three or more planets in one sign; some define it as a gathering of three or more planets in conjunction. Others describe it as a convergence of three or more planets in both conjunction and the same sign. Personally, I consider four planets in the same sign to qualify as a stellium. Over time, you will decide for yourself. Think it through, do your research, and form your own conclusion. As with so much in astrology and in life, strict rules are often elusive.

In Guidepost 8, we discussed the Sun, Mercury, and Venus coming together in a triple conjunction in relation to the concept of idealism. This should never be considered a stellium. Although this gathering certainly emphasizes the importance of the house in which they reside, because these three are so often together, I would never consider this a stellium. I think of them simply as friends gathering for tea.

But imagine what happens if Mars, Saturn, or Neptune joins that little tea party. Now a true stellium has taken shape. And as more planets join in, the complexity of the stellium deepens and expands.

In order to be called a stellium, the gathering must, I believe, consist of a minimum of four planets in a single sign. A planet in an adjacent sign that is conjunct a planet within the gathering may influence the stellium, but don't consider that planet to be a part of it. Those out-of-sign planets are either rushing to join the group and haven't quite made it, or they have just escaped.

Mission or Quest?

Because a stellium is a gathering in one sign and we are using the Whole Sign house system, your eye will immediately be drawn to the house involved. To me, this kind of planetary huddle suggests that individuals have a mission or a life purpose that is bigger than they are. Before they reach or understand this purpose, they are on a quest to find it.

The mission itself is outlined by the house the stellium is in. The quest is the path the individual must take to flesh out what is required to fulfill this overriding mission. Often the quest will take the majority of the individual's life as they travel the path to a full understanding and implementation of their purpose. They are apt to meet challenges and helpers along the way. The planets themselves and the aspects they make beyond the walls of the stellium will provide clues as to the challenges and the helpers they will meet.

One problem with a stellium is that it can function as such a powerful focus that it creates a blind spot, perhaps resulting in someone being unable to see the forest for the trees. When someone is so thoroughly immersed in any one thing, it can be hard to see anything outside of that focus. Hence the old adage that fish don't know they are in water.

When you encounter a significant stellium, don't try to absorb its meaning all at once. Stand aside to gain an overview; look at the gathering as a whole. Consider the planets involved, as well as the sign and house they are in. Does it feel like a gathering of teens out for a joy ride, thinking only of themselves and the fun they seek? Does it feel like a gathering of grandmothers joined together for a humanitarian cause? Does it feel like soldiers going off to war? A ballet troupe preparing to go on stage? Find a way to wrap your mind around what this gathering is all about and what it is trying to accomplish. If you were sending out an invitation to this gathering, what would it say?

As you untangle the intricacies of a stellium, try to determine whether those whose charts you are considering are still on a quest to identify their mission, or if they have found it and are now working to accomplish it. You cannot determine this with the chart alone; you will need to ask questions. Most people will be on the preliminary quest for the majority of their lives. Very few discover or understand their mission early in life—and sadly, some never do. However, with the perspective of astrology, they will surely find it much earlier.

Analyzing a Stellium

Many budding astrologers have been stopped in their tracks by a truly impressive stellium. You may even wonder if there is an error in the chart when you first see a gathering of six or more planets grouped together. It can leave you scratching your head, uncertain about how to find your way into the heart of that planetary gathering, which is clearly the focus of the chart and of the life being lived.

When analyzing a stellium, it is important to get a feel for it by considering the planets involved. Consider carefully the role they are playing by the sign they are in. Get a feel for what they are trying to accomplish by the house they occupy. Once you have a good sense of the gathering itself, think about the movement occurring between the planets at the moment the chart represents. Looking at any chart with the movement of the planets in mind will give you a powerful perspective on the way in which the chart works. This is particularly important when working with a stellium.

Because the chart is a snapshot of one moment in time, it can be all too easy to engage with it as a static two-dimensional image. Your understanding will grow exponentially as you envision the motion that occurred before and after the click of the camera—the snapshot of the moment of birth. Consider the speed with which each planet is moving, how recently each has joined the stellium, and how soon they are preparing to leave. If any of the outer planets (Uranus, Neptune, or Pluto) are involved, they may have been in this particular sign for a very long time. If the Moon is involved, it may have just stepped through the door. Look to your ephemeris to determine if any of them are about to become retrograde or have just returned to direct motion. Ask yourself: Who is gaining on whom? Who is moving away from whom? Who is anxious to join? Who is in a hurry to leave?

Consider what the motion suggests. Have several quick-moving planets recently passed over a slow-moving one? Think about the conversation that happened as the faster planets joined with the slower one. What did the faster planets pick up from the slower one that they are now bringing forward with them? Think of the faster planets as "picking up" the energy of the slower one, changing their own energy in the process and bringing the new energy into a new story ahead. When a faster-moving planet approaches a slower one, it is reaching for the energy that it will "pick up" through progression in the months and years following the birth.

Continue this investigation until you feel fully familiar with the characters in the stellium and what they are up to. What conversations are they engaged in? Get creative with the ideas that the planetary movements provide. By allowing your mind to play with these connections, you will gain a tremendous amount of clear, intuitive, subtle, and obvious information and insight.

Has Mercury just passed over Mars? In this case, the mind has picked up and absorbed assertiveness and that person is ready for action and will possibly struggle with anger. Is Mercury approaching Jupiter? In this case, the mind is reaching toward enthusiasm, expansion, and possibly humor, which will be gained in the months and years following the birth. What if Mars has passed over Jupiter? Perhaps anger and assertiveness will be imbued with self-righteousness.

Each planet within a stellium carries a distinct, yet entwined, tale. Consider a chart where the Sun, Mercury, Venus, Mars, and Jupiter have all passed over Uranus shortly before birth. The core of the life (Sun), the mental processes and the ability to express them (Mercury), the personal values regarding love and resources (Venus), the energetic drive and ability to take action (Mars), and the belief system and rewards (Jupiter) will all be infused with the energy of innovation for the betterment of the collective (Uranus). That in itself gives you a lot of information, and there is a great deal more to come as you investigate each planet's individual journey.

External Forces

You must also consider the planets that are impacting the stellium from outside its confines. If a planet is in a close aspect to any planet in the stellium, consider that its impact likely extends to the entire gathering, even though some may be beyond your usual orb.

If the stellium you are working with consists of Jupiter, Venus, Mars, and the Moon all in Leo in the 10th house, you may decide that it feels like a dance troupe on stage. Now imagine Mars in Taurus forming a square aspect from the 7th house. The individual's internal dance troupe is being challenged by an assertive or angry relationship. Perhaps a partner is making angry demands that hold the individual back from full public expression, or a dance partner is assertively pushing the person to the limit, thereby leading to an acceptance and embracing of the mission through action and determination.

Once you have a firm grasp of and feel for the stellium itself and how it is impacted by outside aspects, it is time to discover how it extends itself into the rest of the chart, and thereby the native's life. Take note of all the houses in the chart that are ruled by the planets within the group. Make sure you are clear about the character of the gathering—the teens looking for a thrill, the grandmothers working toward a cause, the soldiers going off to war.

Now turn your attention to how this gathering is going to bring its energies to the houses that it rules. Perhaps the native's career path is impacted by the teenagers. In that case, the development of maturity will be necessary while maintaining the bright-eyed enthusiasm of youth. Perhaps intimate partnerships are ruled by the soldiers going off to war and negotiation skills will be necessary to bring more peace to partnerships. A mature understanding can bring the tools of war to peacetime and put them to work building and protecting, rather than tearing down.

Josephine Baker's chart provides an interesting example of how all these factors and forces work together in a stellium (see Figure 15). Born into poverty in Missouri in 1906, Baker became a well-known Black entertainer and civil rights activist. After being rejected by American audiences because of her race, she performed as a dancer, singer, and actress in France during the 1920s, gaining renown for her wildly uninhibited style. Ultimately, she became one of the most celebrated figures of the Jazz Age and used her platform to advocate against racism and inequality.

Later in life, Baker adopted twelve children from various racial and cultural backgrounds, calling them her "rainbow family." Her efforts and determination to create a diverse and happy family defied traditional norms and clearly showed her belief in and commitment to equality. She lived a remarkable life and made powerful contributions in the fields of both entertainment and social justice. Take a moment to watch some film footage of Baker, who starred in four movies. Seeing her dance and hearing her speak will bring this chart to life more vividly than any words can.

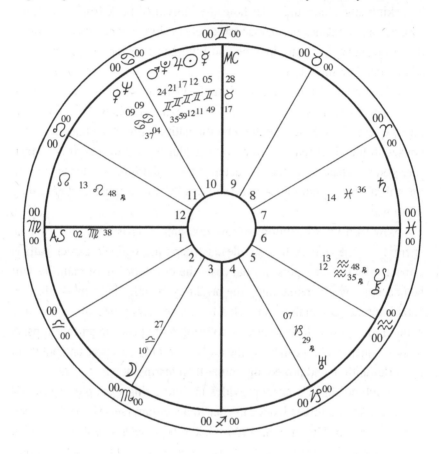

Figure 15. Chart of Josephine Baker, born June 3, 1906, at 11:00 AM CST in St. Louis, Missouri.

Josephine's chart contains a five-planet gathering in Gemini in her 10th house. There is a wide orb between the planets on each end of this configuration, but the stellium itself holds them together. Think about the path these planets have traveled before the moment they were captured in Baker's chart. None of them are retrograde; none have recently been retrograde; and none will turn retrograde soon. Therefore, you can simply consider direct motion at typical speed for each of them. As your eye follows the clockwise path of planetary motion, it becomes clear that Mercury led the gathering into the morning sky, with the Sun, Jupiter, Pluto, and Mars following close behind.

Now consider the movement of Jupiter, Pluto, and Mars through the zodiac. Move your gaze counterclockwise, while considering the speed of each planet. Because Mars moves so much faster than Jupiter or Pluto, you know that Mars has passed over each in the days or weeks before Baker's birth. What does this tell you? Because Mars is in Gemini, it will use its voice as a tool to express what it has "picked up" before birth from its meetings with both Jupiter and Pluto. This expands (Jupiter) and empowers (Pluto) the voice (Gemini) of Mars. Thus you can expect this woman to have a very powerful voice. But where will she use that voice and to what purpose?

With her stellium in Gemini and the 10th house, you can safely anticipate that Baker's mission involves how she uses her voice as a tool of her career and/or social reputation. At the very least, she will bring her voice to a public mission. And in fact, the world knows her by the mission of her voice, which she presented in the public sphere. You can gather more information about the mission, the gift, and the challenge of this stellium as you bring its influence beyond the borders of the 10th house through planetary rulerships.

Mars has been expanded (Jupiter) and profoundly empowered (Pluto) through its recent path and its interactions with both Jupiter and Pluto. Ask yourself where Mars will extend its influence and bring its expansive power. Look to the houses that are ruled by Mars—the houses that hold the signs that Mars rules (Aries and Scorpio). Aries appears in her 8th house, and Baker will need this empowerment to navigate the beliefs and values of others. Scorpio inhabits her 3rd house, and she will use this immense empowerment to communicate with both her voice and the way in which she navigates her immediate environment. Bringing the consideration of these two houses together, you see that her empowered, sometimes combative and overtly sexual, voice pushes the buttons of "other people's values" (8th house). How she navigates those values will be very important.

Consider how those with values unlike her own responded to her delightful gifts as she expressed them to the world with her Gemini voice.

She clearly took many powerful actions in her navigation of other people's values, from moving to Europe to adopting twelve multi-racial children.

As Mars passed over Pluto and gathered its energy, it left something behind as well. Drive, leadership, and determination have been embedded within Pluto's ability to destroy and empower. Scorpio is ruled by Mars and co-ruled by Pluto, bringing an incredibly powerful intensity to the 3rd house, which is ruled by both. With both ruler and co-ruler conjunct in the 10th house ruling her 3rd, Baker's voice is her action and empowerment. Don't forget that Mars also represents the action taken to move sexual energies. Think about that as you watch Baker perform on stage. Think as well about Pluto as the catalyst and Mars as the sexual aggressor. Baker's very public voice was a catalyst in forcing the public (10th-house stellium) to face and contend with a woman's sexuality in a very Gemini manner.

It is fascinating to see how the impact of this very public stellium is brought to the 4th and 7th houses by Jupiter's rulership. It is clear, as well, how its impact changes throughout the course of Baker's life. Quite often, a Jupiter-ruled 4th house tells of individuals who live far away from the world or culture into which they were born. Jupiter's rulership of the 7th may speak to marriage or other significant relationships with those from other lands. Jupiter's sign and house placement will tell you what has brought that person far afield and established contact with the potential partner or partners. In Baker's case, her public voice, in all its forms, brought her far from the place and conditions of her birth. She engaged in multiple relationships with men and women in foreign lands. In 1937, Josephine renounced her American citizenship and became a French citizen. Moreover, her "rainbow family" is a clear reflection of the expansion over time of her understanding of what home, family, and relationships can be.

Baker's journey is an inspiring story. Her Gemini stellium puts her expansive, powerful, sexual voice and expression on public display. Her large, intense, and assertive communications pull her far from her family roots, and allow her to give voice to issues that are, to this day, deeply uncomfortable to many. Clearly her mission in life was to bring the power of her voice to the world.

GUIDEPOST 17

Dispositors

The dispositor of a planet in a natal chart is the planet that rules the zodiac sign in which the planet is placed. In other words, it is the ruling planet of the sign in which a planet is positioned. Dispositorship involves the connection between two planets by virtue of their placements in particular signs, and helps you understand the influence one planet has over another due to its rulership of the sign in which the first planet is located.

In fact, the concepts of rulership and dispositorship are closely connected, since they both derive from the relationships between planets and signs, and help us understand how different planetary energies are expressed and interact within the chart. But while planetary rulers derive their energy from the connection between a planet and a sign, dispositors derive theirs from the relationships between planets within a specific chart.

There is often confusion regarding the difference between the chart ruler and its final dispositor. The chart ruler is always the planet that rules the sign of the Ascendant (see Guidepost 7). We will clarify final dispositors in this guidepost.

Who's Running the Show?

When a planet is disposed by another planet, it is *directed* by that planet. When we find Mars in Gemini in a natal chart, Mercury, as the ruler of Gemini, is the dispositor of Mars. This relationship creates a dynamic in which the dispositor (in this case, Mercury) has an influence over the expression of the planet it disposes (in this case, Mars). In essence, any action that Mars takes must be "in service" to Mercury. In order to fully understand Mars in this chart, we must understand the placement and condition of Mercury.

Consider Mars in Leo. In this scenario, the Sun disposes Mars. Regardless of what sign the Sun is in, it is the force that directs the actions of Mars from behind the scenes. In a sense, Mars is in service to the Sun. Its activities and functioning will depend on, and be influenced by, the energy that it receives from the Sun. Mars in Leo will behave very differently if the Sun that it must serve is in Sagittarius rather than Capricorn. When Mars serves a Sagittarius Sun, the Sun is disposed by Jupiter, the ruler of Sagittarius. When the Sun is in Capricorn, it is disposed by Saturn, the ruler of Capricorn. Imagine how differently Mars will behave when it is directed by or in service to a Sun that is being directed by Jupiter rather than Saturn. Jupiter brings joviality and an expansive nature to the Sun, which will pass that influence along to Mars. On the other hand, if the Sun is disposed by Saturn, the serious ambition and restrictive nature of the Sun will be passed on to Mars.

One way to wrap your mind around the concept of dispositorship is to envision each planet as a particular character living in its ideal home. When a planet is disposed by another planet, it must answer to the character and live in the home of that planet. So when Mars is in Leo, it must answer to the confident leader and live in a warm, opulent mansion with floor-to-ceiling windows. Mars will, of course, bring along some tools and weapons, and will have to be careful not to break any windows or question the leadership of the Sun.

You can apply this interpretation to the Sun, the Moon, and all the personal and social planets.

- The character of the Sun is warm and bright, a leader with powerful vitality and confidence. The ideal home of the Sun is a large mansion with lots of windows—very bright and warm.

- The character of the Moon functions on instinct. The Moon is domestic, protective, nurturing, and moody. An ideal home for the Moon will be a cozy cabin with a basket of kittens by the wood stove, a larder full of comfort foods, and family photos of the past four generations on the wall.

- The character of Mercury is quick-thinking and understands technology. Mercury is talkative, curious, and full of information and ideas. An ideal home for Mercury is an office or communication center where computers and communication technologies are the central feature.

- The character of Venus is artistic, relationship-oriented, sensual, pleasure-seeking, and attractive. The ideal home for Venus is beautiful inside and out, with a lovely view, beautiful colors and textures throughout, and a closet full of comfortable and elegant clothing.

- The character of Mars is courageous. Mars is driven by passion, competition, conflict, and determination. The ideal home for Mars is a fortress with an armory and workshop full of tools, weapons, and heavy equipment.

- The character of Jupiter is expansive, jovial, and optimistic. Jupiter is always reaching for wisdom or looking for a party. The ideal home for Jupiter is very large and contains a library with bookshelves reaching to the ceiling, with maps and memorabilia from around the world covering the walls.

- The character of Saturn wears a buttoned-down tightly restrictive suit. Saturn is authoritative, stable, serious, and disciplined. The ideal home for Saturn resembles a government office or a boardroom—a place where rules are made and order is kept.

When Mars is in Cancer, it must answer to the nurturing character of the Moon and live in the cozy cabin with the kittens. Unless Mars needs to protect those kittens, let's hope that the weapons were left behind. When Mars is in Capricorn, it must answer to Saturn, the disciplinarian, and live in government offices.

Think about how these various dispositors will result in Mars being expressed in very different ways in the native's personality.

Mercury, by virtue of rulership, brings its intellect to the natal houses that hold both Gemini and Virgo. By extension, Mercury brings this influence to any planets that are in Gemini and Virgo. The houses that hold these signs and any planets in them will be colored by whatever sign Mercury inhabits. When a planet is said to rule a sign, that planet in rulership has an oversized impact on any planet currently within that domain.

Working with this interplay of planetary energies is a bit like engaging in a treasure hunt. You search for the planet or planets that have the greatest power in order to discover the hierarchy between them. I know this sounds complicated, but you will quickly get the hang of it and the results will greatly deepen your understanding. Besides, treasure hunts can be a lot of fun.

Final Dispositors

A final dispositor is a planet located in its domicile that governs all other planets in a natal chart. All the planets in the chart are in service to this one planet. Using traditional rulerships, begin with any planet in the chart and identify the ruler of the sign it's in. Then follow the chain of rulership from one planet to the next, continuing this process until you reach a planet in its own sign. If the chain of disposition from all planets in the chart leads to a single planet that is in its domicile, that planet is the final dispositor. This is the planet in charge, the planet that exerts ultimate influence and authority over all the others. This is the boss, the leader steering the ship of the native's life.

However, not all charts have a final dispositor. If no planet resides in its own sign, there is no final dispositor. Moreover, if you find two planets in each other's signs, creating a mutual reception (see below), or if the chain of rulership forms a loop, there is no final dispositor.

A chart with a final dispositor typically belongs to an individual who is highly focused and displays an unwavering commitment to their goals, channeling their energy through the planet that is the final dispositor with remarkable concentration and determination. Identifying the final dispositor helps in understanding the planet that holds the most significant sway in shaping the person's character and life path. Most natal charts do not have a final dispositor, making it a unique and influential feature when it occurs.

Mutual Reception

When you determine that there is no final dispositor in a chart, start looking for a mutual reception. A mutual reception occurs when two planets each reside in the sign of the other. In this case, each planet disposes the other. As an example, consider a chart with the Moon in Capricorn and Saturn in Cancer. In this situation, anytime the Moon is activated, Saturn is called on for support or guidance. Conversely, when Saturn is activated, the Moon is called upon. This creates a circular feedback loop that links the two planets together.

In this scenario, consider what it feels like for the Moon to live in Saturn's authoritative home, where rules are made and order is kept. The Moon is hyper-aware that Saturn, as the landlord, is keeping a close eye on what is happening in its domain. The Moon will be careful not to anger or alienate Saturn. How will the Moon use its nurturing domestic instincts? Will it bring the basket of kittens into Saturn's authoritative home?

By the same token, how does Saturn—dressed in a conservative suit and prepared to set standards and make rules—feel about being sent to live in the Moon's cozy cabin full of comfort foods and memories of the past? Saturn is aware that the Moon is the landlord and must be kept informed of and content with the goings-on in this nurturing domain. As these two planets come to understand the environment in which they find themselves residing, they learn how to utilize their own resources, as well as those they find in that environment. This, in practical terms, means that, even if the planets involved never actually meet, they will get to know each other very well. They learn how best to manage themselves in order to navigate their relationship with their landlord.

The Moon learns that the kittens can indeed grow fat and happy when kept on a strict schedule. The Moon comes to understand that an ordered environment can be comforting and that ambition can be emotionally satisfying. Saturn learns to loosen up restrictive clothing and enjoy a simple bowl of soup by the fireside. Saturn may even use ambition to create a home-based business—making soup on that wood stove, or breeding kittens, or selling antique furniture from generations past.

In a mutual reception, two planets get to know one another by inhabiting each other's domain. As each learns to respect and function in a world that is unfamiliar and yet linked by rulership, an interesting relationship develops. They help each other adjust, adapt, and function in ways that push them into unfamiliar, but supported, territory.

When you find a mutual reception in a chart, you know that you are dealing with an individual who holds multiple focuses and sees both sides of certain situations more easily. There may be more than one distinct side to the personality, with one or the other dominating in different circumstances.

Loops and Chains

Dispositors link planets together. In a dispositor loop, one planet leads to another, which leads to another and then another, and then finally leads back to the first. There will be at least three or more planets involved in a dispositor loop. In a dispositor chain, the links continue until you reach a planet that does not dispose any other. When there is no final dispositor, this chain can end in one of two ways.

With a long dispositor loop, no one planet is in charge, as everyone answers to the next until the loop comes full circle. In a sense, the native's life is being run by committee rather than being led by a team or a top boss. But long dispositor chains, whether or not they end in a loop, can get complicated. Think of these links as forming a chain of command. When working with long dispositor chains, you have to allow your focus to soften and feel the connections as you watch the chain weave a pattern around the chart from one area of life to another. In this way, you get a feel for the movement of energy within the chart and within the native of the chart.

When I think of long dispositor loops and chains, I remember a children's game from my early childhood called "Telephone," in which a group of children stand in a circle, passing whispered messages or phrases from one to another until they have gone around the entire loop. The last person to receive the whispered message says it out loud. Often, the resulting message has been altered and distorted beyond recognition. I remember laughing uproariously as messages totally unrelated to their original intent emerged. This game demonstrates how communications can break down, and the effects of potential inaccuracies when relaying information.

One way to avoid confusion and misinterpretations when considering dispositorships is to draw a dispositor tree.

Dispositor Trees

Dispositor trees are graphical representations used to visualize the connections and relationships between planets and their dispositors in the natal chart. They can be especially helpful in showing, at a glance, the planetary chain of command or the hidden hierarchy of the chart. When you find long loops or chains in a natal chart, you know you are dealing with individuals who potentially struggle with internal confusion and a resulting lack of focus. On the positive side, this person is likely to be quite flexible and have various interests, with multiple dimensions within their personalities. Drawing a dispositor tree can help you understand some of these complexities.

There are a few simple guidelines to follow when drawing these trees:

- A planet that rules a sign disposes all planets in that sign.

- The three outer planets are never used as dispositors and are always at the end of a chain.

- Dispositor trees generally have a top tier, a middle tier, and bottom tiers, although some may have only two tiers and others may have more.

- A planet in its own sign will always be in the top tier.

- Mutual receptions belong in the top tier.

- Any loop belongs in the top tier.

- The planets in the top tier have the most power and influence.

- A natal chart can have multiple trees.

- A tree can have all the planets in it, or a single planet.

A dispositor tree shows which planets are pulling the strings (top tier), which planets are playing a supportive role (bottom tiers), and which planets are providing a link between the two (middle tiers).

When you come across a planet in its own sign with no other planets in the sign(s) it governs, you've identified a tree with no branches. No one answers to this planet and it answers to no one. You can expect this planet to exhibit its energy in a pure, unadulterated manner. It may be highly independent of the rest of the personality—not well integrated and a bit of a wild card. When this happens, look for similarities to an unaspected planet.

When drawing a dispositor tree, look first for planets in their domicile/rulership and place any you find in the top tier. You may find more than one planet in its rulership, or you may find none in this category. Then look for mutual receptions. If you don't find any, look for a loop. Perhaps the best way to demonstrate this is by looking at some examples.

First, let's look at the chart of Ruth Westheimer, born June 4, 1928, at 4:00 AM CET in Frankfurt, Germany. She is better known as Dr. Ruth (see Figure 16). A brief summary of this woman's long and fascinating life exposes the basic planetary theme of her chart. Torn away from her family by war at the age of ten, Ruth later became a sniper in the Israeli army, during which time she was severely wounded. She went on to focus her education and career around sex and sexuality. These are all Mars-related themes, so it is perhaps not surprising that Mars is the final dispositor in her chart.

When you look through her chart for a planet in the sign of its rulership/domicile, you find Mars in Aries. There are no other planets in domicile, so you don't need to look further. Place Mars at the top of your tree (see Figure 17 on page 246).

Ruth's Jupiter, representing her beliefs, and Uranus, representing the unique cultural time in which she was born, also reside in Aries and the 11th house. The potent force of her beliefs (Jupiter) and the distinctive cultural context into which she was born (Uranus) are in direct service to Mars. She has no planets in Scorpio, so these Aries planets are alone in their direct service to Mars.

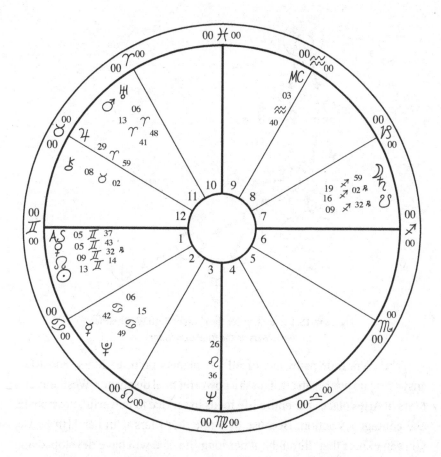

Figure 16. Chart of Ruth Westheimer, born June 4, 1928, at 4:00 AM CET
in Frankfurt, Germany.

Because Uranus is one of the three collective outer planets, it will not dispose others. Jupiter disposes both Saturn and the Moon (in Sagittarius). Because there are no planets in Saturn's ruling signs of Capricorn or Aquarius, look to Cancer to find planets disposed by the Moon. Both Mercury and Pluto are in Cancer, so place them beneath the Moon in your tree. Both the Sun and Venus are disposed by Mercury, and Neptune, at the end of the line, is disposed by the Sun. All these placements yield the dispositor tree shown in Figure 17 on page 246.

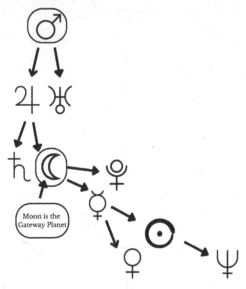

Figure 17. Dispositor tree for the chart of Ruth Westheimer, with Mars as the final dispositor.

The dispositor pathways of all the planets point to Mars, and Mars answers to no one but itself. This is a powerful final dispositor. Westheimer's Mars in Aries places her entire life focus in service to powerful, passionate, and courageous action. Because dynamic, hot Mars is in her 11th house, you can expect that, throughout her long life, she will have developed and exhibited great courage, as well as the ability to take direct action for the sake of her goals and the community that ultimately supports her.

Consider how much courage it took for a young woman only four and a half feet tall to train to be a sniper in the Isreali army! And how much courage did it take for her, in her role as Dr. Ruth, to talk about sex in a direct, forthright manner in America in the 1960s? In November 2023, she was appointed by the governor of New York as the state's honorary ambassador to loneliness. Dr. Ruth passed away on July 12, 2024, at the age of ninety-six, as I was doing the final edits of this book.

Next, let's look at an entirely different chart—one that contains a mutual reception and a single-planet tree. Robert Frost, born March 26, 1874, at 7:00 AM LMT (Local Mean Time) in San Francisco, California, was a highly acclaimed poet known for his use of common language and realistic representations of rural life in New England. He was the first poet to receive four Pulitzer Prizes for Poetry, and was awarded the Congressional Gold Medal for his work in 1960. He was named poet laureate of Vermont in 1961, explaining why I read his works a great deal in my early schooling in rural Vermont in the early 1960s.

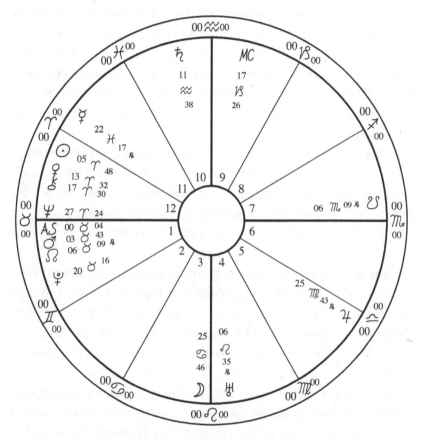

Figure 18. Chart of Robert Frost, born March 26, 1874, at 7:00 AM LMT (Local Mean Time) in San Francisco, California.

Frost's chart provides us with an example of two mutual receptions, and two single-planet trees (see Figure 18). This is an unusual chart, in that he actually has four trees—two without branches—and two mutual receptions—one with branches and one without. Since he is a poet, let's begin by looking at the mutual reception that holds Mercury, the planet associated with the written word. Mercury resides in Pisces disposed by Jupiter in Virgo, which, in turn, is disposed by Mercury. So each disposes the other. Consider the quick-thinking character of Mercury inhabiting the expansive imaginative space of Jupiter's home (Pisces). Mercury answers to Jupiter.

As Mercury absorbs the energy of Jupiter's environment, it is aware that there is something important to say. This native must allow the human condition of compassion and suffering (Pisces) to expand his voice (Mercury), bringing forth words of wisdom (Jupiter). In turn, Jupiter must answer to Mercury. As larger-than-life Jupiter adjusts to its position in Mercury's arena of analytical precision, it understands that great care must be exercised to develop the craft of writing by means of effort, detail, and focus (Virgo).

This simple mutual reception shows the cadence and beauty of this man's words, as his poetry reflects the very way in which his mind worked. Accentuating the importance of this mutual reception, two planets stand in opposition to each other straddling the 5th and 11th house polarities. This clearly shows the potential of his expansive creativity to allow for the adoration of the larger social community.

The other mutual reception in this chart is fascinating as well. Venus in Aries and Mars in Taurus highlight how Frost bucked the traditional gender roles of the culture and time in which he lived. In the early 1900s, poetry was certainly considered a feminine endeavor. If Frost were alive today, it would be interesting to have a conversation with him about his experience and his perspective on gender-role expectations.

As for the two single-planet trees, the Moon in Cancer in the 3rd house of communication speaks for itself. The Cancer Moon's tender emotional nature is going to need to be expressed. This is indeed a wild card, as single-planet trees tend to encourage acting independently and speaking the truth in simple unadulterated words. With Saturn, also a single-planet tree, inhabiting the 10th house and ruling both the 9th and the 10th, suggesting strength and undiluted ambition in the outer world, this native will simply be unable to keep those words to himself. As you examine the dispositor trees generated by this chart (see Figure 19), remember what are perhaps Frost's most famous lines:

How to Read and Interpret a Birth Chart

Two roads diverged in a wood, and I—
I took the one less traveled by,
And that has made all the difference.

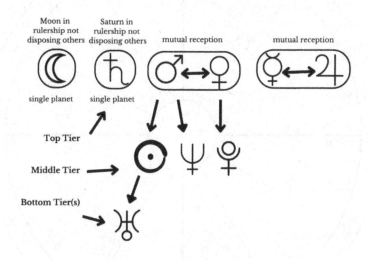

Figure 19. Dispositor tree for the chart of Robert Frost, showing
two mutual receptions and two single-planet trees.

Finally, let's look at the chart of Chaz Bono, born March 4, 1969, at 12:55 AM PST in Los Angeles, California (see Figure 20 on page 250). This chart demonstrates a dispositor loop. We already know a little bit about this writer, musician, and LGBTQ activist from our discussion in Guidepost 7.

The dispositor loop in this chart is actually quite simple, involving only three planets. Therefore, Chaz's life is run by a three-planet commit-tee. Those are the only planets in the top tier; there are no single-planet or alternate trees involved. Mars answers to Jupiter, who answers to Venus, who answers to Mars. These three are in equal standing at the top of the tree. Be sure to consider the condition and essential dignity of the planets involved in this committee (see Figures 1 and 3, pages 40 and 45).

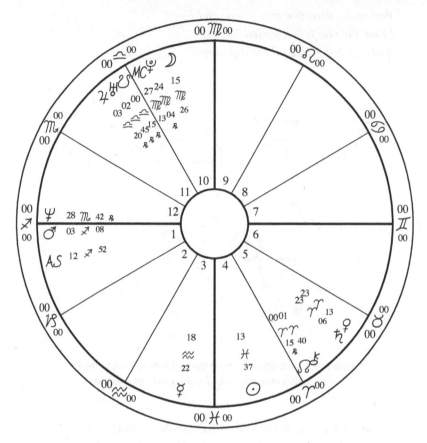

Figure 20. Chart of Chaz Bono, born March 4, 1969, at 12:55 AM PST in Los Angeles, California.

Mars and Jupiter are content enough in the signs they are in, but, in Aries, Venus is in her detriment. I think of Venus as being a bit cranky and under the weather in this position, even before taking into account that she is standing hip-to-hip with Saturn. Jupiter in Libra is doing its best, not only to please the other two, but also to show Mars (Sagittarius) that there are other perspectives that may help Venus to find a place of comfort. Given that Jupiter is standing shoulder-to-shoulder with Uranus, these ideas are not only expansive, but have a powerful innovative twist, as well as being ahead of their time. This is displayed clearly in the dispositor tree of this complex person (see Figure 21).

How to Read and Interpret a Birth Chart

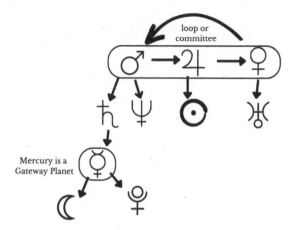

Figure 21. Dispositor tree for the chart of Chaz Bono, showing a dispositor loop.

I encourage you to create a dispositor tree for every chart you analyze. With time and practice, it becomes a quick and efficient method for understanding the internal hierarchy of any individual. Consider the planets as internal characters that influence and guide the person's life. Ask yourself: Who holds the key to this life? Understanding this will help you provide the best support for clients as they navigate life's journey.

Final Thoughts and Acknowledgments

The seed of this book was sown over thirty years ago when I first developed the habit of writing in the early morning hours as the rest of the world slept.

My 12th house, six-planet Leo stellium, squared by Saturn in Scorpio (3rd house), and trine my Moon in Aries (8th house), tells the tale of my life and of my work. It has required a substantial internal journey of introspection, deep healing, and release to enable that seed to sprout, let alone flourish into some semblence of maturity.

Within the pages of this book, I present some of what I have absorbed in more than fifty years of study and practice. The work of astrology has transformed my life into something remarkably and unexpectedly beautiful. I firmly believe that understanding ourselves through a deep exploration of our personal natal charts represents a pure and profound form of soul alchemy.

This book springs from a deeply personal act of love, as all authentic expressions of creativity do. It has taken me well into my sixth decade to realize that I am best equipped to give of myself through writing, and it is through my writing that I can ultimately accept the support of others.

Now, as I approach the culmination of this writing project, my love and gratitude toward those who have stood by my side are boundless. I'm immensely grateful to my cherished students and my valued clients. To my dear children, Angela Eileen Gale and Elliot Thor Lajza, thank you for your patience when constantly exposed to the intricate language of astrology. I have always felt supported by you. To my siblings—Jo Anne Kulberg, Gail Farrington-Sprague, and Mark Farrington—you each hold a powerful and special place in my heart. Dave Battick, my steadfast companion, has been an unwavering source of support, encouraging me to allow the natural world and the great outdoors to support my process.

I'd also like to extend my heartfelt appreciation to several influential teachers—Noel Tyl, Steven Forrest, Mark Learner, and Toni Stone.

Throughout the process of bringing this book to fruition, I have been indebted, as well, to the invaluable support of Jennie Date, Noelle Letteri, Amy Whitehorn, Paula Diaco, and David Brizendine. My friend and time-twin, Alora, has continuously assisted in smoothing the path we travel together in this life. To Janet and Mary Jo, your camaraderie has been an invaluable gift in times of need. I've learned as much from each of you as from any teacher or book I've encountered. And I cannot forget to thank my dear feline companion, Kairos, who has been by my side, complaining or purring through every word I have written.

Finally, to all those whose names are not mentioned here explicitly, but who have played a part in this journey, your contributions are deeply appreciated.

Bibliography

Burk, Kevin. *Understanding the Birth Chart: A Comprehensive Guide to Classical Interpretation.* Llewellyn Publications, 2003.

Edington, Louise. *The Complete Guide to Astrology: Understanding Yourself, Your Signs, and Your Birth Chart.* Rockridge Press, 2020.

Forrest, Steven. *The Book of Pluto: Finding Wisdom in Darkness with Astrology.* Seven Paws Press, 2012.

Forrest, Steven. *The Inner Sky: How to Make Wiser Choices for a More Fulfilling Life.* Bantam Books, 1984.

George, Demetra. *Astrology and the Authentic Self: Integrating Traditional and Modern Astrology to Uncover the Essence of the Birth Chart.* Ibis Press, 2008.

George, Demetra. *Ancient Astrology in Theory and Practice—A Manual of Traditional Techniques, Volume I.* Rubedo Press, 2019.

Green, Liz, and Howard Sasportas. *The Luminaries: The Psychology of the Sun and Moon in the Horoscope.* Samuel Weiser Inc, 1992.

Lineman, Rose, and Jan Popelka. *Compendium of Astrology.* Para Research, 1984.

Martin, Clare. *Alchemy: The Soul of Astrology.* The Wessex Astrologer, 2020.

Meyer, Michael. *Handbook for the Humanistic Astrologer.* Doubleday, 1974.

Meyers, Eric. *The Astrology of Awakening, Volume 2: Chart Application and Counseling.* Astrology Sight Publishing, 2016.

Oken, Alan. *Rulers of the Horoscope.* The Crossing Press, 2000.

Reed, Theresa. *Astrology for Real Life: A Workbook for Beginners.* Weiser Books, 2019.

Rudhyar, Dane. *The Lunation Cycle: A Key to the Understanding of Personality.* Servire/Wassenaar, 1967.

Rudhyar, Dane. *The Practice of Astrology as a Technique in Human Understanding.* Servire/Wassenaar, 1968.

Rudhyar, Dane, and Leyla Rael. *Astrological Aspects: A Process-Oriented Approach*. Aurora Press, 1980.

Schwartz, Richard C. *Internal Family Systems Therapy*. Guilford Publications, 1997.

Schwartz, Richard C. *No Bad Parts: Healing Trauma and Restoring Wholeness with the Internal Family Systems Model*. Sounds True, 2021.

Taylor, Carole. *Astrology: Using the Wisdom of the Stars in Your Everyday Life*. DK Publishing, 2018.

Tyl, Noel. *Synthesis and Counseling in Astrology: The Professional Manual*. Llewellyn Publications, 1998.

Index

G

Gandhi, Mohandas, 188–189
Gemini
    as air element, 28
    keywords and personifications, 147
    the Moon in, 73
    as mutable sign, 30
    as outward (yang) orientation, 31
    in planetary rulership, 42
    rising and Ascendant, sample chart, 121
genders (orientations), 30
generational planets, 24, 44
George, Demetra, 39
grand cross, 62–63
grand trines, 217–227
    defense mechanisms, 220–223
    elemental energy, 217–218
    formation of, 217
    separated grand trines, 223–227
    upsides and downsides of, 218–220
Grandin, Temple, 80

H

Hand, Robert, 35
Handbook for the Humanistic Astrologer
    (Meyer), 11
Harry (Prince), 195
Hefner, Hugh, 189–190
hemispheres, 52–55
horary astrology, 8, 10
horizon, 52–54
house classifications, 61–64
    functional houses, 63–64
    grand cross, 62–63
    opposition and polarity, 62, 63
house systems, 20–22
houses
    described, 18–20
    empty, 48–50
    rulership of, 46–48
    of wealth, 63
houses (1st through 12th)
    idealism in the chart, 137–141
    keywords, surface-level and deeper-level,
        149–152
    placement of the Moon and rulership,
        76–90
humanistic Western astrology, 11–13

I

idealization, 133–141
    in charts of the twelve houses, 137–141
Imum Coeli, 54
individual houses, 63

The Inner Sky (Forrest), 160
Internal Family Systems therapeutic model,
    223–224
Internet, astrology information online, 2–3
IO Series, 35
islands, unaspected, 194, 198–199

J

Jackson, Michael, 171–172, 214–215
Jefferson, Melissa Viviane. *See* Lizzo
Jones, Marc Edmund, 11
Joplin, Janis, 129–130, 192–193
Jupiter
    at Aries Point, 207
    in aspect to the Sun and Moon, 110–111
    aspects between Moon and Jupiter, 96
    character of, in dispositorship, 239
    keywords and personifications, 145
    and planetary rulership, 42–44
    as social planet, 24
    unaspected, 191–193
juxtaposition, 62

K

Kahlo, Frida, 177
Kennedy, Rosemary, 75
keyword notebook, 143–144, 160
keywords, 143–160
    for aspects, 152
    example of using keywords, 152–156
    example of using keywords and aspects,
        156–159
    for planets, 144–146
    for signs of zodiac, 146–149
    for the twelve houses, 149–152
King, Billie Jean, 87–88, 128–129
King, Martin Luther Jr., 177
Kübler-Ross, Elisabeth, 130–131

L

Lady Gaga, 83
Laing, R. D., 89–90
Lennon, Julian, 74
Leo
    as fire element, 27
    as fixed sign, 30
    keywords and personifications, 147
    the Moon in, 74
    as outward (yang) orientation, 31
    in planetary rulership, 41–42
    rising and Ascendant, sample chart,
        123–124
Lewinsky, Monica, 48–50
Libra

About the Author

Laurie Farrington has been studying astrology since early childhood. She began her professional practice more than thirty years ago. Laurie, a master astrologer, consultant, writer, teacher, and mentor, lives on the beautiful wild coast of Maine. Follow her on Instagram @laurie.farrington_astrolore.

To Our Readers

Weiser Books, an imprint of Red Wheel/Weiser, publishes books across the entire spectrum of occult, esoteric, speculative, and New Age subjects. Our mission is to publish quality books that will make a difference in people's lives without advocating any one particular path or field of study. We value the integrity, originality, and depth of knowledge of our authors.

Our readers are our most important resource, and we appreciate your input, suggestions, and ideas about what you would like to see published.

Visit our website at *www.redwheelweiser.com*, where you can learn about our upcoming books and free downloads, and also find links to sign up for our newsletter and exclusive offers.

You can also contact us at *info@rwwbooks.com* or at

Red Wheel/Weiser, LLC
65 Parker Street, Suite 7
Newburyport, MA 01950